Patterns in Human Geography

An Introduction to Numerical Methods

DAVID M. SMITH

Patterns in Human Geography

An Introduction to Numerical Methods

David & Charles Newton Abbot
Crane Russak & Company, Inc New York

First published 1975 by
David & Charles (Holdings) Limited
Brunel House Newton Abbot Devon
(ISBN 0 7153 6968 7)

Published in the United States of America by
Crane, Russak & Company, Inc
347 Madison Avenue
New York, New York 10017
(ISBN 0-8448-0764-8)
Library of Congress Catalog Number 75-21520

Set in 10 on 12p Times Roman and printed in
Great Britain for David & Charles (Holdings) Limited
Brunel House Newton Abbot Devon
 by Redwood Burn Limited, Trowbridge & Esher

Published in Canada
by Douglas David & Charles Limited
132 Philip Avenue North Vancouver BC

Contents

Contents

Introduction

The arrangement of man's existence on the surface of the earth is the subject matter of human geography. Approaches to human geography have undergone great changes in recent years, with increasing attention to theory, model building, and the analysis of large volumes of numerical information. Central to these changes has been the so-called 'Quantitative Revolution', through which conventional statistical methods have been applied, modified and extended in geographical research. The ability to use numerical methods has now taken its place alongside the traditional skills of fieldwork and map interpretation as an essential element of a geographer's range of techniques.

A number of excellent texts on quantitative geography are now available, and there are many books on statistics for the social or behavioural sciences to which reference can be made. However, these works are often too advanced for the introductory-level student and non-academic reader, and they are generally more concerned with the application of standard statistical measures and tests than with the rather special problem of geographical description. The purpose of this book is to provide an introduction to a wide range of commonly used numerical techniques, applied in a descriptive context in human geography. The emphasis is on demonstration through illustration and example, rather than on the derivation of formulae. The strong dose of inferential statistics, probability theory or matrix algebra which typifies textbooks on quantitative methods is deliberately avoided here, in favour of a less formal exposition aimed at a more intuitive grasp of the principles involved. The primary objective is to breach as painlessly as possible the mental blockage which separates students and others from an appreciation of numerical techniques.

9

Introduction

It must be emphasized from the outset that this book is *not* intended to be a practical guide for research workers. The discussion of many matters is brief and to some extent simplified, particularly in the case of statistical inference and hypothesis testing. Before attempting research applications, the reader is strongly advised to consult *at least two* specialist textbooks on statistics or quantitative geography; resolving the confusion arising from the uncomfortable discovery that few texts explain things in the same way is part of the process of understanding how to use a technique as opposed to knowing roughly what it can do. Brevity of treatment of certain topics is necessitated by the attempt to cover so many techniques, up to and including factor analysis. To go as far as factor analysis is admittedly rather risky in an introductory text, but this method has been used so often in recent years that every reader of geographical literature needs some familiarity with what it does.The treatment of this and other 'advanced' techniques here is based on the belief (not shared by all quantitative geographers) that a little learning, though possibly dangerous, is preferable to total ignorance.

This approach has some disadvantages, of course. The only way to complete competence in the application of numerical methods is through an understanding of the mathematical and statistical basis on which they rest; there is no short cut, and to try to find one is an exercise in self-deception. However, not all students (or teachers) need an advanced level of comprehension and operational competence. With limits to the time and effort which can be devoted to this subject, a broad familiarity with a wide range of techniques may be more useful, particularly when a single course may be the student's one and only exposure to numerical methods. This kind of general survey can also provide an effective first step in the direction of a more thorough technical training in the use of quantitative analysis as a research tool. In addition, such a treatment may be helpful to non-geographers aware of the changes in human geography in recent years, who may find some applications for the new techniques of spatial analysis in the fields of planning, commerce and so on.

The main purpose of this book is thus to explain as simply as possible how human geographers now use numerical methods in a descriptive context. In the process, a wide variety of techniques are introduced, and demonstrated by means of illustrations and examples. An *illustration* is here a worked application using simple imaginary data, to show the step-by-step procedure for calculating some measure, while an *example* is an actual research application or one using data from a real-world situation. Most of the examples are from the author's own research or, like the illustrations, have been especially developed for teaching purposes; they are drawn from a number of different countries, and cover many different facets of human existence. A deliberate attempt has been made to demonstrate the application of numerical methods to geographical problems closely connected with contemporary social issues. There are many maps and diagrams to clarify the procedures and display the results, at the same time showing that in the computer age the traditional graphic methods still have their uses.

The emphasis throughout is on geographical *description*. But this is not to say that the contents of this book have no relevance in the search for explanations of geographical patterns, for accurate description is a necessary prerequisite to any attempt to explain. Description forms an important part of hypothesis testing or the use of models, where it is required to compare some theoretical expectation with the real-world pattern. In fact, it is impossible to consider descriptive techniques in total isolation from the wider research context in which they are used, the purpose of which is usually to explain something. Description also has a vital part to play in applied human geography or the design of preferable alternative spatial arrangements for man's activities on earth, for this obviously requires accurate information on the existing patterns as well as the capacity to specify clearly those to replace them.

The chapters which follow differ somewhat from the usual arrangement of statistics texts in their order and content. The discussion proceeds from preliminary matters concerning the type of data the geographer uses, through a brief consideration of the map as a descriptive device, to simple descriptive statistics and means of comparing sets of numerical observations. This is

Introduction

followed by a chapter on scale transformation and the combination of data – matters largely neglected in existing texts. A review of more direct measures of areal distribution patterns comes next, leading into the idea of geographical surfaces. Then comes a chapter on the measurement of association, including correlation methods, followed by a brief discussion of measures of networks and patterns of movement. Finally, there is a lengthy chapter on areal classification and the identification of regions. A short epilogue raises some general problems associated with quantitative analysis in human geography, and attempts to set them in a broader academic and societal context. Each chapter has its own set of technical and application references, grouped together at the end of the book as a set of Selected Readings.

Acknowledgements

This book grew gradually over a period of years, the unintended outcome of a partnership of necessity between a teacher and his students. As the teacher attempted to explain and the students struggled to understand, the devices found most effective for expository purposes emerged by trial and error. The author's unwitting collaborators were geography students at Southern Illinois University between 1966 and 1970, and at the University of Florida from 1970 to 1972, and the book owes much to their reactions to the lectures, notes and exercises reflected in many of the pages which follow. Particular gratitude is due to Tso-Hwa Lee, who as a student and associate assisted with a number of the illustrations and examples, and also contributed his considerable skill as cartographer and computer programmer. Other one-time research assistants whose labours find their way into various parts of the book include Wayne Wiedeman, David Kolzow, Philip Frankland, Steven Gladin, Robert Gray and James Skinner. Many of the maps and diagrams were prepared in the Cartographic Laboratory, Southern Illinois University, under the supervision of Daniel Irwin and Tso-Hwa Lee. Special thanks are due to the Department of Geography and Environmental Studies, University of the Witwatersrand, for the cartographic and other facilities which enabled the author to complete this project during the tenure of a visiting appointment in 1972–3, and to the Department of Geography, University of New England, where revisions were undertaken with similar assistance during the latter part of 1973. Special acknowledgement is due to the efforts of a number of reviewers, who provided helpful and often conflicting evaluations of the manuscript at various points in its preparation; the author alone must accept responsibility for advice rejected, most of which

Acknowledgements

was to be more rigorous. David Hillier gave valuable assistance with checking proofs. Finally, thanks go to Margaret Smith, who read the manuscript as a more practical and less numerate social scientist and thus provided a measure of its worth.

David M. Smith

Armidale, NSW, November 1973

1. Compiling Geographical Information

Human beings arrange their lives in geographical space. They exist and perform their activities at specific locations, and they move or distribute things in certain directions. They thus give character to places or areas, differentiating and connecting them with respect to various aspects of the human condition. The geographical expression of man's existence can be thought of very simply as a geometry of points, lines and areas. Production locations, places of residence, settlements and so on form patterns of points or *nodes* around which life is organized. Lines of communication and transportation form *networks* of movements and interaction. Human differentiation of geographical space forms systems of *regions*, or areas distinguished by some particular characteristics bestowing homogeneity or functional cohesion. The man-made landscape is a collage of these nodes, networks and regions.

The analysis of this geometry of spatial form is the basic task of human geography. But before the existing situation can be explained, or improved upon, it has to be accurately described. This implies a careful process of observation in which the results can preferably be expressed in numerical form, for the precise description of human geographical patterns is basic to their eventual understanding.

Observing Human Activity

Knowledge begins with observation. We perceive the world around us with our eyes and other senses, and we arrange these observations in a certain relationship to each other so that they 'make sense'. Repeated observation of the same object or event brings familiarity; repeated observation of a particular association of objects or events creates an expectation. Knowledge imposes order or predictability on the world, reducing uncertainty and helping to make the unexpected consistent with experience if not always entirely expected. It gives us a feeling of security, knowing roughly where we ourselves stand in the complex reality of life. It also gives us a capacity to control our individual circumstances to make life better.

How do we go about making observations of the world around us? Obviously, if we want to build up precise and systematic information rather than simply random impressions, some methods of observation will be preferable to others. The cardinal rule in scientific inquiry is that observations should be taken in a way which would lead others to obtain the same results. This is often quite easy to accomplish; for example, such properties as the height and weight of a person can be accurately found by independent observers because there are appropriate *measuring instruments* available and agreed *scales of measurement*. But in observing many other properties of human beings – for example, how they behave, feel or think – the process is much more difficult.

Something of the range of methods of observation and measurement in human geography can be explained by a simple illustration. Suppose that someone visited five cities (*A*, *B*, *C*, *D* and *E*) at known locations, and wished to find out about four things: whether they have a university, whether they are 'attractive', what political attitudes are held, and how much industry there is. The first question is answered in advance by a directory of universities in the library. The attractiveness of each city is established relative to the others by visual observation and subjective judgement. Political attitudes may be measured by asking each of a sample of fifty people to give the national government a score anywhere on a scale of 1 to 10 (where 1 means 'strongly dislike' and 10 means 'strongly like'), and then totalling the results. The amount of industry is found by visiting the Chamber of Commerce and asking how many people are employed in factories. Finally, the geographical position of each city is established by taking a four-figure grid reference on a map. The observations which result might be set down in a notebook as follows:

City *A* (grid ref: 15 85) – no university; quite attractive; government scores 350 points; 33,254 industrial workers.

City *B* (grid ref: 53 76) – has university; more attractive than *A*; government scores 265 points; 25,943 industrial workers.

City *C* (grid ref: 90 45) – has university; more attractive than *A* and *B*; government scores 140 points; 66,608 industrial workers.

City *D* (grid ref: 52 32) – no university; least attractive; government scores 230 points; 50,121 industrial workers.

City *E* (grid ref: 18 23) – has university; less attractive than *A* but more than *D*; government scores 420 points; 17,780 industrial workers.

These observations can be expressed in a somewhat more useful manner if they can be converted into a table of numbers (Table 1.1). The presence or absence of a university is measured simply by giving the numeral 1 to a city if it has such an institution and 0 if it has not. The attractiveness of each city has been judged in relation to others, and they can thus be placed in rank order giving 1 to the most attractive and 5 to the least attractive. The government scores have been converted back to an average position on the 1 to 10 scale by dividing the total points for each city

Table 1.1: Numerical Observations on Four Conditions in Five Imaginary Cities

City	Grid Reference	University 1 = has 0 = has not	Attractiveness Rank Order	Politics Average Score	Industry Employment to Nearest 100
A	15 85	0	3	7·0	33,300
B	53 76	1	2	5·3	25,900
C	90 45	1	1	2·8	66,600
D	52 32	0	5	4·6	50,100
E	18 23	1	4	8·4	17,800

by the number of people interviewed (i.e. 50). The number of industrial workers has been rounded to the nearest hundred, because the figure fluctuates from day to day and the exact numbers given by the Chamber of Commerce will be liable to error.

Measurement involves assigning numbers (or symbols) to objects in accordance with variations in a given property or condition. Four different scales of measurement are represented in Table 1.1: nominal, ordinal, interval and ratio. Each of these scales can be thought of as a different rule of measurement, which provides successively greater information about the condition which has been observed.

The *nominal* scale simply identifies observed differences without putting a quantity to them: it means, literally, 'naming'. In the illustration above each city is given a numeral 1 or 0 according to whether it has or has not a particular attribute. They could also have been given the symbols UD, MB or CB, for example, according to whether they were Urban Districts, Municipal Boroughs or County Boroughs. Nominal scaling establishes the existence or otherwise of a condition, but does not permit us to say that one thing is greater than or less than another. It is thus the lowest or weakest level of measurement.

The *ordinal* scale involves ranking. We can say that on a given property one thing or place is greater than or less than another – one city is more or less attractive than another – though we cannot specify by how much. Thus we can say of the attraction of the five imaginary cities, $C > B > A > E > D$ where $>$ means 'is greater than', or $D < E < A < B < C$ where $<$ means 'is less than'. But the difference between any two adjoining cities in this sequence must be assumed to be the same.

The *interval* scale allows the difference between adjoining pairs in sequence to vary. Thus the difference between the government's score in the two cities in which it is most popular (A and E) is 1·4, whereas between the two cities where it is least popular (C and D) it is 1·8. We can say that the difference between one pair is greater or less than the other, e.g. $(E-A) < (D-C)$, and also that they are in a certain ratio such that $E-A = x(D-C)$ where x is any number (in this case $\frac{7}{9}$, or 1·4 ÷ 1·8). But we cannot say, for example, that one observation is twice as great or three times as great as another. The government is not necessarily twice as popular in city B where it scores 5·6 as in C where it scores 2·8 because there is no true zero on an interval scale: it would be meaningless to say that a government has zero popularity or a city zero attractiveness. The measurement of temperature is the usual illustration of this; on neither a Fahrenheit nor a Centigrade scale is there a true zero (the choice of 32° of frost or the freezing point of water are both quite arbitrary), so we cannot say that 40° is twice as hot as 20° on either scale.

The *ratio* scale preserves the ratio between numerical observations as well as between intervals. Thus industrial employment in city C really is twice that in city A, or $C = xA$ where x is 2. This is because the condition of no industrial employees is a true zero. Ratio scales thus measure the difference (or 'distance') from a true zero, while *interval* scales measure difference from an arbitrary zero; otherwise the rules of number assignment are the same. Many important conditions in human geography are measured on a ratio scale – for example, levels of production, demographic characteristics, and monetary values.

All measurement scales involve placing observations along some dimension or dimensions. The difference between them is further demonstrated in Figure 1.1a, where the information about the five imaginary cities is plotted on four scales. The first simply shows the two points representing 'has' and 'has not', the second shows the equal intervals implicit in a ranking scale, while the third and fourth show the irregular intervals and the zero points on the interval and ratio scales. The first two are, in fact, *discrete* scales, where observations can be placed only at certain positions, whereas the last two are *continuous* scales because any position on the line could conceivably be occupied.

One set of information about the five cities in Table 1.1 not considered so far is the grid references showing location in geographical space. They are measurements in just the same way as the numbers assigned to the other conditions, establishing position on the two-dimensional map representing the surface of the earth (Figure 1.1b). This position is identified within a system of

Patterns in Human Geography

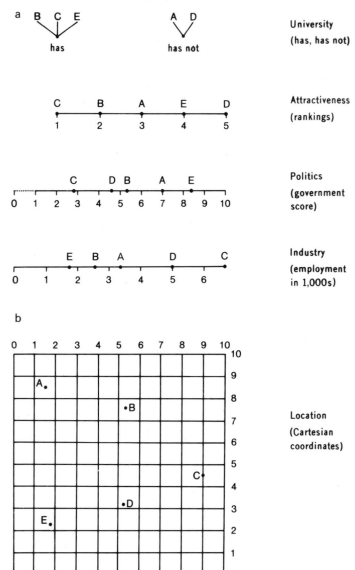

Figure 1.1   Measurements on five attributes of five imaginary cities.

Cartesian coordinates, a regular rectangular grid with an arbitrary origin or zero point. Coordinates measure on an interval scale, while distances between places (e.g. miles) are on a ratio scale. Most human geographical conditions are discrete, occurring only at specific points, compared with continuous spatial variables such as temperature or atmospheric pressure which are important in physical geography. It is the two dimensions required to define location which distinguish information on geographical position from that concerning single properties of place. Giving a number to a condition at a specific geographical location can be thought of as measurement in three dimensions.

The case of the five cities discussed above raises the question of the 'instrument' of measurement as well as of the scale. A different method was used to make the observations for each of the conditions considered. Finding out about the universities in a library source may be thought of as documentary research, judging the attractiveness of the city involved visual observation, establishing political views required attitudinal research, and obtaining employment figures required access to existing numerical data. Attractiveness and politics were measured 'in the field', while observations on the other two conditions were obtained from secondary sources.

What kind of instruments are involved in these measurement processes? Human geography has generally relied on two main methods of compiling primary data: visual observation, and asking questions of people. In the former case the actual observer may be regarded as the instrument, the eyes taking things in, the brain filtering the information, and the hand holding the pen which records the results. In the latter case the instrument may be a verbal question or written questionnaire, designed to elicit a certain response from the individual being surveyed or observed. Traditionally, human geography placed heavy emphasis on direct visual observation in the field as a primary source of information, but systematic surveys are becoming increasingly important just as in other social sciences. Such major data sources as the population census and industrial employment returns are, of course, compiled from vast numbers of responses elicited in surveys where some kind of questionnaire is used. Obviously, this kind of data collection is more accurate than visual observation, which is highly susceptible to subjectivity and differences of individual perception. Judging the attractiveness of five cities by visual observation is hardly likely to produce results which would be duplicated exactly by other observers; to do this requires that the criteria of attractiveness be specified exactly, and that precise measuring instruments be available.

Much information derived from questionnaires is based on a sample or sub-set of the total population. This was so for the political information in the imaginary case above. If a sample is used, the numerical information that results is only an estimate of the true value; the government popularity scores in Table 1.1 are estimates for each city based on samples of fifty people. A properly conducted sample survey is very likely to give results close to those which would have been derived from questioning the entire population (see Chapter 3). As sample surveys become more important as a source of geographical information on human conditions, the design of questionnaires is a matter of great importance.

Human geography, and indeed the social sciences at large, have very few instruments which compare with those in the physical sciences. There are no equivalents of the thermometer or barometer. The most exact kind of measurement is probably that of location itself, where position in geographical space (grid reference) is established by very sensitive physical survey instruments. The development of the 'remote sensing' of human activity by the use of air photography, space satellites and so on represents an important recent innovation in the geographer's instrumentation. However, the nature of man is such that we can never expect to measure things like his happiness, self-esteem and attitudes as accurately as his height, weight, and location – and perhaps we will never wish to.

Description via Maps and Matrices

The orderly arrangement and display of a set of observations can be thought of as a *description* of a segment of reality. Man first put together his observations of the world as verbal descriptions. This reached a high form of art in early twentieth-century human geography, and in the work of such regional novelists as Arnold Bennett and D. H. Lawrence, who could evoke a feeling for place which no set of numbers could reproduce. Traditionally geographers have relied on the *map* as a means of description, with the points, lines and areas (regions) defining human activity readily depicted on a piece of paper. But with the growing interest in quantitative methods in the past two decades, greater emphasis is now being placed on numerical description, and the map is being replaced by the *matrix* as the human geographer's basic information system.

A matrix is simply a table, in which numerical information is inserted. Table 1.1 above shows observations on the five imaginary cities in matrix form. Although these facts could have been displayed on a map or maps by various kinds of symbols, the table of numbers is more precise and easier to read accurately. Arranging information in matrix form has the additional advantage that the data can be directly manipulated in various ways by the use of algebra, to give row and column totals, averages, and so on.

Any set of geographical observations which can be mapped can also be put in a matrix. The general form of a *geographical data matrix* is illustrated in Figure 1.2. Along the vertical axis are the units of observation – places, locations or areas – which may be thought of as numbered in sequence $1, 2, 3, \ldots, j, \ldots, n$, where j stands for any individual unit and n is the total number under consideration. These units might be cities, regions, counties, census enumeration districts, or locations identified by coordinates. Along the horizontal axis are the conditions on which observations are taken, numbered in the sequence $1, 2, 3, \ldots, i, \ldots, m$, where there are m conditions any of which can be represented symbolically by i. They may also be referred to as *variables* or *attributes*,

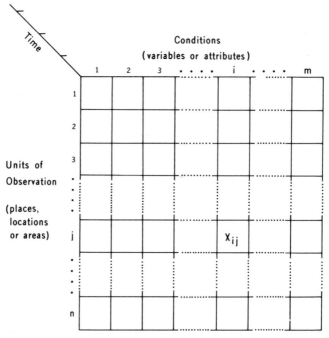

Figure 1.2   The geographical data matrix.

and could be anything from number of pigs kept to quality of life. The term attribute is sometimes reserved for conditions measured on a nominal scale, so the presence of a university would be an attribute, while number of industrial workers is a variable. Some conditions may be geographical *constants* rather than variables, if they occur to the same extent in all units of observation.

Each square, or *cell*, in the matrix will be occupied by a number. Thus the content of cell *ij* will represent the incidence of condition *i* in place *j*, which may be expressed by the symbol X_{ij}. This can indicate the presence or absence of an attribute measured on a nominal scale, the rank of a unit of observation if ordinal measurement is used, or the magnitude of the observation on a variable using an interval or ratio scale. The skill of measurement involves putting the best or most accurate numbers in the matrix.

The geographical data matrix can contain all the 'relevant'

24

information on a given part of the world. A column of numbers represents a single distribution pattern, or how the incidence of a particular condition varies between areas or locations. A row indicates the character of a particular place – perhaps its employment structure or its demographic profile. A third dimension can be added to represent the situation at different points in time. The data in the matrix could of course represent changes over time rather than actual magnitudes observed.

Any geographical pattern, be it one of points, lines, or areas, may be depicted as a matrix (Figure 1.3). In Figure 1.3a five settlements identified on a map by points in geographical space are differentiated by symbols representing the presence of three features. This is readily transformed into an *attribute matrix* in which 1 indicates the presence of any feature and 0 indicates its absence. Figure 1.3b shows lines of communication connecting the same five settlements. This may be transformed into a *connectivity matrix* with locations on both axes, where 1 indicates a direct road link and 0 indicates no direct road. Figure 1.3c shows the territory under study divided up into administrative areas for the purpose of compiling production data, and four overlapping regions of agricultural specialization are superimposed. The numerals 1 and 0 in the *areal classification matrix* indicate whether or not a given area lies in a given region.

In each of these three cases the matrix version uses a nominal scale of measurement. This need not necessarily be so, however, if additional data are available. In the first case, observations on the level of production of the factory, the number of children in school, and the number of villains in prison would enable a ratio scale to be used. The same would be true in the second case if there were data on volume of goods moved or people travelling along the roads. And in the third case each cell in the matrix could contain a measure of the output of the product in question.

Looking at geographical patterns in matrix form helps to focus attention on three important practical problems arising in any investigation. These are how the conditions to be observed are selected (the horizontal axis), how the study area is to be subdivided (the vertical axis), and what units of measurement should

Patterns in Human Geography

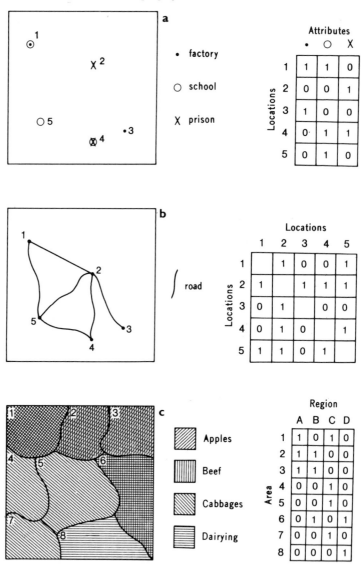

Figure 1.3 Transforming different geographical patterns into matrices.

be used (the content of the cells). Each of these problems may be discussed briefly.

The Choice of Variables and the Classification of Phenomena

The conditions or variables to be included will be determined primarily by the nature of the research problem. The scope may be wide or narrow, ranging from perhaps a hundred demographic and socio-economic variables, if a fairly comprehensive picture of the human geography is required, to a single attribute like the presence of a university in a more narrowly focused investigation.

Compiling data in matrix form involves *classification*. Individual observations, whether they be factories or fields of corn, births or incidences of crime, must be allocated to classes on the basis of common properties. There are two ways of classifying: subdividing a population or grouping individuals. In both cases the classification will be hierarchical in nature, with many minor classes capable of amalgamation into larger and more general classes. This is illustrated in Figure 1.4, where an imaginary population is classified in two different ways. Once individuals are given the two attributes of colour (Black, Brown or White) and residences (Urban or Rural), they can be allocated into more general classes on the basis of either of them.

The essentials of a well-designed hierarchical classification may be exemplified by the Standard Industrial Classification (SIC) used by the Bureau of the Census in the USA. All industrial establishments are classified according to the type of activity in which they are engaged, and are allocated to a specific category or industry. These are defined by a group of related products which are usually made from similar materials and by similar processes. In the SIC applied in the *Census of Manufacturing 1967*, manufacturing industry is divided into twenty-one 'Major Industry Groups', each with a two-digit code number from 19 through 39. The Major Groups are divided into 'Industry Groups' with a three-digit code number of which there are 150 in all, and these are themselves subdivided into 422 'Industries' with four-digit

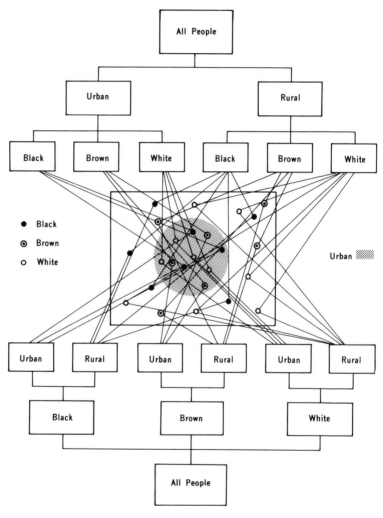

Figure 1.4   Two different classifications of an imaginary set of people, based on the properties of colour and area of residence.

codes. Thus Major Group 20 (food and kindred products) has its first Industry Group designated by the three digits 201 (meat products), which has as its first Industry code 2011 (meat packing plants). At the four-digit level some industries are further subdivided into 'Product Classes' with a five-digit code (beef not canned or made into sausage is 20111), and then into 'Products'. Thus there are six levels in the hierarchy, or seven counting the individual plants or units of observation.

The number assigned to any industry enables it to be quickly related to the larger groups to which it belongs. If a particular range of activities is the subject of an investigation, individual categories from any or all levels of the hierarchy can be combined, the only constraint being that categories at the lowest or most detailed level obviously cannot be split up. The more detailed the classification at its lowest level, the more flexibility it provides in building up exact definitions of groups of activities which may have to be identified for some research purpose.

There are two main problems arising from the use of this kind of 'standard' classification. The first is that it may change over time, as it is refined in the light of experience or changing circumstances. For example the use of artificial fibres in textile mills formerly concerned exclusively with cotton now makes it unrealistic to talk of 'the cotton industry', a change recognized in the 1958 revision of the British Standard Industrial Classification by the amalgamation of the cotton and man-made fibres categories. Such changes can make year to year comparisons impossible. It is important to know the details and history of a classification system, for otherwise it is easy to make erroneous comparisons over time.

The second problem arises if international comparisons are being made, for different countries may use different standard classifications. The British SIC, for example, is quite different from that used in the United States, having only fourteen major manufacturing categories and only one complete further level of subdivision. The major groups are known as 'Orders' and have a Roman numeral code from III to XVI, while the subdivisions, or 'Minimum List Headings', have three-digit codes in Arabic numerals which bear no relation to the Roman codes of the Orders to which they belong. Thus Minimum List Heading 211 (grain milling) is the first subdivision of Order III (food, drink and tobacco). If a comparison is sought between the food industries in the United States and Britain, either tobacco must be subtracted from British Order III or the USA Major Industry Groups 20 (food and kindred products) and 21 (tobacco manufacture) must be combined. Even then there is no guarantee that individual establishments will have been allocated according to identical criteria in both countries. Similarity of description is no guide to the criteria used; for example the British Order IV ('chemicals and allied industries') includes petroleum refineries, but the USA Group 28 ('chemicals and allied products') does not. The adoption of a single standard classificatory system throughout the world would clearly be a great advantage.

While in some fields of inquiry, such as industrial geography, description can sensibly proceed from a given classification, in others the establishment of a classification may still be a research objective. Only when knowledge of different phenomena reveals common properties or mutual associations can they be allocated to the same class, and this requires careful observation and measurement. Classification and understanding are closely inter-twined; some understanding of properties and relationships within a set of phenomena is needed before classification can be attempted, and classification should itself advance such under-standing.

The Geographical Units of Observation

All geographical information on human existence is built up from individual observations – the household census return, a response to an attitudinal survey, a consignment of freight, a crime recorded, and so on. Usually, the occurrences are aggregated for particular geographical units or territories, and these totals or some appropriate ratios then become the data with which the geographer works. Very often there is no choice but to use given aggregate areal data, because records of the individual observations are not available. This is true of census returns and other sources of 'official' data on which a large proportion of human geographical analysis is based. Data of this kind are often published for different levels of aggregation, however, and the level at which to work can be chosen in accordance with the objectives of the investigation and the detail required.

Areal classifications used in official data collection and publication generally follow a hierarchical structure similar to that used in the classification of phenomena. Geographical space is broken down into successive levels of smaller areas, or conversely individual observations or sets of observations are amalgamated for successively larger areas. In the United States, for example, census data on a wide range of social and demographic conditions may be available at as many as eight different levels: (1) the nation as a whole, (2) four major regions, (3) nine geographical divisions, (4) fifty states, and (5) over 3,000 counties; then counties with urban areas are further subdivided into (6) census tracts, (7) enumeration districts and (8) blocks (Figure 1.5). In addition to the choice of level of aggregation offered, such a system enables a researcher to build up his or her own geographical units from any number of smaller ones which may be selected. Thus economic regions can be constructed from groups of counties, and urban community areas can be formed from groups of blocks or enumeration districts.

A major shortcoming of administrative areas as units of observation is that they vary considerably in size and shape. The counties, parishes and other civil divisions of Britain are an obvious case in point. In the United States, the western states and counties are much larger than in New England, and American counties can vary in shape from perfectly square in northern Texas to extremely long and narrow in parts of the Appalachians. This affects geographical description, for a large area may have a large occurrence of some condition simply because of its size or because of the way the boundary is drawn. A group of small or narrow areas may give an exaggerated impression of inter-area movement (e.g. journey-to-work patterns) simply because so many boundaries are

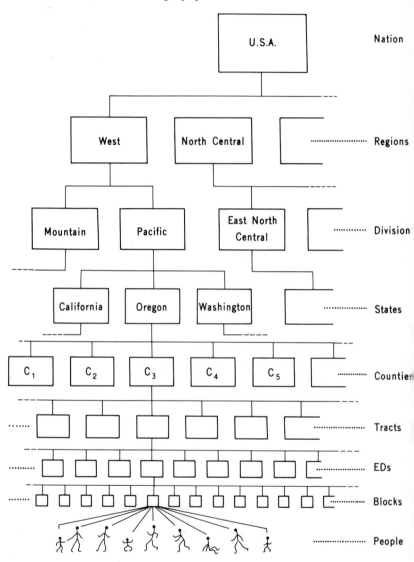

Figure 1.5   A portion of the hierarchical areal subdivision of the USA
used for aggregating census data.

32

crossed. There are also technical problems in the analysis of numerical data compiled for geographical areas, for measures of areal distribution are sensitive to the size of the units of observation and can give different results at different levels of aggregation.

Few of the systems of areal classifications used for compiling official figures on social or economic affairs have been designed specifically for this purpose. Generally they follow some established system used for the organization of local government. Such areas may have no social or economic significance, and their boundaries may have been laid down well before human activity assumed its present spatial form. Sensible definitions of relevant study areas can thus be difficult if official data sources have to be used. One way out of this problem is for the investigator to collect his own information, and aggregate individual observations according to whatever areal classification seems most appropriate, though this can be extremely laborious and time-consuming.

The only really satisfactory solution to this problem is for official data to be compiled so as to give research workers much more freedom to organize information according to their own choice of areal units. The ideal arrangement would be for all demographic, social and economic data to be recorded and stored by individual observations, each with a grid reference to identify location. Computers could very quickly aggregate such figures for any specified area or areas. A satisfactory alternative would be to compile information for very small areas of regular size and shape, which could in their turn be amalgamated into close approximations of any larger area for which information is needed. In a number of countries numerical data are already being compiled and made available for relatively small grid squares, or 'quadrats'. In Germany the Land government of Hamburg conducted its census on this basis in 1961, Sweden is collecting data on the basis of a new system of land registration which gives every parcel of land in the country a grid reference correct to ten metres, and in Britain figures from the 1971 census are compiled for hundred-metre squares based on the national grid. Similar systems are in operation in cities in both Europe and North America, as a means of organizing data for use in urban planning. These new methods of compiling and storing information in 'data banks', incorporated into a modern computer system, can go a long way towards solving the problem of unsuitable geographical units.

The Measurement Criteria

Having set up or accepted some classificatory system and an area subdivision, how is the relative magnitude of specific conditions to be measured? Using industrial activity as an example again, the various alternatives include number of persons employed, value of output, capital invested, and number of plants. Accurate information may be available for all of these, but each may give different results. For example, in Table 1.2 the industrial 'significance' of certain parts of the world is measured by two commonly-used criteria. Value added in the process of manufacture (i.e. the contribution of capital and labour) has North America as the clear leader with over a third of world industry, and also under-

Table 1.2: Shares of World Industry Measured by Two Different Criteria

Area	Value Added		Labour Employed	
	billion $	%	millions	%
North America	225	34·8	26	10·4
Western Europe	175	27·1	57	22·9
Eastern Europe and USSR	150	23·2	51	20·3
South East Asia	50	7·7	83	33·1
Latin America	23	3·6	17	6·9
Middle East and North Africa	9	1·4	6	2·3
Sub-Saharan Africa	7	1·1	8	3·1
Oceania	7	1·1	3	1·0
World Total	646	100·0	251	100·0

Source: Based on L. A. Hoffman; *Economic Geography*, Ronald Press, New York, 1965, 332–3.

lines the importance of Europe and the USSR. But the employment of labour places North America in fourth place and South East Asia first. North America, Europe and the USSR account for 85 per cent of the world's industry by value added, but only a little more than half by labour employed. These differences arise from the greater labour intensity of manufacturing in the less developed parts of the world.

In the United States the *Census of Manufacturing* provides a choice of nine measures of industry. These are the total number of establishments, establishments with twenty or more employees, total number of employees, total payroll, total number of production workers, man-hours worked by production workers, wages of production workers, value added by manufacture, and value of new capital expenditures. In Table 1.3 four of these have been used to calculate the percentage distribution of manufacturing by regions. They give the same general impression of where industry is concentrated, but there are some differences; for example, the order of the two leading regions (Middle Atlantic and East North Central) is reversed when number of establishments and total

Table 1.3: The Percentage Distribution of Manufacturing in the United States as Measured by Different Criteria

Region	Number of Establish- ments	Total Employ- ment	Value Added	New Capital Expenditure
New England	7·9	8·5	7·0	5·6
Middle Atlantic	26·2	23·5	22·7	18·3
East North Central	22·2	26·3	29·3	28·3
West North Central	6·6	6·0	6·1	5·8
South Atlantic	11·4	12·7	11·0	13·8
East South Central	4·6	5·4	4·9	6·6
West South Central	6·5	5·2	5·7	8·1
Mountain	2·7	1·7	1·8	2·2
Pacific	11·9	10·7	11·5	11·3
USA	100·0	100·0	100·0	100·0

Source: United States *Census of Manufacturing,* 1963.

employees are compared, and the dominance of the latter over the former is greatest under new capital expenditure.

Industry is fairly easily measured, for numbers employed and value of production can be readily counted. The same is true of demographic features such as number of people, births, marriages and deaths. But many other aspects of human existence are much more difficult to measure, for little if any reliable geographical information exists in numerical form; examples would be such abstractions as the quality of life, happiness and freedom. Here it is not a question of which of a number of existing measures to use, but how to define a concept and then design some appropriate measuring device or instrument. In such cases the theoretical context of the investigation is the logical generator of claisification and measurement decisions, and it is to this that the discussion must now turn.

The Research Context

When a matrix of data is compiled, with a suitable areal sub-division, classification of phenomena, and system of measurement, we have a geographical description. Each observation or number – the content of each cell – is a geographical fact. These facts may be of interest for their own sake, satisfying curiosity about our fellow men and women and the world they inhabit. But compiling geographical facts is seldom an end in itself; it is simply one step in the direction of increasing our understanding of the nature of human existence. It is but one part of a process of research which helps to build a systematic body of knowledge of how man arranges his activities on the surface of the earth – knowledge which not only explains things but also enables us to take action to improve the quality of life.

Geographers, like other scientists, follow various routes to explanation and understanding. Some may begin with the collection of facts on a concept or aspect of life which arouses curiosity, then seek empirical or observed relationships which might be expressed as laws, and finally attempt to put these together with other laws to form theory. For example, data might be collected on the location of crime committed in a certain city, this might be compared with the occurrence of other conditions, and the repeated observation of a close association between crime and social problems like poverty, alienation and racial discrimination might lead to a 'theory' of the geographical incidence of crime. Such findings might not constitute a theory in the sense in which this term is used in the physical sciences, but probably represent the highest form of generalization to which the social scientist can aspire. Others begin with some kind of theory, use it to generate hypotheses or possible explanations for geographical patterns, and then test these against observations of the real world. For example, spatial economic theory may lead to the expectation of a certain geographical pattern of industrial activity, observations are taken on the actual pattern, and a comparison between the two either confirms the validity of the theory or suggests some modification.

The research design, and its conceptual or theoretical framework, determines the kind of information required. This gives the scientist an alternative to the random collection of facts about everything and anything, and a basis for selection from the masses of numerical data made available by government agencies and others. It is society's need for *useful* knowledge – knowledge that can be applied in improving the human condition – that generates criteria of relevance for the selection of the research topic.

Two actual geographical problems may be described briefly, to show how the need for particular numerical information arises. This will place the various aspects of observation and measurement raised earlier in this chapter in a specific research context, and reveal some of the practical difficulties that must be faced.

The first problem is that of finding the best place to build a new factory. Industrial location theory tells us that if the anticipated revenue is the same everywhere (i.e. it is a geographical constant), the best place will be where the total cost of producing a given output in a given period of time is minimized. Total cost is the sum of the costs of the required quantities of all the 'inputs' (capital, labour, materials, etc.) required in the production process. This may be expressed as a simple equation as follows:

$$TC_j = \sum_{i=1}^{m} q_i U_{ij}$$

where TC_j is total cost at a location j ($j = 1, 2, \ldots, n$),

$\quad q_i$ is the required quantity of an input i, assumed to be the same at any location,

$\quad U_{ij}$ is the unit cost of input i at location j,

and $\displaystyle\sum_{i=1}^{m}$ means add up the result of the expression $q_i U_{ij}$ for all inputs in the series $1, \ldots, i, \ldots, m$, where m is the number of inputs involved. (Σ, i.e. the Greek capital letter sigma, is the conventional symbol for summation.)

The expression above is, in fact, a symbolic representation of how total cost comes to vary between locations, under simplified circumstances in which much of the complexity of the real industrial world is assumed away for convenience. It is a specific statement of a segment of the theory from which it is derived, and, when coupled with a means of solution, can be regarded as a *mathematical model* of some spatial economic process. It embodies three essential ingredients of any such model – variables, parameters and relational statements. The *variables* in this case are the unit input costs (U), which vary between locations in accordance with their availability, or supply and demand. The *parameters* are numerical constants, namely the quantities (q) of inputs needed as determined by production techniques which are assumed to be the same everywhere. The *relational statements* are simply the operations such as addition and multiplication which express the way in which the variables and parameters are connected.

The best location will of course be where TC_j is minimized. The form of geographical matrix required to solve this problem is indicated by the model. There will be n rows where n is the number of possible locations or those which some initial investigation has shown to be worth considering, and there will be m columns where m is the number of input classes determined to be relevant to the problem. The cells of the matrix will be filled by the unit costs measured in monetary terms. A second matrix will be needed for the required quantities, or 'input coefficients'. This will have the same number of rows and columns as the first one, but as the coefficients are in this case assumed to be spatial constants one row of figures is sufficient. When the data have been compiled, the one matrix is multiplied by the other, the results are summed by rows, and the locational row with the lowest total is the best place to build the factory.

Table 1.4 provides an example of spatial data matrices used in this manner. It is required to evaluate the relative merits of three regions in the USA as possible locations for the production of aluminium, with four major inputs needed. The first matrix tabulates the cost of each input in each region, the second (a single row) contains the input coefficients in the appropriate units

Table 1.4: Matrices of Numerical Data on the Manufacture of Aluminium in Three American Regions

Data	Region (j)	Inputs (i)			
		1 Alumina (tons)	2 Power (1000 kwh)	3 Labour (man-hours)	4 Carbon (cwt)
U_{ij} ($\$$)	1. Tennessee	48·50	4·90	1·35	1·95
	2. Texas	47·00	4·20	1·45	1·87
	3. Northwest	53·18	3·00	1·72	2·20
q_i (units)	all regions	2	18	16	10
q_iU_{ij} ($\$$)	1. Tennessee	97·00	88·20	21·60	19·50
	2. Texas	94·00	75·60	23·20	18·74
	3. Northwest	106·36	54·00	27·52	22·00
			TC		
$\sum_{i=1}^{4} q_iU_{ij}$	1. Tennessee		226·30		
	2. Texas		211·54		
	3. Northwest		209·88		

Source: data adapted from J. V. Krutilla, 'Location Factors Influencing Recent Aluminium Expansion', Southern Economic Journal, 21, 1955, 273–88.

Note: the input coefficient (q) relates to one ton of finished product.

per ton of output, the third is the product of the first two and shows the cost of the required quantity of the inputs, while the fourth (a single row) lists total input costs per ton for each region. The Northwest offers lowest production costs, by virtue of its cheap electric power.

The research problem generates the nature of the information required, but filling the matrix with accurate data may raise severe measurement difficulties. Although in the case of industrial input costs the units of measurement (money) are predetermined, the lack of effective instruments makes the compilation of comparative cost data a time-consuming and hazardous task. Even when some information may be available from official or industry sources (e.g. wage rates and material costs) they may not accurately reflect what a new firm would have to pay for the input in question. And some items which should be entered into the cost equation, for example the 'external economies' arising from location in an existing industrial agglomeration, are almost impossible to express in monetary terms. Data on the input coefficients may be difficult to obtain because of industrial secrecy. Thus in the field of industrial location analysis, where there are already well-developed theory and highly sophisticated models, the optimum solution of practical problems is often prevented by basic measurement deficiencies.

The second research problem is different from the one just considered, in that there is no adequate theory to start from. The task is that of identifying geographical variations in the 'quality of life', which involves translating a highly abstract concept into numerical terms. It is obviously very difficult to contemplate the direct measurement of the quality of life, social well-being, or welfare, for like most aspects of human existence they cannot be measured with a ruler or pair of scales. Yet placing individuals or groups on a quality-of-life scale by some appropriate measurement rule may seem a sensible objective. The nearest method to direct measurement is attitudinal research, but suitable survey instruments have yet to be perfected. The best alternative at present is to attempt to define the concept by certain properties, on which something approaching direct measurements can be obtained.

Quality of life means different things to different people. To some it may be largely reflected in the money they make and their material possessions, to some it may mean a healthy body and an educated mind, and to others it may come more from a feeling of belonging or identification with some group or cause. Once personal survival is assured, the quality of life is largely a matter of individual preference and perception, and there is no theory of society to say who is right or wrong. However, some attempt can be made to define the concept operationally, because there is at least some consensus on the necessary ingredients.

Suppose the quality of life could be adequately defined in terms of the following general conditions: (1) income and wealth, (2) the environment, (3) health, (4) education, (5) social order, (6) social belonging, and (7) recreation. This could be regarded as a first step in giving concrete identity to the initial abstract concept. But in order to measure each of these seven criteria they themselves would have to be defined, for none of them have a very precise meaning as they stand. The expression 'the environment' might be taken to cover the quality of the general physical environment (e.g. air and water), the built environment of the neighbourhood, and the immediate environment provided by the home. Each of these can then be subjected to measurement: for example, certain properties of housing on which data are obtainable for geographical areas from the census can stand for the quality of the home environment in a given territory. This process is illustrated in Figure 1.6. Once each of the major criteria has been defined and suitable variables identified, the required data matrix can be specified. The rows or areal subdivision will be determined by the scale of the investigation, e.g. whether the concern is with regions, cities or local communities. The columns or variables to be measured will represent the most relevant properties for which suitable data can be obtained. The units of measurement will vary, perhaps including monetary units under income, people under health, test scores under education, incidences of crime under social order, social integration indices under social belonging, and possibly areal units of park space under recreation.

The major difficulty in filling the matrix is maintaining what is sometimes termed the 'internal validity' of the concept, avoiding

41

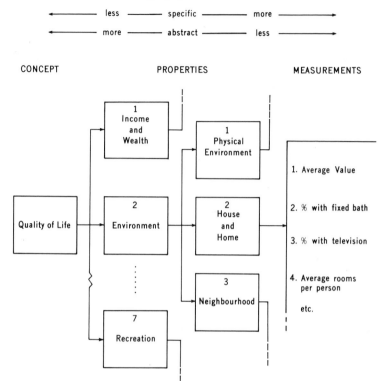

Figure 1.6   Stages in the translation of an abstract concept into operational terms.

distortion in the process of making it operational. Many of the final variables used may be imperfect substitutes, called 'surrogates' or 'proxies', for the actual properties which it is desired to measure. For example, the quality of the home environment is obviously not a direct reflection of its monetary value. Similarly levels of education in a city are not directly measured by public expenditures or pupil–teacher ratios – indices of input or effort which often have to be substituted for output or achievement.

Because of the problems of operational definition and measurement, society is often ill-informed about variations in the quality of life. Recent years have seen a growing interest in this question, however, with the gradual realization that the production and consumption of goods is not the be-all and end-all of human existence. In more advanced industrial nations the emphasis is shifting a little, from economic growth to social progress as the major national concern. To know whether progress is being made, or whether things are getting better or worse, requires the measurement of a wide range of conditions which impinge on the quality of life, and the development of some general 'social indicators' comparable with the economic indicators which we use as barometers of the economic climate. The design of suitable instruments to 'monitor' social climate or social health, by taking observations on the quality of individual or group existence and placing them on some scale, is one of the major research problems in the social sciences. To do this for groups of people defined by area of residence seems the ultimate challenge to the human geographer's descriptive skills, in our current era of preoccupation with 'social relevance'.

Some Concluding Remarks

The description of spatial patterns of human existence by converting observations into numerical data belongs to the contemporary quantitative approach to geography. (The only real difference between 'numerical' and 'quantitative' is that the latter, strictly speaking, applies to measurement on an ordinal, interval or ratio scale, so the two terms can be used virtually synonymously.) However, there is some confusion between numerical methods and quantitative geography on the one hand, and other contemporary approaches concerned with developing theory and building models on the other. The two are certainly not the same, and to assume that any work full of numbers and equations is necessarily theoretical is to bestow a status that may not be deserved.

The discussion in the previous section should have made some of the distinction clear. A *theory* can be thought of as a high-order intellectual structure within which the facts established by observation and measurement, and their relationships, are fitted together into some logically consistent body of knowledge. Theories give order and meaning to our experience of the world, or, as Harvey puts it in his book *Explanation in Geography*, they make the unexpected expected. A *model* may be any simplification or abstraction from reality, such as a classification, a statement of relationships, or even a physical replica like a relief model or a model railway. In social science it is something which physically or symbolically replicates part of man's world, in a way which can contribute to its comprehension. The simple mathematical statement of the industrial location problem described above is a particular kind of model: one which makes a theory specific, or the sort of thing that a theoretician offers when invited to 'put up or shut up' (Abraham Kaplan, *The Conduct of Inquiry*). All quantitative analysis takes place within the context of some kind of theory or model, explicit or otherwise, for this is what sets the measurement process in motion.

Another aspect of contemporary geography closely related to numerical or quantitative analysis is the use of statistics. Like the term model, *statistics* has a variety of meanings, one of which is its colloquial usage to refer to any numerical information (e.g. population 'statistics'). The term is used more strictly to refer to the science of drawing sound conclusions from limited observations, or the mathematical study of probability. There are two branches: *descriptive statistics* which is concerned with summarizing a set of numerical observations according to some rule, and *inferential statistics* which has to do with inferring relationships between sets of observations. Statistical methods are very important in the manipulation and analysis of numerical data in human geography, and are considered further in subsequent chapters. But all numerical analysis is not statistical in the strict sense.

This chapter has set the scene for the discussion of various methods which can be used to describe geographical patterns of human existence numerically. But before proceeding a word of warning is in order. There are very few devices in this field which are not subject to major technical constraints, regarding both the uses to which they can legitimately be put and the precision of the results which are obtained. Many of the difficulties arise from the nature of the subject matter and the problems of accurate measurement. In addition the arbitrary areal classifications often used to collect numerical data can impose an immediate restriction on the value of computations performed on the material, just as an arbitrarily chosen level of classifying phenomena imposes limitations on the usefulness of the results of any research based on it. All this adds weight to the obvious need to improve the nature of the data available to the student of human geography. If full advantage is to be taken of developments in new techniques of spatial analysis, it must be accompanied by increases in the range and quality of numerical data.

Quantitative methods have been very much in vogue in geography for more than a decade. In addition to their evident value as means of bringing greater precision to both description and interpretation, these techniques have in varying degrees the less desirable attribute of ease of abuse and misuse. The formulae, and the computer programmes designed to solve them, involve a purely mechanical manipulation of a set of numbers. The results obtained can be no more accurate than the information on which they are based, and no more meaningful than the research context in which they are employed. Computer scientists use the guiding acronym GIGO – 'Garbage In, Garbage Out' – and this can be applied to any research involving numerical manipulation. The chapters which follow review a range of techniques in use in human geography, with demonstrations of their application to actual research problems, and a recurrent theme is that they have to be used with very great care. It may well be that continuing experimentation will eventually lead to the discrediting of some of the methods discussed, as further limitations to their usefulness are revealed. Similarly, new ones will be devised, perhaps designed more with the particular needs of human geography in mind. Whatever the exact contents of this bag of tools at any one time, it is necessary to see them just as tools – as means of achieving specific objectives and not as ends in themselves. The important thing about any tools is not to have them out all the time but to know what they can do, when they may sensibly be used, when they need sharpening, and when they should be replaced.

45

2. Mapping Numerical Information

The most obvious way of describing a geographical pattern is to map it. A map can be thought of as a simple model of geographical reality, scaled down in size and with various properties represented symbolically. Once a matrix of numerical information has been compiled, it can be displayed cartographically in a variety of ways to provide a visual impression of the patterns which the data portray. Maps can also be used to display the results of calculations performed on an initial set of measurements, as subsequent chapters will show.

Maps still have a very important part to play in modern geographical research. Mapping numerical data can add information, by showing the relative location of the incidents which the numbers represent. For example, a line on a map representing a road between two places tells us more than the numeral 1 in a cell of a connectivity matrix, particularly if the road is not straight. A map can also illustrate spatial forms – the geometry of a transportation network, the regularity of a point pattern, or the concentration of large observations in a particular area.

But maps also have their shortcomings. Some information is lost when interval or ratio data are represented by symbols, and even location in geographical space may be more accurately depicted by a numerical grid reference than by a point on a map. Maps are also liable to subjective interpretations, so that two observers can easily come to different conclusions from examining the same pattern. For example, the simple question of whether a particular set of points is clustered, regular or random requires a more powerful tool than a map to answer objectively. Similarly, visual comparison between maps is an unreliable way of accurately determining the correspondence between different patterns.

Methods of Mapping Numbers

Numerical information can be depicted on maps by various kinds of symbols, lines, and patches of shading or colour. These correspond with the system of points, networks and differentiated areas which are the physical expressions of man's spatial existence. They have been introduced already in the first chapter, in the three imaginary patterns transformed into matrices in Figure 1.3.

The simplest kind of symbol is a dot. *Dot maps* can be used to portray data measured on a nominal scale: a place either has or has not a particular attribute, and a dot represents the 'has' condition or the numeral 1 in an attribute matrix. The same information can be depicted by any other kind of symbol, such as squares, triangles, or even simple artistic representations of real objects like an aeroplane to show the location of an airport. Dot maps can also be used for ratio data, each dot representing a given number of occurrences. The distribution of population and production is often portrayed in this manner, with one dot for, say, 1,000 people, 100 pigs or 10 acres under a particular crop. For example, Figure 2.1 depicts the location pattern of elastic web manufacturing in England, with each dot representing one factory. In the absence of data on employment or production, this method of mapping provides a satisfactory picture of the pattern, and reveals the regional concentration in the East Midlands.

If data relating to points (or areas) are available on ratio scale, symbols of different sizes can be used instead of dots. In these *proportional symbol maps*, squares, circles, bars or lines are drawn proportional in size to the magnitude of the occurrence. In the case of squares, the lengths of the sides should be proportional to the square root of the numbers they show, so that the areas covered by the symbols (the square of the length of the side) are proportional to the numbers depicted. Using circles, the radius (r) of the symbol is proportional to the square root of the number; the area of a circle is πr^2, π (Greek letter pi) being ignored because it is a constant which occurs in every single case being mapped. Examples of proportional symbol maps will be found below (Figures 2.3,

47

Figure 2.1 A dot map showing the location of elastic web manufacturers in England. (Source: D. M. Smith, 'The Location of Elastic Web Manufacturing in England and Wales', *East Midland Geographer*, December 1964.)

2.5 and 2.6). Sometimes representations of spheres or cubes are used, but this is not a very effective way of showing numbers cartographically because the volume of a symbol is difficult to judge visually. In some maps, the actual numbers are printed, but the visual impression of pattern is less effective than when proportional symbols are used.

Networks such as transportation and communication systems are easily portrayed on maps by lines. If it is required to show volume of movement such as goods shipped, people carried, or telephone calls made, the lines can be proportional in thickness to the quantities involved. An example of this type of *flow map* is provided by Figure 2.2, which shows bus traffic in Swaziland. Although the actual volume of movement cannot be judged with perfect accuracy from the scale on a map of this kind (i.e. some information is lost), the general geographical pattern and the relative importance of the major development corridor between Mbabane and Manzini is shown clearly.

Subdivisions of geographical space, such as economic regions or political units, can be shown by patches of contrasting shading or colour. The information depicted in this way will be on a nominal scale, as was shown in the agricultural regions example in Figure 1.3. Shading is also used to map information on a ratio or interval scale. In these *choropleth maps*, observations are allocated to classes defined by a certain range of values and different densities of shading are used to represent each class. If the map is drawn properly the density of shading is roughly proportional to the quantities being depicted, with heavy shading showing high values and light shading low ones or *vice versa*. Population density and rate of change is often mapped in this way, as are the results of various kinds of transformations into proportions, indices or other ratios.

A difficult decision in the use of choropleth maps is the number of classes and their intervals. This becomes a compromise between the desire to preserve as much information as possible (i.e. to use many classes), and the need to have the different levels of incidence clearly revealed by the shading (to use few classes). General opinion in cartographic circles is that no more than about ten

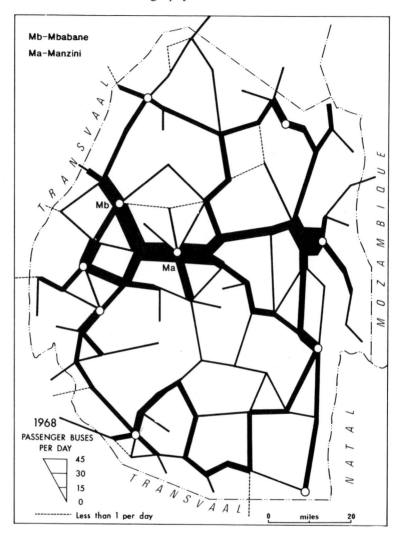

Figure 2.2   A flow map showing bus traffic in Swaziland. (Source:
T. J. D. Fair, G. Murdoch and H. M. Jones, *Development
in Swaziland: A Regional Analysis*, Witwatersrand
University Press, 1969.)

different grades of shading can be used effectively on the same map, and that the viewer has difficulty in distinguishing between more than seven or eight. The number of categories can be increased by the use of colour. Class intervals can be regular or varied, depending on the data. If possible, they should run between 'bunches' of similar values rather than through them. Drawing a frequency distribution of the values to be mapped (see next chapter) can help in determining appropriate classes.

There are important distinctions between density shading and proportional symbol maps, which are not always fully understood by those who depict numerical data cartographically. If some absolute quantity – such as number of people – is being shown, a circle or other proportional symbol should be used, even if the numbers refer to classes (e.g. 1,000–1,999, 2,000–2,999, and so on) rather than being on a continuous scale. To show population size by different densities of shading is misleading because a large area will show up more prominently than a small one with the same population simply by virtue of size of the area on the map. When choropleth mapping is used in a system of territories of unequal size, the variable depicted should be either a direct function of area, such as population per square mile, or completely independent of area like rate of population change.

An example of poor numerical mapping will help to clarify this. Each year *The Times* newspaper prints a map showing national wealth throughout the world measured by Gross Domestic Product. The European part of the map published in 1972 is as reproduced in Figure 2.3a, and this was accompanied by the information in Table 2.1. The map itself does not in fact depict wealth, but merely provides a key to the location of nations and their population size category. The use of density shading to show population size is obviously misleading; for example Russia (not all of which is included on the European map) has a large population by virtue of its area, and Denmark has a small population partly for the same reason. If European Russia was split up into smaller nations like Western Europe, each would have a relatively small population and that part of the map would be shaded lightly, while if Western Europe was one nation it would have a

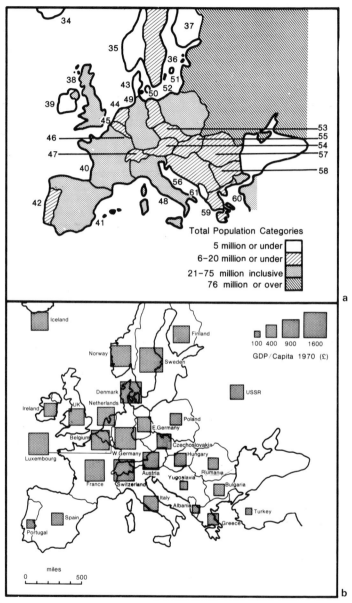

Total Population Categories

5 million or under
6-20 million or under
21-75 million inclusive
76 million or over

a

100 400 900 1600
GDP/Capita 1970 (£)

Iceland
Finland
Norway
Sweden
Denmark
USSR
UK
Netherlands
Ireland
Poland
E.Germany
Belgium
Czechoslovakia
Luxembourg
W.Germany
Hungary
Austria
Rumania
France
Switzerland
Yugoslavia
Bulgaria
Italy
Albania
Turkey
Spain
Greece
Portugal

miles
0   500

b

Figure 2.3   Two cartographic methods of depicting national wealth in
Europe, measured by Gross Domestic Product. (Source:
top map from *The Times*, 25 September 1972.)

very large population and would fall into the heaviest shading
category. Another problem with this map is that although it was
headed 'National Wealth', neither the shading nor the numbers
on it (a national identification code) refer to GDP.

A better method of mapping national wealth is illustrated in
Figure 2.3b. Here GDP is shown by proportional squares, which
put the stated subject matter on the map and have the additional
advantage of allowing each country to be named. This map could
be accompanied by a table of population figures, listed exactly and
not in the four categories used in the original presentation, if this
information is required. National wealth could have been shown
by density shading, but such a map would still be unsatisfactory
because large countries such as Russia would be represented by

*Table 2.1: National Wealth in Europe, Measured by Gross Domestic
Product per Capita (£) 1970*

Nation		GDP/capita	Nation		GDP/capita
34	Iceland	1004	48	Italy	758
35	Norway	1317	49	West Germany	1467
36	Sweden	1812	50	East Germany	667
37	Finland	917	51	USSR	596
38	United Kingdom	887	52	Poland	427
39	Ireland	539	53	Czechoslovakia	672
40	France	1314	54	Austria	897
41	Spain	432	55	Hungary	562
42	Portugal	285	56	Yugoslavia	259
43	Denmark	1393	57	Rumania	418
44	Netherlands	1080	58	Bulgaria	394
45	Belgium	1196	59	Greece	405
46	Luxembourg	1397	60	Turkey	169
47	Switzerland	1477	61	Albania	198

Source: *The Times*, 25 September 1972.

Note: The numbers before the nations are identifications relating to
Figure 2.3a.

patches of shading unrelated in area to the variable being mapped. The proportional squares preserve as much quantitative information as possible on the map without inserting the numbers themselves. But even these symbols are related to the political subdivisions, in both size and location, and different boundaries could produce a different pattern.

Variation in size of geographical units of observation seriously restricts the value of numerical mapping as a true representation of geographical pattern. Even maps using proportional symbols suffer to some extent, for areas may have large incidences partly because of size. But the problems are more severe with choropleth mapping, where the pattern of shading can be largely determined by the form of data collection units, which may be quite irrelevant to the conditions being measured. One way around this is to compile data for systems of regular grid squares or quadrats, as was mentioned in Chapter 1, and to map it on this basis. This method has been adopted occasionally to build up industrial employment figures from the individual plant returns of HM Factory Inspectorate, using the one-kilometre grid squares on Ordnance Survey maps as units of observation and summing the employment for plants in each square. The *Atlas of London and the London Region* published in 1968 contains a series of maps of land use and factory location in certain industries using 500-metre grid squares. An example of quadrat choropleth mapping of industrial data is provided by Figure 2.4, where employment in hosiery manufacturing in the East Midlands is depicted in much more detail and with greater clarity than could be achieved by the alternative of using census data compiled by local government areas. The main problem with this method is the time required to compile data on this basis, compared with the ease with which figures for local government areas can be extracted from the census.

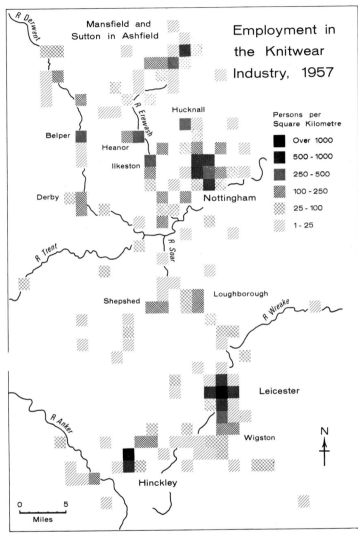

Figure 2.4   An example of quadrat choropleth mapping: employment
in hosiery manufacturing in the East Midlands. Figures for
individual plants have been aggregated for quadrats of
four square kilometres. (Source of data: HM Factory
Inspectorate, District Registers.)

Mapping Multiple and Continuous Variables

The cases of numerical mapping illustrated so far all involve only one variable. And their occurrences are discrete, in the sense that they apply to a limited number of points or areas separated by distance or boundary lines. To portray the content of a data matrix with two or more attributes or where there is an infinite number of possible occurrences is simple enough if nominal data are involved, for different symbols can be placed anywhere and superimposed if necessary (as in Fig 1.3). But if the data are measured on a ratio or interval scale some new technique will be needed.

The difficulties that arose in the mapping of national wealth by *The Times* occurred partly because it was required to say something about two conditions – GDP and population. In the original (Fig 2.3a) population was mapped and GDP tabulated, while in the proposed alternative (Fig 2.3b) GDP is mapped and population would have to be tabulated. But there is a way of showing them both together, using symbols drawn in proportion to the nation's population and shaded according to the level of GDP per capita (Fig 2.5). This method has the advantage of portraying the condition of national wealth both absolutely and on a per capita basis. In the case of two circles with the same shading the larger circle represents more absolute wealth, while in two circles of the same size the heavier shading shows more per capita wealth. Some information is lost by grouping GDP levels into classes and the use of shaded circles requires considerable drafting skill if they are to be easily read, but every map has its limitations as a representation of reality.

To map a matrix of data with more than two variables requires yet other techniques. Two that are frequently used are *bar graphs* with bars representing a different variable, and *divided circles* (sometimes called 'pie diagrams') in which the size of the segments represents the magnitude of different conditions. Examples are provided in Figure 2.6, which shows the cost of three fuels used in the production of electricity in the USA, and their relative contributions to the total output. The top map shows cost per million BTU generated, with the height of the bars representing cents. The bottom map shows the proportion of total production of electricity accounted for by each of the fuels, by segments of circles of the same size. Although such maps are not always easily read, those illustrated do show the general correspondence between relatively low cost of a particular fuel and relatively high share of total production.

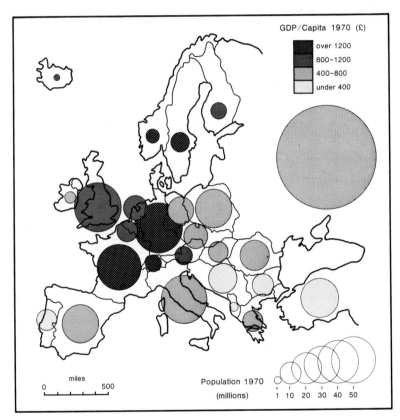

Figure 2.5   Mapping two variables simultaneously: another solution to *The Times* national wealth and population problem in Figure 2.3a.

57

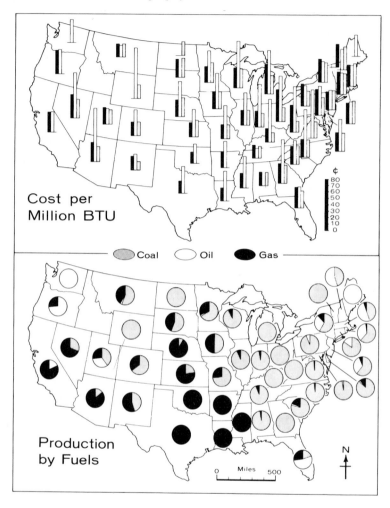

Figure 2.6   Mapping a data matrix with multiple variables by bar and
pie diagrams: the cost and contribution of three fuels in
the United States steam-driven electricity generating
industry. (Source of data: National Coal Association,
Bituminous Coal Facts, 1968.)

Another method of portraying a geographical data matrix with a number of columns is by using a sequence of maps. This is particularly appropriate if the variables are the incidences of the same condition at different points in time. Figure 2.7 shows four stages in the evolution of the location pattern of the hosiery industry in the East Midlands (previously illustrated in the quadrat map, Fig 2.4). The geographical limits of the old 'framework knitting' district under the domestic industry are shown, and the maps indicate the gradual spread of the industry into most parts of this district under the factory system of production initiated in the middle of the nineteenth century.

Construction of a choropleth map showing more than one variable is hazardous, and the outcome can often be confusing when different kinds of shading are superimposed on one another. An exception is in cases where the variables can be regarded as additive, i.e. where the incidence of each condition might reasonably be summed. As an example, mortality rates from the three leading causes of death are mapped in Figure 2.8, for an eighteen-tract area in an American city. Individual choropleth maps have been drawn, and then superimposed to focus attention on the areas of high mortality. Map overlays of this kind have been used with great effect by the landscape architect McHarg in his book *Design with Nature*, to portray the geographical coincidence of social problems and constraints on physical development. However, it may be preferable to combine data on a number of conditions in a composite numerical index of health, social well-being or development potential before mapping, a possibility explored further in Chapter 5.

The examples so far have all portrayed patterns either as discrete distribution represented by symbols or as a series of 'steps' coinciding with breaks between different shading categories. But some patterns in human geography can be regarded as continuous three-dimensional surfaces, similar to the surface of the earth, temperature or rainfall. In such cases *isopleth maps* may be used. These involve the interpolation of lines joining places with the same value on the variable in question (like contours on a relief map) from a number of discrete incidences at 'control points'

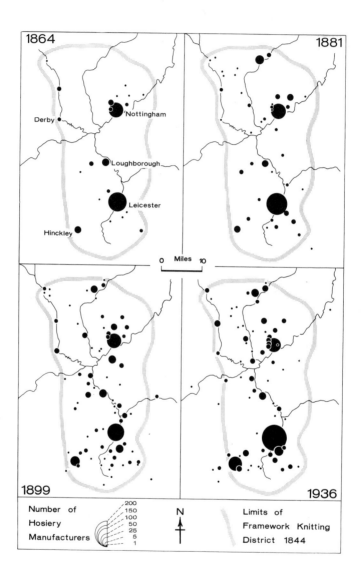

Figure 2.7   Mapping time-sequence data: changes in the distribution
              pattern of the hosiery industry in the East Midlands, 1864
              to 1936. (Source: D. M. Smith, 'The Location of the British
              Hosiery Industry since the Middle of the Nineteenth
              Century', *Geographical Essays in Honour of K. C.
              Edwards*, Department of Geography, University of
              Nottingham, 1970.)

which can be considered a sample of an infinite number of possible points.

Drawing an isopleth map requires considerable skill. A sensible choice of 'contour' interval must be made with reference to the number of control points. Generally the fewer control points the fewer isopleth levels will be justified, because interpolating many isopleths from data for very few points will obviously give a largely spurious impression of accuracy. Some rules of thumb exist for the correct number of classes in a frequency distribution (see Chapter 3), and these could be followed in both isopleth and choropleth mapping. The process of interpolating isopleths once the interval has been determined involves making an assumption that the magnitude of the variable changes regularly with distance between control points.

Some conditions in economic geography can be drawn as three-dimensional surfaces; at any point in the geographical space there is some possible value for such variables as cost, revenue and profit. In Figure 2.9 an urban land-cost surface has been inter-polated from data for a number of representative locations within a German city, as an example of a map of 'cost topography'. The concept of areal distribution as three-dimensional surfaces is very important in human geography, and is dealt with in detail in Chapter 7.

Mapping by Computer

Recent advances in computer technology have led to the develop-ment of what is sometimes referred to as 'automated cartography'. When programmed in a certain way and fed with geographical

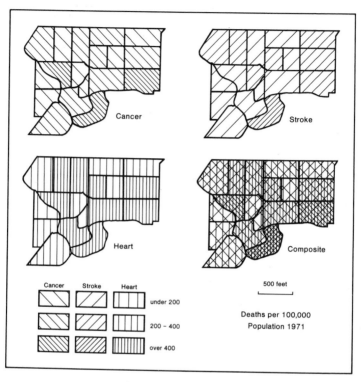

Figure 2.8   The composite mapping of variables by an overlay
technique: death rates from the three leading causes in
part of central Tampa, Florida. (Source of data:
Hillsborough County Health Department.)

information, computers can draw maps. The advantage of computer maps over conventional hand-drawn maps is their accuracy
and speed of production; their main disadvantage is that computers are not very good artists, though their skills are rapidly
improving. The range of computer cartography and graphics is
now quite considerable, and only a sample of applications can be
considered here.

The best known and most frequently used method of computer

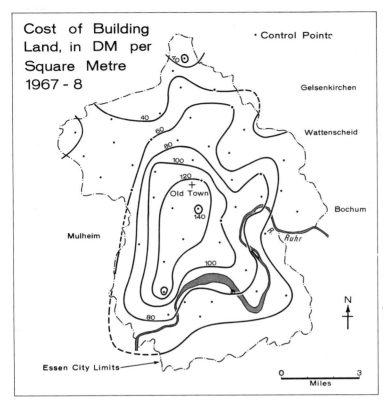

Figure 2.9   Depicting a geographical pattern as a three-dimensional
surface by isopleths: land costs in Essen, West Germany.
(Source of data: City of Essen, 1968.)

mapping is the SYMAP system developed at Harvard University.
It produces shaded maps by printing or overprinting different
alphabetical or numerical characters to produce the required
density. The most common application is an isopleth-choropleth
combination, with isopleths interpolated from discrete data and
the different levels or classes shaded according to their values. The
result resembles a relief map with successively heavier shading for
higher land.

63

In order to produce a computer map, certain information or 'input' is required. The outline of the area to be mapped must be specified by grid coordinates, and the location of control points is determined in the same way. Then the computer needs the numerical values of the observation at each control point. Also required is information on where and how to write a title, the north point, scale and so on, and instructions concerning the desired number of isopleths and their intervals. When all this information is fed to the computer in the correct form, along with the program required to interpolate isopleths and produce the map, the desired 'output' is generated on a printer.

In Figure 2.10 the land-cost surface for Essen shown in Figure 2.9 has been redrawn by computer. Whereas the human cartographer chose regular isopleth intervals (40, 60, 80, etc.) the computer simply took the range of the data (39·00 to 140·00) and split it into an instructed number (five) of classes of equal size (39·00–59·20, 59·30–79·40, etc.). The class limits become the isopleth values on the computer map. Despite these differences, the patterns shown on the two maps are similar. The main departures occur round the edges, for the computer interpolates from the values of points within a certain 'search radius', and at the edge there may be few points. The cartographer can use his judgement in such cases, but the computer cannot.

In addition to the map, the SYMAP computer output contains some useful information about the conditions under study (Fig 2.10). First, certain comments about the subject matter can be printed, for example details of the source of data. Then the class limits are specified, followed by a frequency distribution diagram showing the number of observations in each class. The original data and control point coordinates will also be printed out, though they are not reproduced here. Each control point is identified on the map by a numeral indicating the class to which it has been allocated.

Figure 2.10   A computer-generated isopleth map of land costs in Essen, produced by the SYMAP system developed at Harvard University. (Source of data: see Figure 2.9; map executed by Randall Bunting.)

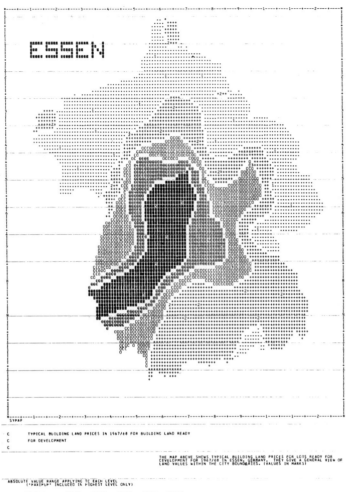

SYMAP

C   TYPICAL BUILDING LAND PRICES IN 1967/68 FOR BUILDING LAND READY
C   FOR DEVELOPMENT
C

THE MAP ABOVE SHOWS TYPICAL BUILDING LAND PRICES FOR LOTS READY FOR
DEVELOPMENT FOR 1967/68 IN ESSEN, GERMANY. THEY GIVE A GENERAL VIEW OF
LAND VALUES WITHIN THE CITY BOUNDARIES. (VALUES IN MARKS)

ABSOLUTE VALUE RANGE APPLYING TO EACH LEVEL
     ('MAXIMUM' INCLUDED IN HIGHEST LEVEL ONLY)

MINIMUM	79.00	59.20	79.40	99.60	119.80
MAXIMUM	59.20	79.40	99.60	119.80	140.00

PERCENTAGE OF TOTAL ABSOLUTE VALUE RANGE APPLYING TO EACH LEVEL

	20.00	20.00	20.00	20.00	20.00

FREQUENCY DISTRIBUTION OF DATA POINT VALUES IN EACH LEVEL

LEVEL	1	2	3	4	5
SYMBOLS					

FREQUENCY

65

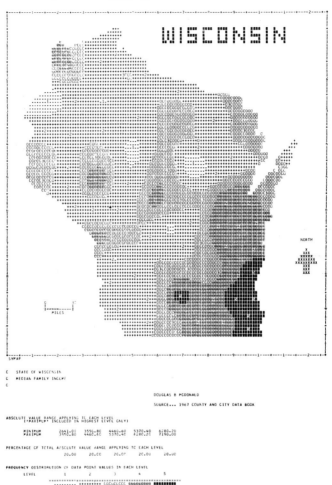

Another example is shown in Figure 2.11, where median family income is mapped by counties for the state of Wisconsin in the USA. The gradual reduction away from the relatively high-income Milwaukee area in the south-east shows up clearly. This map differs from Figure 2.10 in one technical respect – the isopleths appearing as white lines on the map of Essen have been suppressed here. The programme also allows the isopleths to be printed black if desired. Various other options within the basic SYMAP package give the user great flexibility in designing maps to special requirements.

Many other types of maps can be produced by computer. One of the most useful is the conventional choropleth map on which areal units of observation are shaded in different densities. Computer mapping systems can also print proportional symbols like squares or cubes. The 'digital plotter', when used in association with a computer, is also a very versatile cartographic instrument, capable of drawing three-dimensional representations of surfaces as well as shading and symbol maps. The plotter works with a pen which draws to an accuracy of one-hundredth of an inch, and can produce maps quite as attractive aesthetically as those of a human cartographer. The capacity to change inks means that a digital plotter can produce multi-coloured maps and diagrams.

An example of a three-dimensional representation drawn by a computer plotter is shown in Figure 2.12. The pattern is that of Gross Domestic Product per capita in the Republic of South Africa. Values have been derived for about fifty areal subdivisions, and the plotter has drawn the surface in such a way that areas with high GDP appear elevated in proportion to their scores on this variable. The Witwatersrand conurbation centred on Johannesburg stands out as the major peak, for more than three quarters of the national wealth is generated there. Lesser peaks correspond with the coastal cities of Cape Town on the left and Durban on the right. The SYMVU system which produced this figure is

Figure 2.11   A computer-generated map of median income by counties in Wisconsin, using the SYMAP system. (Source of data: *Census of Population*, 1960; map executed by Douglas McDonald.)

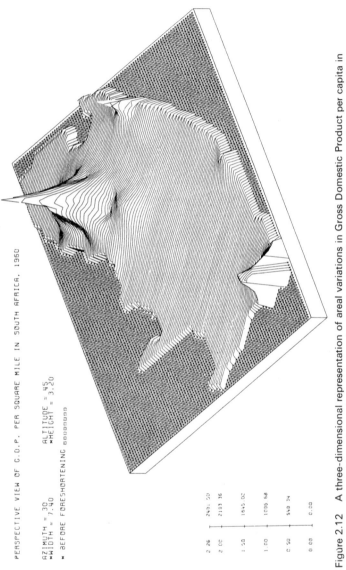

Figure 2.12   A three-dimensional representation of areal variations in Gross Domestic Product per capita in South Africa, drawn by computer plotter using the SYMVU system. (Source: Courtesy of John Browett and the Urban and Regional Research Unit, University of the Witwatersrand.)

versatile enough to allow the user to specify both the direction and angle of view as well as the vertical scale. It is but one of a number of similar computer graphic methods of three-dimensional data display now available to the geographer.

The main practical limitation on the use of computers and plotters for displaying numerical information is financial. The initial programming and data preparation, and the required computer time, make single maps expensive to produce. The methods illustrated here would normally be used only if a sequence of maps of different conditions for the same set of areas is required, as in the case of an atlas. A number of experimental local atlases of computer-generated maps have appeared in recent years (see Selected Reading at the end of the book).

Distance and Areal Scale Transformation

Any map can be thought of as a *projection* of part of a sphere on to a flat piece of paper. Some information is lost in the process of transformation from three dimensions of measurement to two, but gain comes from the fact that a map is easier to use than a globe. There are four important properties which map projections attempt to preserve: relative distance, direction, area and shape. At least one of these is sacrificed in any map, though for small areas this loss is not significant. The choice of projection is dependent on the purpose of the map, and the properties required to portray its information correctly. For example, an equal-area projection would be required to show areas under different crops at a world or national level, while to show linear distances between places an equidistant projection would be preferred.

Choice of an unsuitable projection can mislead, by distorting one or more of the properties relevant to the subject matter of the map. For example, the Mercator projection greatly exaggerates both distance and area towards the poles, in order to preserve direction. Its use to convey the subdivision of the world into political units is improper (though it is still found in some well-known school atlases); it shows Greenland roughly the same size as Africa and Ellesmere Island in the Canadian Arctic larger than

Western Europe. Some world maps may at one time have been drawn on this projection so as to exaggerate the size of Canada and hence of the area coloured red to represent the former British Empire. Today, it is the size of the USSR which would most impress the observer of a Mercator world map.

But the transformation or distortion of 'true' geographical scales can serve a useful purpose in certain circumstances. Distances are conventionally shown true to their length on a scale of miles or kilometres (*absolute* distance), but it may be more appropriate to measure them in other units (*relative* distance). To the daily commuter or the manufacturer shipping goods to market, it is the time or cost involved in overcoming distance that matters, rather than the mileage. A map of Britain with places located in relation to their travel time or cost from London would clearly be a gross distortion of the 'reality' shown in a conventional map, yet it might be more real in a certain context. Euclidean geometry, on which our usual concepts of distance are based, may be quite unsuitable for portraying the geometry of spatial economic systems on relevant scales without some such transformation.

Social distance may also differ greatly from absolute distance. To the black American born in the ghetto on the 'wrong' side of Main Street and the railway line, the white middle-class suburb in which he might like to live could as well be thousands of miles away in terms of actual accessibility. If he makes it 'across the tracks', he really has come a long way. The South African government, in attempting to confine black Africans to segregated townships and so-called homelands, has greatly increased the social and political distance between whites and blacks, making the latter legally aliens in the land of their birth, simply by drawing new lines on the map. Yet out of economic necessity daily contact between the races remains strong, with blacks *de facto* occupying most of the same physical spaces as whites – streets, shops, factories and houses (as servants) – though there is segregation in public facilities. People who spend much of their time in close physical proximity may not be 'close' in other senses. How the realities of this kind of 'distance' relationship can best be portrayed on a map is a major challenge to cartographic ingenuity.

Geographical
Space

☐ 100 Square Miles

Ten States with
Most Electoral Votes

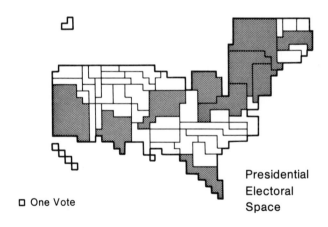

Presidential
Electoral
Space

☐ One Vote

Figure 2.13   A cartogram showing American 'Presidential election
space', compared with a conventional geographical view
of the country. (Source: cartogram based on *Newsweek*,
9 October 1972.)

71

Just as distances (and directions) can be transformed, so can areas and shapes. A common device in recent years has been to redraw national maps with the counties or states proportional in size to population, or (at election time) number of electors, instead of proportional to absolute area. These are sometimes referred to as *cartograms*. In Figure 2.13, the USA is mapped with the area of each state proportional to the number of votes in the electoral college which officially elects the President. A comparison with the conventional map shows that some of the larger states are of only minor significance in 'presidential political space'. The major urban-industrial axis extending from Illinois in the west to Massachusetts in the east is relatively small in conventional geographical space, but almost large enough to elect the President in political space. The ten states with the largest number of electoral votes are shaded on both maps. Together these account for almost half the total of 538 votes, i.e. half the surface area on the bottom map. Carrying these major populous states guarantees a candidate's election to the Presidency, yet they cover only a small proportion of the total physical area of the USA.

However we portray the world on maps, the individual may perform his own scale transformations in accordance with his personal perceptions. Such geographical properties as distance and area may be seen quite differently by different people. In Dallas, Texas, there are postcards on sale purporting to depict the Texan's view of the United States, which comprises an immense piece of territory forming Texas with small and obviously insignificant places representing various other states around the edges (Figure 2.14). The city of Dallas itself is 'Big D'. Whether all the people of Dallas or Texas really perform these mental scale transformations is debatable. But in general the near and familiar – the territory of personal identification – does assume disproportionate importance or size in the minds of many of us, as we view a world most of which is beyond our direct experience.

Maps can thus perform a variety of descriptive roles in contemporary geography. They can provide simple ways of portraying numerical information, both in its 'raw' state and after some analysis or transformation. As a component in a large computer-

Figure 2.14   A Texan's view of the United States. (Source: from a
postcard produced by Hosts International, Dallas.)

based system of data storage and retrieval, machine-drawn maps
can offer rapid display of spatial patterns which can be instantly
updated as new information is fed in. Maps can also show how
individuals distort their own geographical circumstances, building
a 'mental map' of their personal perceptions of space and distance –
the 'real' world in which their daily lives are organized. Which of
the various versions of reality should appear in our maps and
atlases is at least as important as questions of cartographic
technique.

3. Summarizing Sets of Observations

The map, like the matrix, involves some simplification of reality. Both arrange geographical facts in a way which facilitates description and analysis, but both are summaries in the sense that some information is inevitably dispensed with in the course of observation, measurement and display. But tabulation or mapping is only a first step, for once the numbers have been compiled or the maps drawn, various calculations can be performed to provide much more concise descriptions of areal variation.

This chapter reviews some of the more common methods of summarizing sets of numerical observations. They involve the measurement of certain basic properties, the derivation of frequency distributions, and the process of estimation from a limited number of occurrences. Although the discussion is largely in a geographical context, the techniques covered are applicable to any numerical data, where the units of observation may be people rather than areas or locations. This chapter thus provides an introduction to general descriptive and inferential statistics. Later chapters will cover techniques applicable specifically to spatial data.

A word of warning is necessary at the outset. A single chapter can hardly do justice to topics on which there are many complete textbooks, and to understand statistics requires knowledge of the theory of probability which is not provided here. However, the discussion of further statistical methods in later chapters should help to fill in some of the detail, and there are many specialized texts which can be referred to on matters beyond the scope of this introductory treatment (see Selected Reading at the end of the book).

Measures of Central Tendency and Variation

Imagine that we are interested in the incidence of two leading causes of death, as they vary among a set of twenty-five towns (or neighbourhoods within a single town). The number of deaths from heart disease (X) and cancer (Y) over a certain period of time is obtained for each town from local records, and expressed as a rate per 10,000 people to allow for (i.e. hold constant) variations in population size. The two sets of figures are as listed in Table 3.1, where i (1, 2, ..., 25) are the towns or units of observation.

Table 3.1: Occurrence of Two Conditions (X, Y) in an Imaginary Set of Areas (i)

i	X	Y	i	X	Y	i	X	Y	i	X	Y	i	X	Y
1	17	5	6	29	7	11	7	6	16	24	10	21	34	27
2	10	4	7	26	7	12	11	6	17	0	15	22	27	1
3	2	9	8	14	8	13	24	23	18	5	11	23	17	6
4	14	13	9	18	18	14	17	5	19	22	2	24	12	4
5	21	34	10	5	8	15	16	11	20	19	3	25	25	5

A glance at the figures shows that in general X has a higher magnitude than Y. The most obvious way of establishing this exactly is by the *arithmetic mean*, which measures 'central tendency' in a set of observations. It may be written:

$$\bar{X} = \frac{\sum_{i=1}^{N} X_i}{N} \qquad [3.1]*$$

where $\bar{X}$ represents the mean for X, and the summation is over all N (1, ..., i, ..., 25 in this case). On average the death rate for heart disease ($\bar{X} = 16.7$) is higher than that for cancer ($\bar{Y} = 9.9$). The arithmetic mean here will not necessarily represent the death rate in all towns taken together, because the individual rates have been calculated from different population bases. However, the

---

* In this and subsequent chapters equations are identified by numbers for ease of reference.

focus of interest is the incidence of conditions as they vary between geographical units of observation, so the mean rate is more useful in this case than the total rate, which could be largely a reflection of a few places with large populations. (The reader aware of the problem of averaging *rates* – explored further at the end of this chapter – may be more comfortable regarding the data in this illustration as absolute numbers).

Another measure of central tendency is the *median*, or the middle value when the observations are placed in rank order. The median of X is the 13th occurrence out of the 25:

Values of X: 0, 2, 5, 5, 7, 10, 11, 12, 14, 14, 16, 17, 17, 17, 18, 19, 21, 22, 24, 24, 25, 26, 27, 29, 34.

Similarly, the median for Y is 7. If there had been an even number of occurrences, the median would have been the average of the two middle values. The median will not necessarily be the same as the mean, though it is often a close approximation where the other values are fairly evenly spread out on either side, as in the case of variable X here.

The third common measure of central tendency is the *mode*, which is simply the most frequently occurring value. For X it is 17, which occurs three times. For Y both 5 and 6 are found three times, so this variable is 'bimodal'. The mode is generally further from the mean than is the median, and is less useful than the other two as a summary measure because frequent values need not be typical of a numerical series.

Although the arithmetic mean is the most often used, it has some disadvantages. One is that it is disproportionately sensitive to extreme occurrences, large or small. In a variable with a few such values the median is more representative of 'average' conditions than is the mean. In the distribution of income, for example, a few millionaires can pull the mean up to a level where most people may be well below it, so 'median income' is the usual summary measure.

The mean (or median, or mode) reveals a certain tendency in the data, but it tells us nothing about the extent to which the individual values vary about some norm or average. With $\bar{X} =$

16·7, all values could be close to this, or they could be widely dispersed. The *range* of the values tells something about their variation – the difference between the highest and the lowest. And it would be quite easy to work out the average extent to which individual values deviate from the mean, i.e. the *mean deviation*. But the usual method of measuring the dispersion about the mean is to calculate the *standard deviation*, which has the advantage of greater ease of mathematical treatment. The standard deviation is usually symbolized by the Greek letter σ (lower case sigma). The equation is:

$$\sigma = \sqrt{\frac{\sum\limits_{i=1}^{N} (X_i - \bar{X})^2}{N}} \qquad [3.2]$$

which simply represents the square root of the mean of the squares of the deviation of individual values from the arithmetic mean for all values.

The calculation of the standard deviation for variable X is set out in Table 3.2. Substituting the required values in the equation above:

$$\sigma = \sqrt{\frac{1850 \cdot 1}{25}} = \sqrt{74 \cdot 04} = 8 \cdot 6$$

Calculating σ for Y in the same way gives an answer of 7·8. So the two standard deviations show that death rates from heart disease within the set of towns tend to vary more from the mean than is the case with cancer.

But this comparison raises a problem. As the heart disease rate is on average higher than the cancer rate, the greater spread about the mean might have been expected. This can be allowed for by calculating the *coefficient of variation* (V) which is the ratio of standard deviation to the mean, i.e.:

$$V = \frac{100 \, \sigma}{\bar{X}} \qquad [3.3]$$

The higher the coefficient, the greater the variation. The results here are 52 for X and 78 for Y, so with differences in mean taken

77

into account the greater variation between the towns is in the cancer rate, despite its lower standard deviation.

The calculation of the standard deviation produces another useful property of a set of numbers – the *variance*. This is simply the square of the standard deviation (i.e. σ^2), or expression [3.2] without the square root sign. The concept of variance and of variation from the mean is basic to statistics and to numerical analysis in general, and will reappear in subsequent chapters.

Table 3.2: Calculation of the Mean and Standard Deviation for an Imaginary Set of Observations

i	X	$X - \bar{X}$	$(X - \bar{X})^2$
1	17	0·3	0·1
2	10	– 6·7	44·9
3	2	– 14·7	216·1
4	14	– 2·7	7·3
5	21	4·3	18·5
6	29	12·3	151·3
7	26	9·3	86·5
8	14	– 2·7	7·3
9	18	1·3	1·7
10	5	– 11·7	136·9
11	7	– 9·7	94·1
12	11	– 5·7	32·5
13	24	7·3	53·3
14	17	0·3	0·1
15	16	– 0·7	0·5
16	24	7·3	53·3
17	0	– 16·7	278·9
18	5	11·7	136·9
19	22	5·3	28·1
20	19	2·3	5·3
21	34	17·3	299·3
22	27	10·3	106·1
23	17	0·3	0·1
24	12	– 4·7	22·1
25	25	8·3	68·9

$$\Sigma X = 416$$
$$\Sigma (X - \bar{X})^2 = 1850 \cdot 1$$
$$N = 25 \quad \bar{X} = \frac{\Sigma X}{N} = 16 \cdot 7 \qquad \sigma = \sqrt{\frac{\Sigma (X - \bar{X})^2}{N}} = 8 \cdot 6$$

Calculating a standard deviation or variance is tedious, but the time can be cut down by using a modification of [3.2] which says the same thing, i.e.:

$$\sigma = \sqrt{\frac{\sum\limits_{i=1}^{N} X_i^2}{N} - \bar{X}^2}$$

[3.4]

This so-called 'machine formula' involves fewer calculations than [3.2] and is best used when working out σ on a desk calculating machine. The machine formula for the variance (σ^2) is, of course:

$$\sigma^2 = \frac{\sum\limits_{i=1}^{N} X_i^2}{N} - \bar{X}^2$$

[3.5]

The standard deviation is not only a commonly used measure of spread about the mean, but also figures prominently in a number of other statistical procedures. The mean and standard deviation in combination are sometimes used as a method of classifying values (or areas), indicating whether they are 1σ above (or below) the mean, 2σ, 3σ, and so on. The use of these two important properties is considered further below and in Chapter 5.

Frequency Distributions

It is very convenient to be able to summarize a set of observations by single numbers. But calculating the mean, standard deviation and coefficient of variation allows only limited statements about X and Y: the former has on average larger occurrences and the latter has greater variation when its generally smaller values are allowed for. Further insight may be gained by working out a frequency distribution. This involves allocating the individual values to classes, usually (but not necessarily) of the same size, and stating the relative frequency with which values fall into the respective classes. Frequency distributions provide a very useful way of summarizing variation in the incidence of geographical conditions, particularly when portrayed graphically.

The first question is: how many classes should there be? There are a number of different rules of thumb relating this to the number of observations (N). For example, if k is the number of classes, then we might say: $k = 1 + 3 \cdot 3 \log N$ (D. V. Huntsberger, *Elements of Statistical Inference*), or $k < 5 \log N$ (C. E. P. Brooks and N. Carruthers, *Handbook of Statistical Methods in Meteorology*). In *Applied General Statistics*, F. E. Croxton and D. J. Cowden suggest that most frequency distributions should have between six and sixteen classes. Clearly there is no 'correct' number of classes, but very few will show relatively little, while very many will produce too detailed a classification unless a large number of occurrences is involved.

The figures for the imaginary death rates X and Y will be used to illustrate the derivation of frequency distributions. As $N = 25$, the Huntsberger formula for number of classes gives:

$$k = 1 + 3 \cdot 3 \log 25 = 1 + 3 \cdot 3 \times 1 \cdot 4 = 5 \cdot 6$$

The Brooks and Carruthers formula gives:

$$k < 5 \log 25, \text{ or } 5 \times 1 \cdot 4, \text{ which is } 7$$

Six would thus be the 'best' number of classes by these criteria; seven is preferred as a matter of convenience.

Next the class limits have to be established. None should coincide with an actual value, so they are generally expressed in decimals if whole numbers are included, e.g. class one might be 0–4·9 and class two 5·0–9·9. Alternatively we could use 0–4 and 5–9, rather than 0–5 and 5–10. To establish class limits and allocate values to the appropriate classes, it is sometimes convenient to list the occurrences in rank order.

Table 3.3 shows the frequency distributions for X and Y, based on seven classes with class intervals of 5. The table includes not only the frequency (f) of occurrence, measured in absolute and percentage terms, but also the class mid-values which will be used in another context later in the chapter. This table shows clearly that the two frequency distributions differ considerably, with Y having most of its occurrences in the first three classes while the X values tend to be bunched in the middle. The percentage fre-

Table 3.3: Frequencies of the Occurrence of Two Conditions in an Imaginary Set of Areas

Class Limits	Class Mid-values	fX	%fX	fY	%fY
0·0– 4·9	2·5	2	8	5	20
5·0– 9·9	7·5	3	12	11	44
10·0–14·9	12·5	5	20	4	16
15·0–19·9	17·5	6	24	2	8
20·0–24·9	22·5	5	20	1	4
25·0–29·9	27·5	3	12	1	4
30·0–34·9	32·5	1	4	1	4

quencies summarize the way towns fall into a particular class: for X, 8 per cent have rates in the range 0–4·9, 12 per cent have 5·0–9·9, and so on.

A mean, median, mode and standard deviation can be calculated directly from grouped data if desired. The mean is found by simply multiplying each class mid-value by the frequency in that class, summing and dividing by the number of observations. Calculating the standard deviation is similarly based on the f and middle-of-class values.

A frequency distribution can be displayed in the form of a bar diagram, called a *histogram* or *ogive*. Columns are drawn with their height proportional to the frequency of occurrences in the class in question. Histograms for X and Y are depicted in Figure 3.1, which confirms the initial impression of Y having a relatively large number of small occurrences compared with X.

A *frequency distribution curve* can be drawn from the histogram, connecting the top of each bar, as a further way of graphically summarizing the distribution of a set of numbers.

An Example

For an example of the application of the techniques illustrated above, the context can shift from an imaginary situation to a real city. In Chapter 2 (Fig 2.8) death rates in the central part of Tampa,

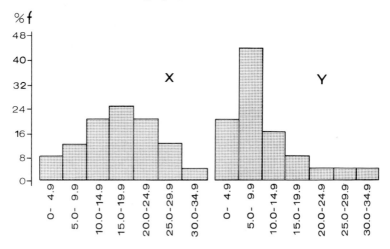

Figure 3.1   Two frequency distributions plotted as histograms.

Florida, were mapped, and considerable variations between areas
were observed. How do the rates of death from cancer, strokes and
heart disease vary through the seventy-one tracts making up the
entire city? The facts could be displayed on maps or in a 71 × 3
data matrix, but what is required here are some simple numerical
summaries.

Table 3.4 lists seven characteristics of the three death rates as
they vary between tracts. The means show that rates are on average
highest for heart disease and lowest for strokes. The medians say
the same thing, but they are all less than the mean. The maximum
and minimum values show a very considerable spread, but the
ranges are not particularly helpful as a summary of geographical
variation because all three maxima are isolated extreme values.
They are found in the same tract in the city centres (the one shaded
heaviest on the composite map in Fig 2.8), where there are the
rather peculiar circumstances of an unstable population prone to
severe social problems. Taking out this tract reduces the maxima
to 552, 415 and 737 respectively, and the ranges to 530, 397 and
737. This illustrates the major disadvantage of the range as a

Table 3.4: Characteristics of Three Death Rates as They Vary Between Census Tracts in Tampa, Florida, 1970 (N = 71)

Characteristic	Deaths per 100,000 Population		
	Cancer	Stroke	Heart Disease
Mean	213	148	362
Median	180	133	295
Maximum	1538	769	2307
Minimum	22	18	0
Range	1516	751	2307
Standard deviation	191	107	293
Coefficient of variation	90	72	81

Source of data: Hillsborough County Health Department.

summary of variation – its sensitivity to a single extreme value. The extremes also help to account for the means exceeding the medians.

The standard deviations show that the degree of variation among tracts is in the same order as the means. But the coefficient of variation shows the cancer rate as greatest, with heart disease next and the stroke death rate least.

Some of the reasons for the differences in summary measures are apparent from frequency distribution (Fig 3.2). Both cancer and stroke show quite regular frequency curves with an obvious bunching of values in a small number of classes. However, the bunching is tighter in the case of strokes, as reflected also in the lower coefficient of variation. Heart disease has a more uneven distribution, and a greater spread as was indicated by its high standard deviation.

Thus some general statements can be made about the spatial incidence of death. The three leading causes clearly have somewhat different patterns of incidence as well as different overall magnitudes. This could suggest differences in causal factors associated with area of residence, which might be investigated in the process of designing improvements in the provision of health care.

Another pattern of health with a rather different distribution of tract rates is shown in Figure 3.3. Unlike the leading causes of death, venereal diseases occur rather infrequently. In almost half

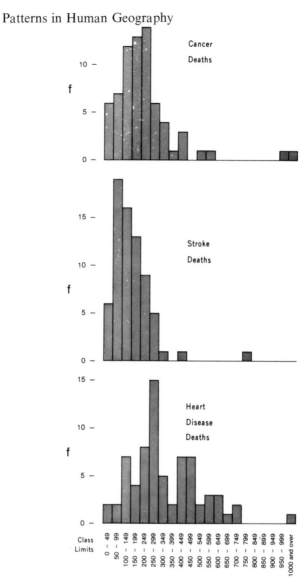

Figure 3.2   Frequency distributions of tract rates for the three leading
causes of death in Tampa, Florida, 1970. (Source of data:
Hillsborough County Health Department.)

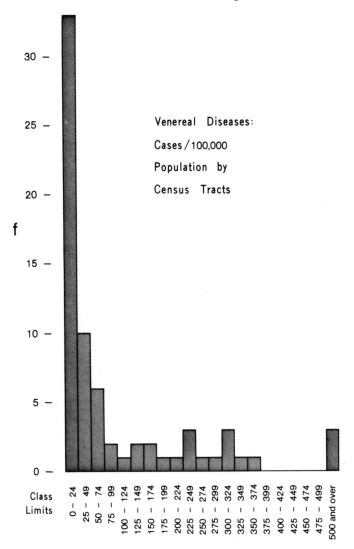

Figure 3.3   A frequency distribution of tract rates for the known
            incidence of venereal disease in Tampa, Florida, 1970.
            (Source of data: Hillsborough County Health Department.)

the tracts in Tampa the rate of recorded cases of VD is under 25 per 100,000 population, while most incidences are concentrated in a very few tracts. The distribution is thus highly distorted compared with those of the death rates. There is now no bunching about the mean of 110, which is well away from the largest (modal) class. In venereal disease the extremes are more important; the elimination of the worst tract brings the tract average down to 95, and the elimination of the worst three tracts reduces it to 72. This condition is severe only in the inner-city slums, where there is a high degree of social disorganization accompanied by ignorance of sources of treatment. As both these factors are within human control, the city government could doubtless have more impact on this health problem than on the three leading causes of death. If the city public health officer wanted to show a drop in venereal disease in his next annual report, he could reduce the tract average, and the rate for the city as a whole, by solving the problem in the few tracts which have high rates of incidence. (By design tract population does not vary greatly, so rates are a fairly accurate reflection of actual numbers affected.) However, the distribution of the incidences of the three leading causes of death shows that to reduce the overall rate (as reflected in the tract mean) substantially would require a reduction in more areas than in the case of VD. Improving health care in just a few tracts will affect the overall rate only slightly.

Estimating from Samples

If there are very many occurrences of some condition it may be impracticable to take measurements on them all. In this case its characteristics may be estimated by use of a *sample*, or subset of the total *parent population* or *universe*. If samples can provide very accurate estimates of the geographical incidence of phenomena, there may be little point in examining the entire population even if this is possible. All the summary measures of central tendency and variation introduced above may be estimated from a sample, as may the form of the frequency distribution. Estimates from samples are known as *statistics*, while the true values for the mean, standard deviation, and so on, are the *parameters* of the population. This use of the term 'parameter' should not be confused with that introduced in Chapter 1 to describe a constant in a model, though both carry the connotation of something which does not vary in a given situation.

The first task in sampling is to determine the appropriate population for which the condition under study should be measured. For example, in using a sample to make a prediction of the pattern of voting in the next election, the population would be restricted to those of voting age on the electoral rolls. If the opinion of Yorkshiremen alone was sought, the population would obviously be confined to that county. Care has to be taken that the population of interest is actually the one sampled; the use of names from automobile registration lists or telephone directories eliminates poorer people and thus biases the results towards the views of the relatively well off.

The next question is how to select the sample. The normal method is to use a *random sample*, or one in which all the elements or observations in the total population have the same chance of selection. This can be done by assigning names or numerals to them all, writing these on pieces of paper, putting them in a hat and shaking well, and then drawing an appropriate number out. But the method generally preferred is to select a subset by code numbers using a table of computer-generated *random numbers* (to be found in most textbooks on statistics). Sampling in geography is generally done 'without replacement', which means that no element selected is, in effect, put back in the hat perhaps to be selected again. A distinction must be made between random or systematic sampling, which is selection according to rules, and unsystematic or haphazard selection. Soliciting information from a few Wiltshire farmers or Panamanian peasants which an investigator just happens to have encountered is not random or systematic sampling. Generalizations inferred from the results of such traditional forms of field inquiry are unlikely to be very reliable – they may simply reflect the condition of those with the time to stand and talk. Attitudinal data obtained from members of a university class in quantitative methods may be similarly un-representative of the population at large.

An example of sampling may be provided, to demonstrate the procedure and introduce an important property of the estimates which result. Suppose that we were to try to estimate the mean tract death rate from strokes in Tampa (see above) from a sample. A table of random numbers generates the identification codes of ten of the seventy-one tracts, and the data for these become the observations from which the sample mean is found. They are listed in Table 3.5 (note that random numbers over 71 or repetitions of earlier ones are disregarded). The sum of the ten observations divided by 10 gives a sample mean of 146·6, which is very close to the true mean of 147·9. But a sample does not always produce such an accurate estimate: a second sample of ten gave 117·8, a

Table 3.5: Estimating the Mean of a Population by Sampling ($n = 10$)

Random Number (tract code)	Observation (stroke death rate)	Reason for Not Using Number
91		no observation
21	99	
72		no observation
44	271	
53	156	
87		no observation
86		no observation
59	126	
37	187	
43	60	
34	201	
82		no observation
5	81	
42	134	
5		repetition
12	151	
	$\Sigma = 1466\cdot$	sample mean = 146·6

Note: the random numbers are from a table in J. P. Cole and C. A. M. King, *Quantitative Geography*, John Wiley, 1968, 677.

third 138·6 and a fourth 150·4. However, if we continue repeating the process until we have a very large number of sample means a pattern begins to emerge. Most of them are found to give quite close estimates, while few depart very greatly from the true mean. To illustrate this a hundred samples of ten have been taken from the stroke data, and the resulting means are plotted on a histogram in Figure 3.4 to show the *sampling distribution* of the measure. The distribution is fairly regular, with a tendency to bunch about the true mean and a tailing off towards both extremes. As further samples are taken the figure would resemble steadily more closely the perfectly regular form of what is termed the *normal frequency distribution*. It is the known properties of this distribution which enable us to judge the reliability of estimates made by sampling.

The concept of a 'normal' distribution is central to statistical

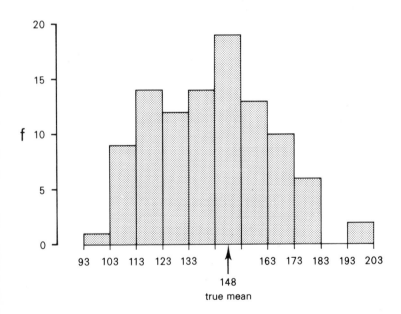

Figure 3.4   The distribution of 100 sample means (*n* = 10), from
stroke death rates for 71 tracts in Tampa, Florida.
(Source of data: as for Figure 3.3.)

analysis. The normal distribution curve is bell-shaped, indicating the infrequent occurrence of extreme values, large or small, and the more frequent occurrence of values relatively close to the mean. This distribution fits observations of a wide variety of natural and social phenomena, as can be verified by thinking of the frequency of occurrence of such a commonplace thing as the height of people: few are over 6′ 6″ tall or under 5′ 0″, even fewer are over 7′ 0″ or less than 4′ 6″, but a high proportion are within a few inches of 5′ 9″. Marks obtained in an examination generally approximate a normal distribution: few students are very good, few are very bad, and many turn in something close to an average performance. Errors of measurement or estimation are usually normally distributed about the true value. An important property of the normal distribution is that the mean, median and mode of the variable in question will be the same value.

If the distribution of some phenomenon is perfectly normal, the proportion of occurrences within a given distance of the mean is known (Fig 3.5). Roughly 68 per cent of occurrences will be within one standard deviation of the mean, 95·5 per cent will be within 2σ and over 99 per cent within 3σ. There is only about 1 chance in 10,000 of a number exceeding the mean by four standard deviations. These facts are very important in *inferential statistics*, which is concerned with drawing sound conclusions from samples.

The size of the sample is, of course, a critical decision. If it is very small the estimates it generates may be poor; if it is larger than the desired degree of accuracy required, unnecessary time and expense will be incurred. The accuracy of the results from a representative random sample increase with the actual number of observations sampled, not with the proportion of the total population. This is because a few extreme cases can greatly distort the results in a small sample, whereas they tend to be compensated for by more representative values in a large sample. If the sample size is large enough it can provide accurate information even if it comprises only a very small proportion of the total population, as for example in the one per cent sample used for certain census purposes.

Sample size depends ultimately on the accuracy of the estima-

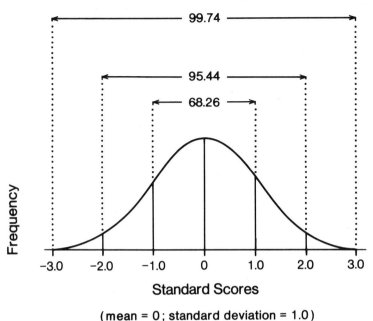

Figure 3.5 The normal frequency distribution, showing percentage
probabilities that an observation will be in particular
sections.

tion required. Statistical theory tells us that if repeated 'large'
samples are taken from any population, the sample means will
tend towards a normal distribution about the true mean regardless
of whether or not the parent population is normal. It also tells us
that the standard deviation *of the sample means* will be the standard
deviation of the parent population divided by the square root of
the sample size. In this context a sample of 30 or more is usually
regarded as large enough (the samples of 10 from the Tampa data
above were too small). Thus a mean derived from a sample of
about 30 observations can have estimates of accuracy placed upon
it, because as part of a normal distribution the probability that it
will be within a certain range of the true mean is known from the
properties of the normal curve.

An illustration should clarify this, and the process of estimation from samples. Suppose that the 25 values for variable X in the death rate illustration at the beginning of this chapter were a 'large enough' random sample from a population of cities. How confident could we be in the mean of X (which was 16·7) as an estimate of the true mean? The standard deviation of a set of means from samples of n observations ($s_{\bar{x}}$) is known as the *standard error of the mean*, and is given by

$$s_{\bar{x}} = \frac{\sigma}{\sqrt{n}}$$
[3.6]

where n instead of N indicates that we are dealing with a sample and x instead of X represents the statistic instead of the parameter. Assume that the standard deviation of the population (σ) is known to be 8·6. Substituting in equation [3.6]:

$$s_{\bar{x}} = \frac{8 \cdot 6}{\sqrt{25}} = \frac{8 \cdot 6}{5} = 1 \cdot 7$$

So the standard error is 1·7. As this is the standard deviation of sample means, and as about 68 per cent of all observations in a normal distribution are within one standard deviation of the mean, there is a 68 per cent probability that the true mean will be 16·7 plus or minus 1·7. Two standard errors (1·96 to be exact) define 95 per cent probability, so there is a 19 in 20 chance that the true mean is $16 \cdot 7 \pm 3 \cdot 4$. These limits on the reliability of the sample estimate are known as *confidence limits*, because we can state how confident we are that the true value is between them. The general form of a *confidence interval* for the mean is:

$$\bar{X} = \bar{x} \pm Z \frac{\sigma}{\sqrt{n}}$$
[3.7]

where $\bar{X}$ is the true mean, $\bar{x}$ is the sample mean, and σ the true standard deviation. The symbol Z is the *standard normal deviate*, or number of standard deviation units defining the required level of confidence on a normal curve, e.g. $Z = 1 \cdot 0$ for 68 per cent confidence and 1·96 for 95 per cent. The smaller the Z value, the narrower the limits and the less confident we are that the true mean is within that range.

In practice, of course, it is highly unlikely that the true standard deviation will be known if the true mean is unknown and estimated by sampling. This case was used simply to introduce the idea of confidence limits. If both the population mean and standard deviation are unknown, the sample estimate of the mean must be related to the *sample standard deviation*. If n is small (i.e. less than about 30) we must refer to a sampling distribution which differs somewhat from the normal curve – *Student's t distribution*. This is more spread out than the normal distribution, reflecting the greater likelihood of departure of sample mean from true mean. In fact, the t distribution changes with sample size, becoming less spread out and more like the normal distribution as sample size increases and the estimate of the true standard deviation improves. The best estimate of σ is actually found by multiplying s by the square root of $n/(n-1)$, which is equivalent to dividing the sum of squares in [3.2] by $n-1$ instead of N.*

The expression for confidence intervals using Student's t thus becomes:

$$\bar{X} = \bar{x} \pm t\, \frac{s}{\sqrt{n}} \qquad [3.8]$$

where s is the standard deviation of the sample. The value for t at a given level of confidence and for a given sample size is found from a table or graph (included in most statistics texts or sets of statistical tables). Returning to the illustration above, with a

---

*Why this is so requires an explanation of the statistical concept of *degrees of freedom*. In any sum of a set of scores, if all but one are known the value of the final one must also be known, i.e. it is not free to vary. Because the calculation of the standard deviation and variance is based on deviations from the mean the sum of which is known (it is 0), when all but one of the values of $X_i - \bar{X}$ are known the final one must also be known. One restriction is placed on the freedom of the n numbers to vary. The degrees of freedom are thus $n-1$ and the use of n in the calculation of the standard deviation and variance will lead to an underestimate of the actual values. Using $n-1$ provides what is sometimes referred to as an *unbiased estimate*. As the sample size increases this correction becomes less important, and in the present example, with $n\ (=25)$ approaching 30 it is ignored. Note that accommodating the loss of one degree of freedom in the t test [3.8] n becomes $n-1$.

sample of 25 at the 95 per cent confidence level, $t = 2 \cdot 06$. From the calculations in section 3.1 the standard deviation of the 25 values for X was $8 \cdot 6$, so the new confidence interval from [3.8] above is:

$$\bar{X} = 16 \cdot 7 \pm 2 \cdot 06 \left(\frac{8 \cdot 6}{\sqrt{25}} \right) = 16 \cdot 7 \pm 2 \cdot 06 \times 1 \cdot 7 = 16 \cdot 7 \pm 3 \cdot 5$$

The confidence interval has widened slightly, from $3 \cdot 4$ to $3 \cdot 5$.

It is now possible to derive a method for calculating the sample size needed at a desired level of confidence. Let the difference between the confidence interval and the sample mean be denoted by d. From expression [3.8]:

$$d = t \frac{s}{\sqrt{n}}$$

which can be rearranged as follows:

$$d\sqrt{n} = ts, \quad \therefore \frac{ts}{d} = \sqrt{n}, \quad \therefore \left(\frac{ts}{d} \right)^2 = n$$

So the sample size n is given by

$$n = \left(\frac{ts}{d} \right)^2 \qquad [3.9]$$

where s is the standard deviation of any sample of size m,

      t is the Student's t value at a given level of probability for a sample size m (if sample size is 'large' Z replaces t),

and d is the distance from the true mean defining the required degree of accuracy.

To use this expression requires an experimental sample. Suppose the 25 observations on X in the illustration above were such a sample, taken to determine the actual sample size needed to estimate $\bar{X}$ to within, say, $\pm 2 \cdot 0$ of the true mean at the 95 per cent confidence level. Knowing that $t = 2 \cdot 06$ with $m = 25$, expression [3.9] can be evaluated as follows:

$$n = \left(\frac{2 \cdot 06 \times 8 \cdot 6}{2 \cdot 0} \right)^2 = \left(\frac{17 \cdot 7}{2 \cdot 0} \right)^2 = (8 \cdot 9)^2 = 79 \cdot 2$$

So a sample of 80 would be needed to be 95 per cent confident that the sample mean was within 2·0 of the true mean. For a confidence interval of 4·0 a sample of 20 would be sufficient. For 3·5 the size would be:

$$n = \left(\frac{2·06 \times 8·6}{3·5}\right)^2 = \left(\frac{17·7}{3·5}\right)^2 = 5·05^2 = 25·5$$

25 is the original sample size which gave the result $\bar{X} = 16·7 \pm 3·5$ in the earlier part of the demonstration.

This simple illustration does no more than introduce techniques for establishing the reliability of estimates from samples. It is deliberately simplified, and reference should be made to specialist texts (see Selected Reading) before attempting research applications. Other aspects of statistical inference will appear in subsequent chapters.

In the end, the degree of accuracy of sample estimates depends above all on the extent to which the sample is truly representative of the population at large. If the population is a heterogeneous body of people, it is important that the distinctive sub-populations within it should be reflected in the structure of the sample. This is achieved by using a *stratified sample*. The significant population 'strata' are identified, their share of the total population worked out, and the number of individuals or objects sampled from each group would be in the same proportions. The bias which can arise from the disproportionate sampling of one ethnic or socio-economic group in attitudinal surveys is eliminated in this way.

The design of the sample frame is very important in geographical research. If the units of observation making up the total population of interest are locations in geographical space (which can be thought of as virtually infinite in number), a sample can be taken in various ways. Random numbers can be used to generate grid coordinates, which identify the locations selected. A systematic sample at regular intervals across the map could also be used. A combination of the two is sometimes adopted to guarantee observations from all parts of the area under study; a sample point is selected randomly from each of a set of grid squares or quadrats with an arbitrary or randomly-generated origin.

Stratified samples are often required in geography. A study of agriculture based on a sample of farms may need a certain number of observations in each major land-use or soils region. If data are being compiled for sets of areal units from a sample of people, there will have to be a certain number from each area. The need to stratify geographically can greatly increase the sample size, and hence the cost of a survey. A sociologist wishing to determine average performance on some educational test in a given city with five social classes proportionally represented might be able to do this from a sample of a couple of hundred, while a geographer wanting an estimate for each of, say, twenty-five social areas within the same city might need as many as a thousand respondents. The cost of conducting large sample surveys is a major constraint on the use of this method of gathering geographical information.

Traditionally, human geographers have not placed very great reliance on sample survey techniques. Much analysis in economic and social geography is performed on entire populations, which are made readily available in published form. However, as interest in some of the more personal and seemingly intangible aspects of life increases, sample surveys are likely to be used with greater frequency, and this requires knowledge of the special skills involved. The most direct way to find out how people see their own existence is to ask them, and the value of the information gathered will depend very much on who is selected and how the questions are put.

The Normality of Distributions

In addition to its role in sampling situations, the normal distribution introduced above provides a general standard against which actual distributions of observations may be judged. If a distribution departs from the symmetry of the normal bell-shape, it is said to be *skewed*. If the bunching is in the direction of the low values, with a 'tail' in the direction of high values, the distribution is *positively* skewed; if the other way round, it is *negatively* skewed. The geographical incidence of many conditions is positively

96

skewed rather than perfectly normal. The three death rates illustrated in Figure 3.2 are all slightly skewed positively. Employment in economic activity in a set of cities is generally distributed in this way, with a few extremely high values representing the specialized cities. In a positively skewed distribution the median will be less than the mean (as in the death rates – see Table 3.4) and the mode will be lower still, while in a negatively skewed distribution the order is reversed. Another characteristic of a distribution is its *kurtosis*, which describes whether it tends to be peaked ('leptokurtic'), flat ('platikurtic') or in between ('mesokurtic'). The properties of skewness and kurtosis are usually sufficient to describe the shape of any frequency distribution.

The normal distribution is often used as a 'theoretical' distribution against which to test some set of observations. Another of a different kind commonly used for a similar purpose is the *Poisson distribution*, which applies when the probability of an event occurring is much less than the probability that it will not occur. The Poisson distribution is very asymmetrical (positively skewed), with most values low but a few extremely high; the VD incidences in Tampa (Fig 3.3) are of this form. Many statistical measures and tests require the data to be normally distributed, or very nearly so. Thus testing data for normality is a necessary early stage in many research projects. Three methods of doing this are set out here, using the imaginary data on death rates X and Y for demonstration.

Once the frequency distribution has been displayed in a histogram, visual examination can give a first indication of whether the distribution is approximately normal. Figure 3.1 above shows that X is clearly more normally distributed than Y. A further quick check is provided by counting the proportion of occurrences within one standard deviation of the mean; in X, there are 16 occurrences between $\bar{X}-\sigma$ (i.e. 8·1) and $\bar{X}+\sigma$ (i.e. 25·3), which is 64 per cent. In Y it is 19, or 76 per cent, so X is nearer the normal 68 per cent than is Y. But this is only a quick initial test, and a more exact method is obviously needed.

The frequency distributions of X and Y worked out by the seven classes above can be tested for normality by a simple graphic method. As a first step the percentage frequencies have to be expressed in a cumulative form. The two *cumulative frequency distributions* are listed in Table 3.6, where the % figures indicate the proportion of occurrences in a particular class and all lower value classes. The cumulative percentages must now be plotted on a special graph paper known as *probability paper*. This has percentage probabilities set out along the horizontal axis, while the vertical axis is regularly divided and is used to plot the class intervals. The paper is designed so that cumulative percentages representing a normal distribution will appear as a straight line when plotted. In Figure 3.6 the cumulative percentages of X fall almost exactly on to a straight line, indicating a distribution very close to normal. Y diverges very considerably from normal, confirming the visual impression gathered from the histograms.

A more accurate test of normality can be obtained by plotting the original individual observations on probability paper in a similar way to the grouped data. This is known as a *fractile diagram*. The observations are ranked, and cumulative percentages are worked out. Each of the 25 observations represents 4 per cent of the total, so the cumulative probability on the first observation (the lowest) is 4, the second is 8 and so on, until the last (highest) reaches 100. If a large number of occurrences is involved, the cumulative percentages need not be worked out for every occurrence – one in ten, twenty, or whatever seems appropriate can be used. In this case the way to find the cumulative percentage for

Table 3.6: Cumulative Percentage Frequencies for the Occurrence of Two Conditions in an Imaginary Set of Areas

Class Limits	Class Mid-values	Cumulative % Frequencies X	Y
0·0– 4·9	2·5	8	20
5·0– 9·9	7·5	20	64
10·0–14·9	12·5	40	80
15·0–19·9	17·5	64	88
20·0–24·9	22·5	84	92
25·0–29·9	27·5	96	96
30·0–34·9	32·5	100	100

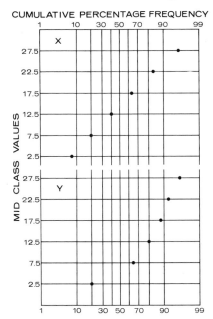

Figure 3.6   Testing grouped data for normality using probability paper.

any given occurrence is to divide its rank by N (i.e. total number of occurrences).

When the cumulative percentage probabilities have been worked out, they are plotted against the values they represent. Figure 3.7 shows X and Y plotted in this way. Again a straight line indicates normality: X closely approximates this, but Y does not. The two lines drawn in Figure 3.7 represent the normal distributions against which X and Y are being measured, with the same mean and standard deviations as X and Y. They are derived very simply by plotting (in the case of X) $\bar{X} = 16\cdot7$ on the vertical axis against 50 on the horizontal axis and $\bar{X}+\sigma$ (i.e. $25\cdot3$) against 84, because the mean is at the mid-point of a normal curve and one standard deviation is 34 per cent further along the scale (see Fig 3.5). Comparing the plotted values with the line shows precisely how the distribution departs from normality.

If a set of data is found to depart considerably from a normal

Patterns in Human Geography

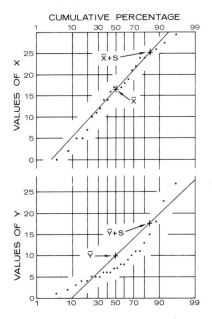

Figure 3.7   Testing ungrouped data for normality in a fractile diagram.

distribution, it may be possible to *transform* it into a normal state, or near enough to use statistical procedures requiring normal data. *Normalization* can be achieved by using any function of the variable which is found to be normally distributed. Two of the most common methods are to replace the original data by their logarithms or square roots. But when a transformation has been made it must be remembered that any conclusions derived from it apply to the transformed values, i.e. to log X if a log transformation has been used, not to X.

As an illustration, assume that the data for our imaginary death rate Y above had to be normalized. The form of its distribution suggests that this could be accomplished by taking the logarithm of each value. The original data with the logarithms are listed in Table 3.7. The transformed data can now be used to produce a new frequency distribution (Table 3.8) which shows the symmetry characteristic of normality. This can be further tested on pro-

100

Table 3.7: A Logarithmic Transformation of an Imaginary Variable

i	Y	log Y	i	Y	log Y	i	Y	log Y	i	Y	log Y	i	Y	log Y
1	5	0·70	6	7	0·85	11	6	0·78	16	10	1·00	21	27	1·43
2	4	0·60	7	7	0·85	12	6	0·78	17	15	1·18	22	1	0·00
3	9	0·95	8	8	0·90	13	23	1·36	18	11	1·04	23	6	0·78
4	13	1·11	9	18	1·26	14	5	0·70	19	2	0·30	24	4	0·60
5	34	1·53	10	8	0·90	15	11	1·04	20	3	0·48	25	5	0·70

bability paper, as in Figure 3.8 which shows a linear trend compared with the previous curve. The distribution of Y is thus found to be very close to 'log-normal'.

Suppose that data are collected for a third cause of death (Z), with the following values when ranked:

2, 5, 7, 9, 11, 12, 13, 15, 16, 17, 17, 18, 19, 20, 21, 23, 25, 26, 28, 30, 33, 36, 39, 40, 49.

When grouped and plotted on a histogram this is positively skewed, but in a different way to cause of death Y. Taking the square roots of each value, and establishing classes of 1·0–1·9, 2·0–2·9, . . . , 7·0–7·9, the distribution becomes approximately normal. The cumulative % data for the transformation are plotted on Figure 3.9, where they can be compared with the original non-linear pattern of the data. A square root transformation is appropriate for a distribution which is moderately skewed, while

Table 3.8: Frequencies of the Occurrence of a Log-Transformed Variable

Class Limits	Class Mid-values (logs)	fY	%fY	Cumulative %fY
0·00–0·24	0·125	1	4	4
0·25–0·49	0·375	2	8	12
0·50–0·74	0·625	5	20	32
0·75–0·99	0·875	8	32	64
1·00–1·24	1·125	5	20	84
1·25–1·49	1·375	3	12	96
1·50–1·74	1·625	1	4	100

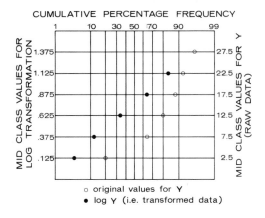

Figure 3.8   Testing original and log-transformed data for normality.

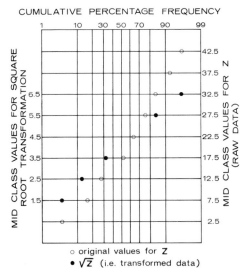

Figure 3.9   Testing original and square root transformed data for normality.

normalization of a more extreme skew requires a log transformation.

Further aspects of the use of distributions and scale transformations, as introduced here, will be taken up in subsequent chapters.

Populations, Samples and Geographical Facts

This chapter has shown that characteristics of sets of numerical observations can be summarized in various ways. The parameters of populations may be measured directly, or they may be estimated from statistics derived from samples. While the parameters are known with certainty except for the contribution of errors of measurement, the inferences from samples are merely statements of probability the accuracy of which is dependent on how the samples are taken and on the element of chance. Knowledge of statistical distributions enables us to place confidence limits on estimates from samples. The discipline of statistics, coupled with the language of mathematics, thus enables us to analyse numerical data and establish geographical facts. It also helps us to separate fact from fiction, or the statistics from the 'lies and damn lies'.

In conclusion, one final matter concerning data as relating to populations or samples may be explored briefly, to reveal some problems arising from the distinctive nature of geographical data. Death rates by census tracts in Tampa were examined above, and means calculated. It has already been pointed out that measures of a geographical distribution will be determined to some extent by the manner in which the area is divided up, so it is quite possible that a different set of tract boundaries could produce a different tract mean rate. Consider the following imaginary data for three tracts:

	popul-ation	cancer deaths	rate/ 10 popn	
tract 1	10	2	2	
tract 2	10	4	4	mean tract rate = $\dfrac{2+4+6}{3} = 4{\cdot}0$
tract 3	10	6	6	

Suppose that tracts 1 and 2 are combined. The data then become:

	popul- ation	cancer deaths	rate/ 10 popn	
tracts 1+2	20	6	3	tract mean rate =
tract 3	10	6	6	$\dfrac{3+6}{2} = 4\cdot5$

Another arrangement could be:

	popul- ation	cancer deaths	rate/ 10 popn	
tract 1	10	2	2	tract mean rate =
tracts 2+3	20	10	5	$\dfrac{2+5}{2} = 3\cdot5$

The change in means with changing geographical aggregation of data is explained simply by the change in relative contributions. Compared with the original arrangement, the first amalgamation gives tract 3, with the highest rate, half the total on which the mean is based, thus raising the mean; the second amalgamation gives tract 1, with the lowest rate, half the total, thus reducing the mean. Hence the overall city rate (4·0) is not necessarily the same as the average of the tract rates.

But suppose the tract rates were a sample. The existing subdivision of the city of Tampa into 71 tracts is one of an infinite number of possible subdivisions, and although it cannot truly be said to have been generated at random it could well have been. It is certainly quite unrelated to the incidence of most of the conditions for which it is used as a data collection frame. Thus it would not be unreasonable to assume that a set of 71 incidence rates comprise a (more or less) random sample of an almost infinite number of possible rates.

If this is the case, then the tract mean cancer death rate of 213 can be regarded as only an estimate of the 'true' mean rate. How confident can we be in such an estimate? Using expression [3.7] from above, with the known standard deviation of the 'sample' of 71 and the value of $Z = 1\cdot96$ at the 95 per cent confidence level, gives the following result:

$$\bar{X} = \bar{x} \pm Z\frac{s}{\sqrt{n}} = 213 \pm 1.96\frac{191}{\sqrt{71}} = 213 \pm 45$$

We can thus be highly confident that the 'true' rate is within 45 either way of the rate calculated from the data for the tracts. A sample of this size gives a fairly accurate estimate. As the sample size (i.e. the number of areal subdivisions) increases, so the accuracy increases. However, care must be taken with this kind of application. Among other things it is important that a certain assumption implicit in the use of the Z distribution has been fulfilled, namely that a random sample has been taken from a normally distributed population, which is not necessarily so in this case.

The geographer using observation units of areal extent and often of arbitrary limits clearly has problems not encountered in research where individual people, for example, are the units of observation. Geographical data are sensitive to the way individual observations are grouped, and to the relationship between contiguous areal units. In the case of cancer in Tampa, at the one extreme would be an arrangement whereby each of the 300,000 or so citizens at the beginning of the year comprised a geographical observation with the attributes 'died' or 'did not die' of cancer during that year. The ratio of the died set to the total population would be the city cancer death rate. At the other extreme would be the entire city as a unit of observation, with total cancer deaths related to total population of course giving the same result. Any areal grouping of people between these extremes can give a different average cancer rate. Which is considered the 'correct' geographical summary fact – the city rate or the average rate for a set of sub-areas – depends on the research context and the use to which the fact will be put.

4. Comparing Sets of Observations

The purpose of summarizing a set of observations is generally to facilitate comparison with another set or with some norm. Compared with one another, any sets of observations can be pronounced similar or dissimilar, but how great a difference is 'significant'? To answer this involves an approach based on inferential statistics. The discussion of estimating from samples in the previous chapter showed that the probability of a sample estimate of a parameter being fairly close to the true value is greater than the probability of it being far off. Conversely, the greater the difference between the two values the less the probability that this can be attributed to sampling error or some random process. In statistics, a *significant* difference is one which cannot be accounted for by chance at a given level of probability or confidence. The smaller the difference, the greater the probability that two means, for example, apply to samples which could have been drawn from the same parent population.

Setting comparisons within an inferential framework may not always be necessary in human geography. Often the observations comprise entire populations, and the question of sampling error does not arise. However, geographical comparisons of this kind are sometimes undertaken *as though* the data were samples, with differences dismissed as insignificant or a consequence of some random process if small enough to have arisen in samples from the same parent population at a given level of probability. The arbitrary definition of areal units of observation alone may be sufficient justification for not treating a set of geographical data as a true universe. In such cases it is important to bear in mind the assumptions which underlie techniques of statistical inference and which govern their validity.

The discussion which follows introduces the idea of testing statistical hypotheses, and demonstrates common methods of comparing differences between sets of observations for significance. As in Chapter 3, the focus is on numerical or statistical distributions and not on areal distributions, though the observational units may be areas. The analysis of *geographical* patterns of variation and comparisons between *areal* distributions begins in Chapter 6.

Testing Statistical Hypotheses

In Chapter 3 we considered an imaginary case comprising two causes of death in a set of areas. Cause X had an average of 16·7, and the 25 observations on which this figure is based may now be regarded as a random sample of a larger population with a known standard deviation of 8·6. The observations might be sample blocks or quadrats within a city. Suppose that, after calculating the sample mean, the local Medical Officer of Health disputed the result, saying that in fact the average incidence in this city conforms to the national norm of 22·0. How would we react to this? We know that the confidence interval at 95 per cent probability is 16·7 ± 3·4, or from 13·3 to 20·1. This suggests that 22 is a rather unlikely true value, so we could reject the claim of the MOH as being wrong, with a high degree of confidence. As we are talking at the 95 per cent confidence level, there is less than a 5 per cent chance that we are incorrect in rejecting 22 as the true average.

This process of making decisions about an estimate involves the testing of an *hypothesis*. We have a value (the average) for some condition, and we are proposing or hypothesizing that this is the true value. The sample information provides a basis for accepting or rejecting the hypothesis, at a given level of confidence.

Testing statistical hypotheses is a rather formalized process, and if mistakes in interpretation are to be avoided it should be done in a particular way. This involves the following stages:

1. Stating a *null hypothesis*, or the proposition to be tested. The

null hypothesis, symbolized by H_o, is that there is no significant difference between the two values being compared. In other words, the estimate could very well be the true value.

2. Stating the alternative proposition, or the *alternate hypothesis*. The alternate hypothesis (H_a) is that which must be true if the null hypothesis is not true, i.e. that there is a significant difference between the two values. H_o and H_a are mutually exclusive, so that we can say: if H_o then not H_a, if H_a then not H_o.

3. Selecting a *statistical test*, or *test statistic*. This is the way in which a decision is made as to whether to accept or reject the null hypothesis. Selecting the most appropriate test involves judging whether the assumptions (such as normally distributed data) made in various tests are fulfilled in the situation under consideration, and making a choice between alternatives.

4. Establishing a *significance level*. This depends on the degree of required confidence that the null hypothesis has not been incorrectly rejected. It is sometimes called the *coefficient of risk*, symbolized by α (Greek alpha), and may be expressed as the probability p (as a proportion of unity) of incorrectly rejecting the null hypothesis.

5. Working out the *region of rejection*. Given a certain significance level, it is necessary to establish the critical values for the test statistic beyond or within which the null hypothesis will be rejected.

6. Conducting the *test of hypothesis*. This involves sampling, or whatever other method may be appropriate, to determine the value of the test statistic, and finding out whether this falls within the region of rejection.

7. Making the *decision*. If the test statistic is outside the region of rejection the null hypothesis is accepted. If it is not, H_o is rejected and the alternate hypothesis is accepted.

In the simple illustration above, the null hypothesis is that the average incidence of the death rate is 22. In other words, we are taking the proposal of the MOH that there is no significant difference between 22 and the true mean. The alternative is that the average is not 22. The statistical test is to compare 22 with the mean of a sample of areas, this being the test statistic. The significance level is 95 per cent confidence, and the test statistic's region of rejection is beyond $Z\dfrac{\sigma}{\sqrt{n}}$ of the sample mean (from expression 3.7), which is 1·96 standard deviations of the sample mean each side of 22. The test finds the sample mean of 16·7 outside these limits, i.e. within the region of rejection, and the null hypothesis is thus rejected in favour of the alternate hypothesis.

Stated formally, all this can be expressed in the following way:

$H_o : \bar{X} = 22$
$H_a : \bar{X} \neq 22$
test statistic: $\bar{x}$
significance: $p = 0·05$
decision rule: reject H_o if $\bar{x} < 18·6$ or $> 25·4$
result: $\bar{x} = 16·7$, $\therefore \bar{x} < 18·6$
conclusion: $\bar{x} \neq 22$

This shorthand description of the process of hypothesis testing helps to avoid mistakes in the logic. All the symbols will be clear except possibly for $\neq$, which means 'does not equal'.

A simple diagram can further explain the process. Figure 4.1 shows a normal distribution curve about the hypothesized $\bar{X}$ of 22. This represents the sampling distribution of the test statistic $\bar{x}$, repeated estimates of which will be normally distributed with a mean equal to the true mean and a standard deviation ($s_{\bar{x}}$) given by the population standard deviation (σ) divided by the square root of the sample size n, from expression [3.6]. The limits of 1·96 $s_{\bar{x}}$ (where $s_{\bar{x}}$ is the standard deviation of the sample means) define the region in which there is a 95 per cent probability of the sample mean being found, *if* the null hypothesis of $\bar{X} = 22$ is true. The shaded areas in the diagram are the areas within which a value for the test statistic $\bar{x}$ will enable H_o to be rejected with 95 per cent confidence, as can be done when $\bar{x} = 16·7$.

It should be noted that this test is of what is known as the 'two-

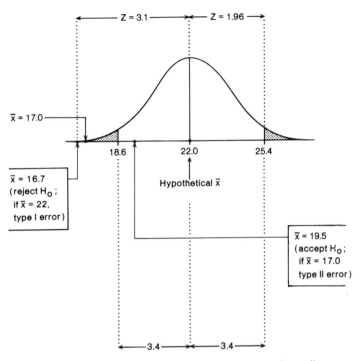

Figure 4.1 Testing a statistical hypothesis against the normal sampling distribution (see text for explanation).

tailed' variety. This means that H_o is rejected if $\bar{x}$ is in either of the two shaded areas representing the tails of the sampling distribution of the test statistic. In some circumstances a 'one-tailed' test is more appropriate, for example, if the null hypothesis was that the true mean was greater or less than a certain value. If the MOH had said that the figure could not be greater than 22 we would then have been able to reject this claim only with a value of $\bar{x}$ in the upper or right-hand tail. This would have raised the level of confidence to 97·5, as one tail contains 2·5 per cent of the distribution instead of 5·0.

As the criterion for rejecting H_o is actually the number of standard deviations in the sampling distribution separating the hypothesized value of $\bar{X}$ from $\bar{x}$, it is generally more convenient to use the following test statistic:

110

$$Z = \frac{\bar{x} - \bar{X}}{\sigma/\sqrt{n}}$$

[4.1]

where Z represents standard deviation units from the mean, and $\sigma/\sqrt{n}$ is the standard error of the mean, or $s_{\bar{x}}$, from [3.6] in the previous chapter. Evaluating this in the present illustration gives:

$$Z = \frac{16\cdot7 - 22\cdot0}{8\cdot6/\sqrt{25}} = \frac{-5\cdot3}{1\cdot7} = -3\cdot1$$

The minus sign simply shows that the sample mean is less than the hypothesized mean. As $3\cdot1$ is greater than Z value of $1\cdot96$ which defines the 95 per cent confidence limits, H_o is rejected. A set of tables showing the percentage of all observations within specific Z values of the mean in a normal distribution enables the exact level of confidence that hypothesized $\bar{X}$ is not true $\bar{X}$ to be found; for $Z = 3\cdot1$, it is $99\cdot8$ per cent. It should be noted that the level of confidence in rejecting H_o increases as $\bar{x} - \bar{X}$ increases. Also, confidence is increased as the sample size increases, for this raises the probability that the sample mean is a close estimate of the true mean.

Two kinds of error are possible in making the decision on any hypothesis. If H_o is actually true it is still possible to reject it. The sample that generated $\bar{x} = 16\cdot7$ above could have been highly unrepresentative purely by chance, and the true $\bar{X}$ could have been 22. Rejecting H_o incorrectly in these circumstances is termed a *type I error*, and the chance of doing this is of course the coefficient of risk (α or p) associated with the chosen confidence level.

The second error is accepting a null hypothesis which is actually false. This is a *type II error*. Suppose that the MOH figure of 22 is false, and what is really true is $\bar{X} = 17$. The region of rejection tells us to reject H_o if $\bar{x}$ is outside the range $25\cdot4$ and $18\cdot6$, but it is possible to obtain a test statistic inside these limits when $\bar{X} = 17$, even though our sample mean of $16\cdot7$ was not. Such a result leads us to accept the H_o that $\bar{X} = 22$. A value of $\bar{x} = 19\cdot5$ would have led to a type II error (see Figure 4.1), and as this is not far from 17 such a sample mean would be quite possible. The probability of a type II error is symbolized β (Greek beta). As the true standard

111

deviation of the population is required to find the probability that any value of $\bar{x}$ would be within a given range of the true population mean, it is in practice difficult to estimate β exactly.

As with the case of estimating from samples discussed in the previous chapter, the true value of the standard deviation is not usually known and it must be estimated from the sample. And for small samples, inferences concerning the population mean must be referred to the Student's t distribution instead of the normal distribution. The test statistic thus becomes:

$$t = \frac{\bar{x} - \bar{X}}{s/\sqrt{n-1}} \qquad [4.2]$$

With a sample size of 25 the two distributions are in fact very similar, changing the confidence interval only slightly.

In any method of testing a statistical hypothesis certain assumptions should be fulfilled. A random sample of observations from a normally distributed population is the most common, and this applies to the t test. The risk of error will increase if the assumptions are not met, and in such cases it may be necessary to set a more stringent confidence level by reducing α or p.

Comparing Means

The method described above tests the likelihood that a hypothesized mean is the true mean of a population, by comparing it with a sample estimate. If the hypothetical mean is also derived from a sample, it is possible to test whether both samples might have been drawn from the same parent population. This is useful, for it enables us to judge the significance of the difference between the average incidence of some condition in two different areas, or different conditions in the same area, where the averages are based on random samples or sub-sets of the total which can reasonably be treated as such. If the two averages are close enough that their respective samples could well have come from the same population, little significance can be attached to the difference.

This test makes use of the variances of the data. If the two variances are significantly different the test may not be appropriate, and as a preliminary the ratio between the variances can be checked by something known as the *F statistic* (see next section). In the unlikely event that the two variances are known to be the same the test is conducted against the normal distribution using the test statistic:

$$Z = \frac{\bar{x}_1 - \bar{x}_2}{\sigma\sqrt{1/n_1 + 1/n_2}} \qquad [4.3]$$

where $\bar{x}_1$ and $\bar{x}_2$ are the two sample means and n_1 and n_2 are the sample sizes. As with expression [4.1] above, the greater the Z value the more likely the null hypothesis of no difference will be rejected. In this case the null hypothesis is $\bar{X}_1 = \bar{X}_2$.

If the variances are unknown so that the population standard deviation σ in [4.3] is unknown, a pooled estimate of the assumed common variance (s^2) has to be made, as follows:

$$s^2 = \frac{(n_1 - 1)\,s_1^2 + (n_2 - 1)\,s_2^2}{n_1 + n_2 - 2} \qquad [4.4]$$

where s_1^2 and s_2^2 are the variances of the two samples. This expression gives a number representative of the average of the two variances, and its square root gives the standard deviation needed in expression [4.3]. If the normal distribution is replaced by Student's t, the test statistic in [4.3] becomes:

$$t = \frac{\bar{x}_1 - \bar{x}_2}{s\sqrt{1/n_1 + 1/n_2}} \qquad [4.5]$$

Using this requires a figure for *degrees of freedom* (*df*), which is given by the denominator in [4.4], i.e. $n_1 + n_2 - 2$.

A simple illustration of comparison between sample means may now be presented. Suppose that it is required to compare the educational attainment levels of two cities. A random sample of 10 school leavers is taken in each city, and they are given an identical test. The results are summarized by means and variances, as follows:

city 1: $\bar{x}_1 = 82$; $s_1^2 = 160$
city 2: $\bar{x}_2 = 74$; $s_2^2 = 128$

Is there a significant inter-city difference between average performance of all school leavers? This can be tested as follows:

H_o: $\bar{X}_1 = \bar{X}_2$
H_a: $\bar{X}_1 \neq \bar{X}_2$

test statistic: $t = \dfrac{\bar{x}_1 - \bar{x}_2}{s\sqrt{1/n_1 + 1/n_2}}$; $df = n_1 + n_2 - 2 = 18$

significance: $p = 0.1$
rejection region: $|t| > 1.734$

The vertical brackets around t recognize that it may be $+$ or $-$ The rejection figure for t at $p = 0.1$ with $df = 18$ is found from tables. To evaluate t requires an estimate of s from expression [4.4] above. Substituting the necessary values:

$$s^2 = \frac{9\,(160) + 9\,(128)}{18} = 144$$

$$s = \sqrt{144} = 12$$

Evaluating t:

$$t = \frac{82 - 74}{12\sqrt{1/10 + 1/10}} = \frac{8}{5.36} = 1.48$$

As t is less than the figure of 1.734 required for rejection, the null hypothesis is accepted. In other words, we cannot be 90 per cent confident that the true city mean test scores are different; there is at least one chance in ten that the two samples could have been drawn from the same population. The actual probability (from tables) is about 85 per cent.

In making comparisons of this kind it is important to remember that both the sample size and the level of confidence used are within the control of the investigator. With a larger sample size or higher p value, a small difference between means can become significant. For example, if the sample size above had been 100 instead of 10 the difference would have been significant at the

99·9 per cent confidence level. This re-emphasizes the important relationship between sample size and confidence in estimates, introduced in Chapter 3.

The method for comparing sample means just described depends for its validity on some important conditions. In addition to random samples from normal populations, it assumes equal population variances, and independent samples in the sense that they do not both refer to the same units of observation. The normality assumption can be tested, and skewness corrected for if necessary, by the methods described in the previous chapter, but if the other assumptions are not fulfilled a modified test must be used. Geographical data often take the form of paired sets of observations, with measurements on two conditions in the same set or sample of areas, and comparison in this case is based on the mean of the *differences* between them instead of on the two sample means. This has the additional advantage of not requiring equal population variances.

A real-world problem may be introduced to provide an example. In recent years many countries have seen a marked increase in the proportion of city dwellers living in flats, and data on this have been compiled for the major metropolitan areas of Australia. How has life in flats changed over the years? To find out whether flats have got bigger or smaller, a random sample of ten municipalities has been drawn, two from each of the metropolitan areas of Adelaide, Brisbane, Melbourne, Perth and Sydney, and the average number of rooms per flat has been found for each municipality in 1954 and 1966 (Table 4.1). We wish to test whether the size of flats has changed significantly in metropolitan Australia.

Instead of $\bar{X}_1 = \bar{X}_2$, the null hypothesis now becomes $\bar{D} = 0$, where D is the difference between each pair of observations in the population of all metropolitan municipalities. If there has been no change, the average of the differences between rooms per flat in 1954 and 1966 will be 0; the greater the departure from 0, the greater the average change. The change observed in the sample is tested by t, where:

$$t = \frac{\bar{d}}{s_d / \sqrt{n} - 1} \qquad [4.6]$$

115

Patterns in Human Geography

Here $\bar{d}$ is the mean of the sample differences, which works out at 0·52 (Table 4.1), and s_d is their standard deviation (0·30). Setting the confidence level at 95 per cent (i.e. $p = 0.05$), the rejection region with $df = 9$ is $|t| > 2.262$. Evaluating t from the expression above:

$$t = \frac{0.52}{0.30/3} = \frac{0.52}{0.10} = 5.2$$

This is well outside the range within which the null hypothesis could be accepted, so we accept $\bar{D} \neq 0$. There has been a significant change (a reduction) in the number of rooms per flat, measured by municipality averages. This can be confirmed from figures for the five cities as a whole, which show an average decrease of 0·54 rooms – a figure very close to that provided by the sample.

Table 4.1: Comparison of Average Number of Rooms per Flat in 1954 and 1966 in a Sample of Ten Municipalities in Australian Cities

City and Municipality		Average Rooms per Flat 1954	1966	Difference (d) 1954 – 1966
Adelaide:	City	3·99	3·64	0·37
	Walkerville	4·21	3·85	0·36
Brisbane:	Greenslopes	4·59	3·68	0·91
	Windsor	4·27	3·84	0·43
Melbourne:	City	3·80	3·82	− 0·02
	Hawthorn	4·32	3·63	0·69
Perth:	Ciaremont	4·29	3·79	0·50
	South Perth	4·24	3·18	1·08
Sydney:	Manly	4·44	4·18	0·26
	Mosman	4·71	4·09	0·62
				$\Sigma = 5.20$
				$\bar{d} = 0.52$

Source of data: G. Clark, 'Urban Australia', in A. F. Davies and S. Encel, *Australian Society: A Sociological Introduction*, Cheshire, Melbourne, 1970, 64–70.

116

The Analysis of Variance

If it is required to compare the means of more than two sets of observations an alternative test is needed: the analysis of variance. This involves calculating the variance *within* the samples and comparing it with the variance *between* or among the samples. If the data are thought of in matrix form with the different samples as columns and the observations as rows, within-sample variance is variance down the columns and between-sample variance is variance across the rows. Both can be regarded as possible estimates of the parent population variance. The ratio of the two is designated F, such that:

$$F = \frac{s_1^2}{s_2^2} \qquad [4.7]$$

where s_1^2 is the greater variance estimate and s_2^2 is the lesser. Thus if the within-sample variance is greater than the between-sample variance, within goes on top and between on the bottom, and *vice versa*.

The F ratio has a sampling distribution which is skewed to the right, unlike the symmetrical Student's t and normal (Z) distributions. Using this statistic establishes the probability that the samples could have been drawn from the same parent population. The greater the difference between the two variance estimates the greater the value of F, and the less likely it is that the null hypothesis of no difference between the samples is valid. A large variation between the samples suggests that different parent populations are involved. Put another way, if the samples are all from the same population and drawn at random, variance measured either down the columns or across the rows should not differ very much. A simple illustration is offered here, to demonstrate the partitioning of the variance, the calculation of the F statistic, and the conduct of the test. This is followed by an actual example, designed to explain the technique more generally and to reveal something of the problems involved in its application.

Patterns in Human Geography

Imagine that an investigation of spatial variations in the yield of a particular crop is under way, and that it is suspected that the differences are related to soil type. It is required to test this hypothesis, with respect to yield in four soil regions. Five farms are selected at random in each region and their yields are found. The null hypothesis is that there is no difference between the true regional average yields. The alternate hypothesis is that there is a difference, which in the context of the investigation would be taken as support for the possible effect of soil type. The test statistic is F, at $p = 0.05$. The degrees of freedom are $n - 1 = 19$, where n is the total number of observations sampled (20).

The data are as in Figure 4.2. They are tabulated below, and a step-by-step calculation of the F ratio follows.*

Data

	Samples				
	Soil A	Soil B	Soil C	Soil D	
	2	3	6	5	
Farms	3	4	8	5	
(observations)	1	3	7	5	
	3	5	4	3	
	1	0	10	2	
sample totals	10	15	35	20	sum (Σ) = 80
sample means	2	3	7	4	

number of occurrences (n) = 20
average of all items ($\Sigma \div n$) = 4
degrees of freedom ($n - 1$) = 19

Step 1 is to calculate the sum of the squared deviations from the average of all items. The squares are:

* This illustration is based on one in M. J. Moroney, *Facts from Figures*, Pelican, 1956 (3rd edition), 372–9. Some of the facts have been changed here.

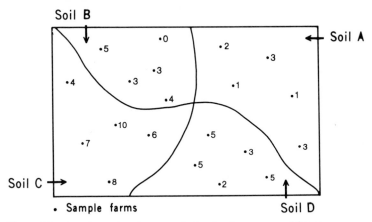

Figure 4.2 Imaginary data for an analysis of variance: crop yields at sample farms in four soil regions.

	A	B	C	D	
	4	1	4	1	
	1	0	16	1	
	9	1	9	1	
	1	1	0	1	
	9	16	36	4	
totals	24	19	65	8	total = 116

The problem is now to partition this total sum of squares into between-samples and within-samples variance.

Step 2 separates out the between-samples variance. This is done simply by eliminating the within-sample variations by substituting the respective sample means for the actual values. The figures for soil A farms thus become 2, 2, 2, 2, 2; for B they are 3, 3, 3, 3, 3; and so on. Now the deviations of each entry in this new matrix from the average for all items (4) are calculated and squared (as in step 1), to give:

	A	B	C	D	
	4	1	9	0	
	4	1	9	0	
	4	1	9	0	
	4	1	9	0	
	4	1	9	0	
totals	20	5	45	0	total = 70

119

Between-sample variance (or 'mean square') is the total of all these squares divided by degrees of freedom. Degrees of freedom are the number of samples less one, which is 3, so variance is $70 \div 3 = 23 \cdot 3$.

Step 3 identifies the within-sample variance. This is done by subtracting from each occurrence in the original data tabulation its own sample mean, i.e. subtracting 2 from all occurrences in soil A sample, 3 from B, and so on. This gives:

	A	B	C	D	
	0	0	-1	1	
	1	1	1	1	
	-1	0	0	1	
	1	2	-3	-1	
	-1	-3	3	-2	
totals	0	0	0	0	total = 0

Variance within samples is calculated from the sum of squares of the deviations of each of the new values from their average (which is 0, therefore each value itself is squared), as follows:

	A	B	C	D	
	0	0	1	1	
	1	1	1	1	
	1	0	0	1	
	1	4	9	1	
	1	9	9	4	
totals	4	14	20	8	total = 46

The total (46) is of course the overall sum of squares from Step 1 minus the between-sample component, or $116 - 70 = 46$. The degrees of freedom required to estimate the variance are the number of occurrences minus the number of samples (because each sample has $n-1$ degrees of freedom), i.e. $20 - 4 = 16$. Within-sample variance is thus $46 \div 16 = 2 \cdot 9$.

Step 4 is the calculation of F, which is the greater of the variance estimates divided by the lesser one:

120

$$F = \frac{23 \cdot 3}{2 \cdot 9} = 8 \cdot 1$$

The rejection region for H_o at the appropriate degrees of freedom (from tables) is $F > 3 \cdot 24$ at $p = 0 \cdot 05$, so the null hypothesis cannot be accepted. In fact, this ratio is significant at the 99 per cent level, and almost at 99·9. So it is highly improbable that the same parent population has been sampled, and highly likely that yield varies with differences in soil type.

Splitting up the variation into its within-sample and between-sample components in any data matrix may now be expressed formally as follows:

$$\sum_{i=1}^{g} \sum_{j=1}^{n} (X_{ij} - \bar{x})^2 = \sum_{i=1}^{g} \sum_{j=1}^{n} (X_{ij} - \bar{x}_i)^2 + n \sum_{i=1}^{g} (\bar{x}_i - \bar{x})^2 \quad [4.8]$$

where g is the number of samples or groups (i.e. the columns in the matrix),

n is the number of observations in the samples (rows in the matrix),

and X_{ij} is the value in the ith group on the jth observation.

The symbol $\bar{x}$ is the mean of all observations, while $\bar{x}_i$ is the mean for the ith sample. The appearance of two summation signs together (i.e. $\Sigma\Sigma$) simply indicates the sum of all items in the matrix, that is, all g columns or n rows. The quantity on the left of the equality sign in [4.8] is the total sum of squares (sometimes written TSS), the first quantity on the right side is the within-sample variation or 'sum of squares due to errors' (SSE), while the remaining quantity is the between-sample variation or 'sum of squares due to groups' (SSG) arising from differences in the means of the populations from which the samples have been drawn.

Calculating SSE and SSG can be accomplished by a less tedious procedure than that used in the simple illustration above. This is done by the introduction of two new terms: the first is a 'correction for the mean' (CM) where:

$$CM = \frac{(\Sigma\Sigma X_{ij})^2}{ng} \quad [4.9]$$

121

Patterns in Human Geography

i.e. the sum of the squares of all items, divided by the total number of observations (ng); the second is the total of all observations in any sample (T) where for the ith sample:

$$T_i = \sum_{j=1}^{n} X_{ij}$$ [4.10]

Now the total sum of squares can be rewritten:

$$TSS = \sum_{i=1}^{g} \sum_{j=1}^{n} X_{ij}^2 - CM$$ [4.11]

The use of the correction item here is identical to the shortcut method of finding the sum of squares in the 'machine formula' for the standard deviation in expression [3.5]. The between-sample component can similarly be written:

$$SSG = \sum_{i=1}^{g} \frac{T_i^2}{n} - CM$$ [4.12]

The within-sample variation is found by subtraction, i.e.:

$$SSE = TSS - SSG$$ [4.13]

The variances or mean squares are found by dividing SSG and SSE by the appropriate degrees of freedom, which are in general:

$$ng - 1 = g(n-1) + (g-1)$$ [4.14]

where $ng - 1$ is df for TSS, $g(n-1)$ is for SSE, and $g-1$ is for SSG.

For an example of the analysis of variance using these methods of calculation, we will return to the problem of flat development in Australia. Suppose that we are interested in occupancy rates, and wish to find out whether the municipality averages vary significantly among the five metropolitan areas. Ten municipalities are selected from each, and their average numbers of inhabitants per flat are listed (Table 4.2). An analysis of variance on these data establishes the likelihood that the five sets of occupancy rates could have been drawn at random from the same parent population, thus enabling us to judge whether the inter-city differences are significant or not.

The null hypothesis is: $\bar{X}_A = \bar{X}_B = \bar{X}_M = \bar{X}_P = \bar{X}_S$, i.e. that the five metropolitan means for all municipalities are the same. The alternate hypothesis is that at least one pair are different from one another. The sum (T_i) for each city group of municipalities is calculated, along with the sample means $(\bar{x}_i)$, the square of the sums divided by sample size (T_1^2/n), and the sum of the squares of the observations (ΣX^2) – see Table 4.2. The correction for the mean from expression [4.9] above is:

$$CM = \frac{(110 \cdot 55)^2}{10 \times 5} = \frac{12221}{50} = 244$$

The total sum of squares of individual observations from the overall mean $(\bar{x})$ from expression [4.11] is:

$$TSS = 274 - 244 = 30$$

Between-group variation, from [4.12], is:

$$SSG = 246 - 244 = 2$$

This leaves within-group sum of squares, from [4.13], as:

$$SSE = 30 - 2 = 28$$

Now, the variances are found by dividing SSG and SSE by their degrees of freedom. From [4.14]:

$$50 - 1 = (5 \times 9) + (5 - 1), \quad \text{or} \quad 49 = 45 + 4$$

So: within-group variance $= \dfrac{28}{45} = 0 \cdot 62$

between-group variance $= \dfrac{2}{4} = 0 \cdot 50$

Conducting the test at $p = 0 \cdot 05$, F of at least $5 \cdot 7$ is required to reject the null hypothesis. The actual value is:

$$\frac{0 \cdot 62}{0 \cdot 50} = 1 \cdot 24$$

Thus H_o cannot be rejected, for the five sets of municipal occupancy rates could easily have been drawn at random from the same parent population. We would therefore be hesitant about attaching any significance to inter-metropolitan differences in the rates; those found among municipalities within the metropolis are a more important source of variation in the data as a whole.

But is it really sensible to dismiss inter-metropolitan variations on the basis of this test? The manner in which the data were selected raises doubts, for the observations were not in fact random samples but the ten municipalities in each city with the highest proportions of flats among all dwelling units. They might therefore be more representative of overall city conditions than random samples would have been. As they stand, the five sets of ten observations reveal municipality mean occupancy rates in two cities (Adelaide and Perth) markedly lower than in the other three (Table 4.2). The analysis of variance has shown that *if* the data were random samples we could not conclude that the true means are not the same, but in reality the average occupancy rates

Table 4.2: Data for Analysis of Variance on Number of Inhabitants per Flat in Australian Metropolitan Areas

Municipality observations $(j; n = 10)$	Cities $(i; g = 5)$					Totals
	Adelaide	Brisbane	Melbourne	Perth	Sydney	
1	2·17	2·18	2·29	2·01	2·17	
2	2·08	2·29	2·13	1·99	2·07	
3	2·31	2·22	2·05	1·95	2·46	
4	2·32	2·23	2·51	2·01	2·09	
5	1·90	2·08	2·22	1·84	2·36	
6	2·37	2·46	2·35	1·54	2·58	
7	2·03	2·52	2·51	2·41	2·39	
8	2·02	2·36	2·41	2·01	2·12	
9	1·79	2·42	2·56	2·36	2·33	
10	1·68	2·35	2·26	2·16	2·63	
T_i	20·67	23·11	23·29	20·48	23·20	110·55
$\bar{x}_i$	2·07	2·31	2·33	2·05	2·32	
T_i^2/n	42·74	53·40	54·24	41·94	53·82	246·14
Σ_i^2	43·21	53·57	54·50	41·68	54·19	247·15

Source of data: see Table 4.1.

for the cities as a whole differ in a manner very similar to that suggested by the data in Table 4.2 (the actual figures are: Adelaide 2·10, Perth 2·03, Melbourne 2·41, Brisbane 2·41, Sydney 2·38). Only if we are dealing with true random samples can we make confident and valid inferences about conditions in the entire populations of areas. The *arithmetic* in the example above is correct, but the *research design* is at fault.

As with other statistical tests, important assumptions are attached to the analysis of variance. These are that the populations sampled are normally distributed, that the population variances are the same, and that the individual observations have been selected at random. The F values associated with different degrees of freedom (i.e. number of groups and their size) hold precisely only if these conditions are met. However, as one statistics text-book puts it, 'in actual practice it has been observed that one or more of these assumptions can be "bent" without appreciable loss in the adequacy of the F test. The researcher strives to meet the assumptions of the F test, but he usually finds that if his data are reasonably close to meeting the assumptions, his conclusions based on the F test are not markedly affected'. (C. I. Chase, *Elementary Statistical Procedures*, McGraw-Hill, 1967, 170.)

Conducted properly, the analysis of variance (ANOVA for short) is one of the most powerful and versatile of statistical tests, and it can be performed in different ways to suit the particular research problem or experimental design. The application shown here is the *one-way* ANOVA with one set of observations for each group, but there is also a *two-way* version in which two conditions might be included, e.g. occupancy rates for two different years in each of the five cities. Unequal sample size can also be accommodated by having a variable n term in the calculations. Fuller instructions as to the conduct of the test will be found in more specialized books on statistics (see Selected Reading), and an examination of some of these is advisable before attempting serious research applications in geography.

One final comment is required on the analysis of variance, with respect to the interpretation of the results of the test. The acceptance of the alternate hypothesis of significant differences between samples does not automatically validate an hypothesized causal relationship, e.g. between crop yield and soil type. An observed association between conditions does not necessarily prove cause and effect, though it may offer supporting evidence. Much depends on whether other possible causal factors have been controlled for – something which is easier in the laboratory than in human geography. Ideally, statistical tests should come at the end of an investigation designed carefully so that a positive result logically substantiates the hypothesized causal relationship.

Comparing Frequency Distributions: The Chi-square Test

Often it is necessary to compare the frequency distribution of two sets of observations. This involves the use of more information about the variables than a comparison of means, for it requires that the data are allocated to classes. Frequency distributions may be compared and tested for significance by the *chi-square statistic*, symbolized by the Greek letter chi (χ). This is one of the most commonly used statistical tests, and has the important property of not requiring normally distributed data. But it must be used with care. It is designed to work on absolute frequencies, and if the data are percentages a modification of the usual method is needed (see H. Walker and J. Lev, *Statistical Inference*, 94–5). Most important is that the test is set out in a formal way, according to the method explained earlier in this chapter.

The chi-square test compares a set of *observed frequencies* (O) with a set of *expected frequencies* (E), and establishes the probability of the difference being the result of chance, or sampling error. Although specifically designed for sample data, it is often used in geography to test whether the difference between sets of data which constitute entire populations is large enough to be considered 'significant'.

To conduct the test, the data must first of all be in the right form. The sum of the expected frequencies should be the same as the sum of the observed frequencies. If less than five occurrences are found in one expected class, classes should be combined, unless the number of classes is greater than two, in which case not more than 20 per cent of the expected frequencies should be less than 5. Observations must be independent, in the sense that one is not influenced by another.

The chi-square statistic is calculated by subtracting the expected frequency from the observed in each class, squaring and dividing by the expected frequency, and summing the results, i.e.:

$$\chi^2 = \sum_{i=1}^{k} \frac{(O_i - E_i)^2}{E_i}$$ [4.15]

where k is the number of classes $(1, 2, \ldots, i, \ldots, k)$. The significance of the result is found by referring to a table or graph of the sampling distribution of the statistic, in which the critical χ^2 value is given at different confidence levels and degrees of freedom. Exact correspondence between the two sets of frequencies makes $\chi^2 = 0$. The probability of a chance explanation of the difference is relatively high with a low χ^2 value and a large number of classes. It becomes less probable as χ^2 increases and as the degrees of freedom are reduced. The degrees of freedom in the chi-square test are generally $k - 1$.

The chi-square test establishes the probability that the observed frequencies could have resulted from a sample drawn at random from a parent population with the frequencies of the expected values. In using chi-square, as in any statistical test, it is important to understand exactly what is being tested, and what can and cannot be inferred from the result of the test. For this reason the null hypothesis, the alternate hypothesis and the confidence level and rejection region should be established and set down initially, before the test is run.

A simple illustration will explain the conduct of the test. Suppose that on the basis of some theory or model it is hypothesized that in a certain region four socio-economic groups will be found in the ratios of 10 professional persons, 30 skilled workers, 40 semi-skilled workers, and 20 unskilled manual workers. Random samples of 100 persons in two cities within this region show the following results:

Class	City A	City B
Professional	17	13
Skilled	51	28
Semi-skilled	22	43
Unskilled	10	16

Neither city has a frequency distribution identical to the hypothesized regional distribution, but are the differences great enough to be significant or could they be attributed to sampling error?

The null hypothesis is of no difference between the true frequencies in the entire population and the expected frequencies on the basis of theory. The test for each city is as follows:

$H_o: fX_O = fX_E$
$H_a: fX_O \neq fX_E$
test statistic: χ^2, $df = 3$
significance: $p = 0.05$
decision rule: reject H_o if $\chi^2 > 7.82$

The symbols fX simply indicate the frequency of some variables X, in this case in the four classes. The calculation for city A are as follows:

	E	O	$O-E$	$(O-E)^2$	$\dfrac{(O-E)^2}{E}$
Professional	10	17	7	49	4.90
Skilled	30	51	21	441	14.70
Semi-skilled	40	22	-18	324	8.10
Unskilled	20	10	-10	100	5.00
					$\Sigma = 32.70 = \chi^2$

The value for χ^2 is well above 7.82, so H_o is rejected and H_a accepted. A similar calculation for city B produces a χ^2 of 2.05, so in this case H_o is accepted. Referring to a graph of χ^2 at 3 degrees of freedom shows that the difference between O and E for city A is significant at the 99.9 per cent confidence level; there is less than 0.1 per cent probability of chance occurrence. For city B the value of the test statistic falls below the 50 per cent confidence level, so the difference between this city and the hypothesized regional socio-economic structure is more likely than not the result of sampling error. These findings might lead an investigator to examine the special circumstances leading city A to depart from the expectation while the other city conforms to theory.

An example using a real research problem may be described briefly. In 1940, Samuel Stouffer put forward the theory of 'intervening opportunity' to help explain population migration, proposing that 'the number of persons going a given distance is directly proportional to the number of opportunities at that distance and inversely proportional to the number of intervening opportunities'. He developed a model to predict the number of families moving given distances, and tested this in Cleveland, Ohio, for the period 1933–5. The data on movement from one census tract are listed in Table 4.3. The fact that his model predicted the observed movement rather closely is obvious, but the question arises as to whether the correspondence is close enough that the difference can be attributed to chance. The χ^2 statistic can test this, if Stouffer's observations can be treated as a random sample – a not unreasonable assumption if the people moving in 1933–5 can be regarded as representative of a wider population of movement over a more extensive time period, or if movement from this one tract is representative of the city as a whole.

The null hypothesis is that there is no significant difference between Stouffer's observations (O) and the expected frequencies from his model. The alternate hypothesis is that a significant difference exists, i.e. that the two sets of observations did not come from identical parent populations. A high degree of confidence is required, so $p = 0.01$. At this level and with 12 degrees of freedom the critical χ^2 value is 26·22, above which H_o must be rejected. The calculation in Table 4.3 shows $\chi^2 = 56.11$, so H_o is rejected and H_a accepted. A table or graph of the statistic shows that the difference is in fact significant at the 99·9 per cent level, so the null hypothesis is rejected very confidently indeed.

We have found that Stouffer's prediction was not so close that its imperfections could be reasonably attributed to chance alone. However, if his model had not seriously underpredicted in just one class ($6-8.9$), the level of significance would have dropped to

129

Table 4.3: Calculation of Chi-Square for a Set of Observed Frequencies
of Movement Over Different Distances Compared with an Expected
Set

Distance Moved (1,000 ft)	E	O	O–E	(O–E)²	$\frac{(O-E)^2}{E}$
0– 2·9	288	253	–35	1225	4·25
3– 5·9	98	92	–6	36	0·36
6– 8·9	46	84	38	1444	31·39
9–11·4	15	22	7	49	3·26
12–14·9	9	15	6	36	4·00
15–17·9	15	22	7	49	3·26
18–20·9	15	17	2	4	0·27
21–23·9	11	11	0	0	0·00
24–26·9	14	8	–6	36	2·57
27–29·9	13	13	0	0	0·00
30–32·9	9	3	–6	36	4·00
33–35·9	6	4	–2	4	0·67
36 and over	12	7	–5	25	2·08

$$\chi^2 = \Sigma \frac{(O-E)^2}{E} = 56\cdot11$$

Source of data: S. Stouffer, 'Intervening Opportunities: A Theory Relating
Mobility to Distance', American Sociological Review, 5 (1940), 845–67,
Table 2.

a point at which the null hypothesis could almost have been
accepted. Following an unsuccessful test, refinements may be made
in the model and another set of expected frequencies generated
which predict reality more closely.

The applications of chi-square presented here for the purpose
of illustration are of the kind where one set of frequencies is a true
expectation on theoretical or other *a priori* grounds. This is known
as a *one independent sample* case, for the expected frequencies are
fixed and assumed to represent a parent population and not a
sample. But if the problem is to compare two sets of frequencies
neither of which can be truly regarded as the expected (i.e. if both
must be regarded as sample data), then a modified calculation is

required. The particulars of this are set down in another context in Chapter 8. In using the χ^2 test it is very important to consider whether the problem is a one or two (or more) independent sample case, as it is only in the former that the method of calculation set out above is appropriate.

Some Other Statistical Tests

The formula for chi-square above [4.15] provides a general method for measuring the 'goodness of fit' between an observed frequency distribution and one derived from theory. This is sometimes written as follows:

$$G = \sum_{i=1}^{k} \frac{(f_O - f_E)^2}{f_E} \qquad [4.16]$$

where G is the measure of goodness of fit, subject to the interpretation that the higher it is the poorer the fit. The expected frequencies (f_E) are usually generated by some sampling distribution or probability function, and the goodness of fit test is in fact identical to chi-square in the way it is conducted.

There are a number of other tests, designed to work on data originally measured on a nominal or ordinal scale. They are referred to as *non-parametric* methods, and have the great advantage that a normally distributed parent population is not assumed. Most parametric statistics have some kind of non-parametric or distribution-free equivalent. Chi-square is the most commonly used non-parametric test in human geography. It is often used in situations where the data are nominal, for example occurrences (dots) on a map, and it is desired to test observed areal frequencies by quadrats or other units against an expected frequency.

One of the simplest non-parametric methods is the *sign test*. This works on sets of paired observations, and uses the property of whether the one is greater ($+$) or less ($-$) than the other. It is applicable where interval or ratio measurement of the differences between the magnitude of two variables is difficult or impossible, and makes no assumption about their distribution. As an example, data have been tabulated for a sample of twenty municipalities from our five Australian metropolitan areas (four from each to stratify the sample geographically), on the number of persons per room in flats at two points in time. The differences are very small, so the best we can probably do is to regard them as accurate enough only to indicate the direction of change. In Table 4.4, a + is given to increases and − to decreases. The null hypothesis is that there is no difference between conditions at the two points in time. If this is true we can expect the same number of + and − signs; if not true one sign will predominate. Counting the number of fewer signs (9 minus) and relating it to sample size ($n = 20$) enables the probability of a significant difference to be found from tables (e.g. S. Siegel, *Nonparametric Statistics*, McGraw-Hill, 1956, 250). At a confidence level of 90 per cent the tabulated value shows that the null hypothesis cannot be rejected, so we judge the change in persons per room between 1954 and 1966 as established by the sample to be insignificant. For larger samples ($n > 25$) a test based on the normal distribution (Z) can be used.

Some non-parametric tests can be applied where the data are in an awkward form. The *Mann-Whitney U test* can be used when one variable is ranked and the other is in frequencies, and when

Table 4.4: *Sign Test Applied to Data on Number of Persons per Room in Flats in a Sample of Twenty Municipalities in Australian Metropolitan Areas*

	1954	1966	sign		1954	1966	sign
1	0·56	0·49	−	11	0·57	0·64	+
2	0·72	0·59	−	12	0·53	0·55	+
3	0·54	0·57	+	13	0·66	0·64	−
4	0·56	0·50	−	14	0·57	0·58	+
5	0·69	0·71	+	15	0·63	0·64	+
6	0·65	0·64	−	16	0·61	0·56	−
7	0·55	0·59	+	17	0·53	0·51	−
8	0·61	0·66	+	18	0·64	0·63	−
9	0·58	0·63	+	19	0·63	0·66	+
10	0·72	0·74	+	20	0·52	0·48	−

Source of data: see Table 4.1.

ordinal data exist for samples of unequal size. It is one of the most powerful non-parametric tests, and provides an alternative to the t test when the assumptions required for the latter are not fulfilled. One example may be described. Within the city of Tampa, Florida, 21 of the 71 tracts were identified in a planning study as 'socially deprived', and it is required to find out whether infant mortality rates are significantly higher here than in the rest of the city. Infant deaths per 1,000 live births in 1970 are known for each of a random sample of 8 deprived tracts and 16 other tracts. Because such local rates are often based on few occurrences they are subject to fluctuations from year to year, so our data might best be regarded as accurate only up to the ordinal scale. Thus there are two samples of different sizes in which we are prepared to do no more than rank observations. In this situation the null hypothesis that the two samples are from the same population can be tested by the statistic U, where the required value is the smaller of those provided by the following expressions:

$$U = n_1 n_2 + \frac{n_1(n_1+1)}{2} - R_1 \qquad [4.17]$$

$$U = n_1 n_2 + \frac{n_2(n_2+1)}{2} - R_2 \qquad [4.18]$$

The sample sizes are n_1 (the smaller) and n_2, and R_1 and R_2 are the sums of the ranks of the items in each sample, derived from a ranking of *all* observations. The data are listed in Table 4.5. Substituting in [4.17]:

$$U = 8 \times 16 + \frac{8(8+1)}{2} - 136 \cdot 5$$
$$= 128 + 36 - 136 \cdot 5$$
$$= 27 \cdot 5$$

and in [4.18]:

$$U = 8 \times 16 + \frac{16(16+1)}{2} - 163 \cdot 5$$
$$= 128 + 136 - 163 \cdot 5$$
$$= 100 \cdot 5$$

Table 4.5: Unequal Samples of Tract Infant Mortality Rates in Two Zones of the City of Tampa

Socially Deprived Areas		Remainder of City	
Rate	Rank	Rate	Rank
51·7	21	32·2	14
0·0	3·5	0·0	3·5
76·3	24	72·4	23
49·2	20	16·9	10·5
15·6	9	0·0	3·5
45·4	18	9·2	7
62·9	22	22·7	12
45·6	19	33·9	15
		13·9	8
		0·0	3·5
		26·3	13
		36·3	16
		0·0	3·5
		42·5	17
		0·0	3·5
		16·9	10·5
$n_1 = 8$ $R_1 = 136·5$		$n_2 = 16$ $R_2 = 163·5$	

Source of data: Hillsborough County Health Department.

So the required U is 27·5. Suppose our hypothesis is that infant mortality in socially deprived tracts is higher than in other tracts. This requires a one-tailed test, for which tables tell us that H_o of no difference or higher rates in other tracts can be rejected at $U < 36$ ($p = 0.05$). We can therefore accept that the deprived tracts as a population have higher infant mortality than those in the rest of the city.

Another useful non-parametric device is the *Kolmogorov–Smirnov test*. This can provide a quick check on the significance of the difference between two sets of frequencies expressed as cumulative proportions. The classes in the two distributions must be the same, but the number of observations in each set need not be equal. The test is based on the quantity D, which is the maximum difference between the two frequencies in any class. As an illustration, the test may be run on the two sets of percentage frequencies for the imaginary data in Table 3.6 from the previous chapter. In cumulative form these are:

$\%fX$:   8   20   40   64   84   96   100 $(n = 25)$
$\%fY$: 20   64   80   88   92   96   100 $(n = 25)$
   dif: 12   **44**   40   24   8   0   0

The maximum difference is 44 (%). Following the procedure described by Siegel (*Nonparametric Statistics*, 127–36) for 'small' independent samples, it is found that a larger value is needed to reject the null hypothesis at $p = 0.05$, so at this level we cannot dismiss the possibility that the two samples could have been drawn from the same parent population.

The critical value in the Kolmogorov–Smirnov test can be found graphically by superimposing the two cumulative percentage frequency distributions. As an example, we may attempt a comparison between the distribution of sub-areal infant mortality rates in Tampa and another city – Sydney. This will be based on entire populations of sub-areal rates, using the test to judge whether any observed difference is 'significant' by the criterion that if the data had been samples it is unlikely that they could have come from the same parent population ($p = 0.05$). For Tampa the data are rates for 71 tracts, while for Sydney they are for 40 local government areas. In both cases the data are allocated to classes with intervals of 10, and the resulting cumulative percentage frequencies are as in Figure 4.3. The two distributions appear quite different, with Tampa values more spread out and exceeding 100 in some cases while all the Sydney values are in the first three classes. The maximum difference can be read off as $D = 37$ (approx.), and tables show that this is well above the value at which the null hypothesis of no difference between the distributions can be rejected.

But is the difference between the cities really as significant as this test implies? When the nature of the data is examined, doubt might be cast on this conclusion. While the Tampa rates are for

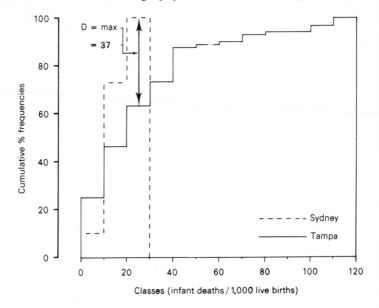

Figure 4.3   Cumulative percentage frequency distributions of sub-areal infant mortality rates in Tampa and Sydney. (Sources of data: Hillsborough County Health Department, and State of New South Wales.)

small areas with similar population sizes and relative socio-economic homogeneity, the data for the Sydney metropolitan area are based on much larger and more heterogeneous areas which in some cases have populations greater than 100,000. The larger the areal unit of observation and the more varied its internal structure, the more likely it is to hide local extremes in infant mortality or any other condition. If the Tampa data had been aggregated for areas of similar size to Sydney, the larger rates in the tail of the distribution would have been lost because they apply only to small neighbourhoods. In fact, the overall infant mortality rate for Tampa (25 per 1,000) is higher than in the Sydney Statistical Division (18), but the differences in the geography of this condition are probably much less marked than the data in Figure 4.3 implies. This example emphasizes once more the sensitivity of numerical description in human geography to the nature of the areal units of observation.

Most of the statistical tests in common use today have been designed for samples of *individuals*, not areas. Like the Kolmogorov–Smirnov test above, they will provide an answer no matter what data are employed; as with the computer, they cannot discriminate between good or bad data or research designs. The geographer using such tests must bear in mind the special limitations of areal data relating to groups of individuals, as well as the conditions imposed by the assumptions underlying specific statistical devices.

This chapter has introduced the idea of comparing sets of geographical observations and conducting tests of significance on the differences discovered. It should be concluded by stressing that descriptive and inferential statistics are complex subjects, on which the advice of a specialist text or a professional statistician is often required to perform competent research applications. Appropriate references are to be found in the Selected Reading at the end of the book. If this chapter has done little else it should have indicated that comparisons, like summaries, must be made with care and interpreted with caution. A quick glance at a list of figures is seldom sufficient basis for firm descriptive statements beginning 'On the average . . .', or 'The difference between . . .'.

5. Transforming and Combining Data

Previous chapters have shown that the geographical incidence of a condition can be measured in various ways. We generate numbers, which can stand as a summary description and which can also be used for comparison with the incidence of other conditions. But many aspects of life cannot sensibly be represented by observations on a single attribute or variable, and it may be necessary to combine information on a number of different conditions. If they can all be measured in the same way combination is easy; number of pigs, bushels of wheat and tons of steel can be summed in a general indicator of production through the common units of their monetary value. But conditions measured in different units or on different scales raise problems. How, for example, might we add people in poverty, infant mortality and crime rates to produce some general social indicator?

This problem can be approached by *scale transformations*, which facilitate the combination (and comparison) of data on variables measured in different ways. The idea of transformation of scales was introduced in Chapter 3, in the context of the normalization of data. In general, a scale transformation comprises any rule which enables one set of observations to be converted into another set which is more useful than the original in a particular context. This chapter demonstrates different methods of scale transformation, and their application to the development of various composite social indicators.

*How Not to Combine Data: The FBI Crime Index**

An example of a bad method of combining information is a useful point of departure. The FBI (Federal Bureau of Investigation) in the United States compiles data on the incidence of various categories of crime throughout the nation, and each year publishes general indices of the level of criminal activity for the country as a whole, for the fifty states, and for many cities. The annual changes in the index are watched with anxiety by government and public alike, as a barometer of the effectiveness of law enforcement and of the maintenance of social order. The reliability of the FBI crime index as a social indicator is thus a matter of some importance.

Whatever the reputation of the FBI for the apprehension of criminals, it is certainly not enhanced by the quality of their numerical analysis. Some of the problems are beyond their control, for they cannot count what they do not observe, and many crimes committed are not known to the local police departments which submit their annual figures to the FBI. But what they do with the data when they get it is very much within the control of the FBI. Once the numbers of crimes have been amalgamated for the required geographical units, they have to be converted into ratios because actual numbers mean little in a comparative context for areas of different size and number of inhabitants. The FBI uses a population base, expressing the level of criminal activity as a rate per 100,000 people. This seems reasonable for crimes against the person because standardizing for population turns incidence into a risk statement which can be thought of as the probability of any member of the population of the area in question becoming a victim of these crimes (though the proportion of the population actually at risk of rape, for example, might vary with age structure). But a population ratio is obviously less satisfactory for crimes against property. What is at risk now is

---

*This case is taken from D. M. Smith, *Crime Rates as Territorial Social Indicators*, Occasional Paper 1, Department of Geography, Queen Mary College (University of London), 1974.

wealth, not people, so local property crime should logically be related to the value of property. The volume of theft can increase over time and geographically, simply because there is more to steal, and it is this condition which should be controlled for in a comparative index of property crimes, rather than population.

The major deficiency of the FBI crime index is to be found in the way figures for different crimes are combined. The general index is based on the incidence of seven types of crime: the 'index crimes' of murder and non-negligent manslaughter, forcible rape, robbery, aggravated assault, burglary, larceny $50 and over, and auto theft. Having been converted into ratios of population as described above, these are then simply summed, and the total for any area is its overall crime index (Table 5.1).

The inadequacy of this method of combining data will be obvious. As a general indicator of criminal activity, this index takes no account of the fact that some crimes occur more frequently than others, and that those occurring less frequently are the ones which the public regard as most serious. In calculating the index for a given area, one incident of each crime is in effect

Table 5.1: The Derivation of the FBI Crime Index for the United States

Crime	Number of Crimes known to Police	Rate per 100,000 Population
Murder and non-negligent manslaughter	17,627	8·5
Forcible rape	41,888	20·3
Robbery	385,908	187·1
Aggravated assault	364,595	176·8
Burglary	2,368,423	1,148·3
Larceny $50 and over	1,875,194	909·2
Auto theft	941,576	456·5
Total number of crimes	5,995,211	
Total crime index (sum of rates)		2,906·7

Source: US Department of Justice, Federal Bureau of Investigation, *Uniform Crime Reports for the United States*, 1971.

equated; in other words, one murder = one rape ... = one auto theft, for the purpose of the FBI statistical analysis. Clearly, if summation is justified, some value other than unity would be desirable for each of the seven crime categories – a figure representing frequency or seriousness.

One of the practical difficulties arising from the derivation of the FBI crime index is in interpreting changes. The general composite index is obviously more sensitive to an increase in the rate of a frequent crime than to the same increase in one occurring less frequently. Doubling the number of auto thefts raises the index far more than doubling the number of murders. The index can in fact go down over time if the number of crimes of violence (relatively infrequent) is going up more rapidly than the number of crimes against property (relatively frequent) is going down. Comparing geographical areas, a city with twice the national auto theft rate and half the national murder rate would, other rates being the same, look worse on the FBI index than a city with twice the national murder rate and half its auto thefts. For the FBI crime index to become a meaningful barometer of social order some method of weighting different types of crime is needed, and this requires scale transformation. We will return to this problem at the end of the chapter.

Linear Scale Transformations

The most usual method of converting a set of numerical observations into a form which can be directly combined or compared with another set is through a *linear* scale transformation, in which the observations plotted on a graph with the original numbers on one axis and the new ones on the other would form a straight line. It can be achieved by adding a constant to all the original observations, subtracting a constant, multiplying by a constant, or dividing by a constant. This can be explained by considering the effect of these operations on a ruler marked with a set of observations. Adding or subtracting a constant is like adding a piece on to the left-hand end of the ruler or cutting a piece off, increasing or decreasing the distance of each observation from zero or the origin of the scale by the same amount. Multiplying or dividing by a constant expands or compresses the ruler, rather like a concertina. In all cases the new observations will be a linear function of the original ones. Thus if X (1, 2, ..., i, ...) is the set of original data, X' (1, 2, ..., i, ...) the new data, and k is a constant, the following expressions all define linear transformations:

$$X_i' = X_i + k$$
$$X_i' = X_i - k$$
$$X_i' = X_i \times k$$
$$X_i' = X_i \div k \qquad [5.1]$$

As each of these transformations does a different thing, one is likely to be more useful than others in any given circumstance. Adding or subtracting a constant changes the ratios between numbers but not their intervals, so these transformations would not be used if the ratios had to be preserved. Transforming data measured on a ratio scale in this way results in loss of information. If we measure height of land from a datum other than sea level we can still say that one place is 100 feet higher than another, but not that somewhere originally measured at 1,000 ft OD is twice as high as somewhere at 500 ft OD. Multiplying or dividing by a constant changes size of intervals but not ratios. Thus changing the scale on a map or converting from miles to kilometres changes units of distance between places (e.g. 100 miles becomes 161 kms), but somewhere originally twice as far from London as Birmingham stays that way.

Linear transformations differ from those discussed in Chapter 3 in the section on normalizing a distribution. They do not change a skewed distribution of values into a smooth, regular curve. To do this requires changing both intervals and ratios between numbers, i.e. a *curvilinear* transformation in which the two sets of observations would form a curve when plotted on a graph with the 'before' and 'after' scales along the axes. Curvilinear transformations can be achieved by raising a set of numbers to a constant power, or by dividing them into a constant, i.e.:

$$X'_i = X^k_i$$
$$X'_i = k \div X_i \qquad\qquad [5.2]$$

The logarithm and square root transformations illustrated in Chapter 3 are curvilinear. The essential difference between these and linear transformations can be confirmed by plotting on a graph the original and log data for variable Y from Table 3.6, and comparing it with a graph of Y against any of the expressions in [5.1], i.e. $Y+k$, $Y-k$, $Y \times k$ or $Y \div k$.

Another important distinction which has to be made is between linear transformations and the common practice of converting absolute numbers into rates and ratios. The most familiar is the percentage rate:

$$X'_i = \frac{100 \; X_i}{Y_i} \qquad\qquad [5.3]$$

where Y represents some other variable such as population. The difference between this and a linear transformation is that Y is a variable and not a constant.

If addition, subtraction, multiplication or division by a constant achieves a linear scale transformation, so they can in combination. A very common form of linear transformation involves both adding (or subtracting) one constant and multiplying by another, i.e.:

$$X'_i = a + bX_i \qquad\qquad [5.4]$$

This is in fact the *linear equation* used as the basis of correlation and regression analysis (see Chapters 7 and 8).

A familiar use of this linear relationship for scale transformation is in the conversion of temperatures. The Fahrenheit and Centigrade scales both measure the same condition, but in different sized units. Between the two points of the freezing and boiling of water, the F scale ranges from 32 to 212 degrees and the C scale from 0 to 100. Degrees C can be converted to degrees F by multiplying C by 9, dividing by 5, and adding 32. This can be written:

$$F = 32 + \frac{9}{5}C$$

143

or by $F = a + bC$ where a and b are the constants 32 and $\frac{9}{5}$. In other words, the conversion is in the form of expression [5.4] above. It is a linear scale transformation.

Now consider the transformation in the other direction, from Fahrenheit to Centigrade. By simple algebra this is:

$$C = (F - 32) \times \frac{5}{9}$$

which is again a linear equation. The F value has a constant subtracted from it, and the result is multiplied by another constant.

As this converts the rather awkward range 32 to 212 into the much more convenient 0 to 100, the general version of this transformation is useful. If variables on a scale with any range can be readily re-scaled from 0 to 100, this would provide one simple method for making measurements on different conditions comparable. Looking at the Fahrenheit to Centigrade conversion formula above, the brackets include the individual F values and the minimum on the range 32 to 212 (i.e. that which is 0 on the other scale), while the other term is the ratio of the two ranges ($\frac{5}{9} = \frac{100}{180}$). This can be written generally as:

$$(X_i - X_{\min}) \frac{R_X'}{R_X} \qquad [5.5]$$

where $X_{\min}$ is the minimum value for the variable X,

R_X is the range of the values of X, or $X_{\max} - X_{\min}$,

$R_{X'}$ is the range into which X is to be transformed, i.e. 100 (or 10),

and X_i and X_i' are the original and transformed variates respectively, as before. This can be made to look more like the basic linear equation [5.4] by changing some of the notation and rewriting. As $X_{\min}$ and $R_{X'}/R_X$ are constants, they can be replaced by k_X and k_R respectively, to give:

$$X_i' = (X_i - k_X) k_R \qquad [5.6]$$

or

$$X_i' = (X_i k_R) - (k_X k_R) \qquad [5.7]$$

This is now the same as the original linear equation, where the constant of addition or subtraction (a) is equal to $k_X k_R$ and the constant of multiplication (b) is k_R. So the final expression for converting from any range to one beginning with 0 and extending to 10, 100, or whatever is required, is:

$$X_i' = a + bX_i \qquad\qquad [5.8]$$

where a is the minimum on the original variable multiplied by the ratio of the original and new ranges, negative if X_{min} is positive,

and b is the ratio of the ranges, i.e. $R_{X'}/R_X$.

This transformation may now be illustrated in a simple imaginary problem, involving the use of a number of different variables to measure 'quality of life' in a set of places. Suppose that an individual is trying to choose between four cities (A, B, C and D) in which he or she might live, and that the major pleasures in life to be considered are dancing, going to the cinema, and drinking in night clubs. All other things being equal, our observer judges the quality of life by access to these facilities. Each city is visited and the number of dance halls, cinemas and night clubs found, with the following results:

	Dance halls (X_1)	Cinemas (X_2)	Night clubs (X_3)
City A	7	21	6
City B	5	8	12
City C	10	12	8
City D	6	1	4

The question posed is, which city is the most attractive by the three quality-of-life criteria, on the basis of the data compiled? One way to answer this might be simply to add across the rows in the matrix; but this would be rather like adding apples and oranges and would automatically give most weight to the facility appearing in the largest number (cinemas), just as the FBI index emphasizes the most frequent crimes. Another method might be

145

to give some subjective weight to each facility (e.g. one point to a cinema, two to a dance hall, etc.) and then sum the results for each city. But in the absence of weights which can be assigned with confidence, it might be better to assume that each of the criteria are of the same importance such that, other things being equal, a city with the highest possible number of dance halls (10) would have the same level of life quality as one with the maximum number of cinemas (21), etc., and the same at the bottom ends of the scales. This is the technique adopted in the present illustration. The values for each of the three variables will be converted into scales with the maximum value arbitrarily assigned the number 10 and the minimum set at 0. This is exactly the same as converting Fahrenheit temperatures into Centigrade. Given values for the minima and ranges, linear scale transformations are derived from expression [5.8] as follows:

Dance halls: $\quad X_{min} = 5, R_X = 5; \quad X_1' = -10 + 2X_1$
Cinemas: $\quad\quad\; X_{min} = 1, R_X = 20; \quad X_2' = -0.5 + 0.5X_2$
Night clubs: $\quad X_{min} = 4, R_X = 8; \quad X_3' = -5 + 1.25X_3$

The results of these transformations may then be added up for each city, to give a composite indicator of the quality of life on the basis of which the cities might be placed in order of preference. The outcome is as follows:

	X_1'	X_2'	X_3'	Total	Order
City A	4·0	10·0	2·5	16·5	2
City B	0·0	3·5	10·0	13·5	3
City C	10·0	5·5	5·0	20·5	1
City D	2·0	0·0	0·0	2·0	4

Thus city C is the first choice. It achieves this position largely by virtue of having a clear lead in dance halls and a middle position on the other two criteria, whereas its nearest rival is poorly served by dance halls and night clubs despite its large number of cinemas. Giving all three facilities one point per occurrence would have made city A first by virtue of its 21 cinemas.

The Development of Intra-city Social Indicators by Range Standardization

The use of a linear scale transformation of the kind explained above may be further demonstrated by a study which attempts to measure the 'quality of life' as it varies within a single city. This involve the development of a number of composite indicators from variables measuring a range of social conditions and their combination into a single set of quality-of-life scores. The study is set in Gainesville, Florida, a college town with a population of about 80,000.*

The first problem is the choice of criteria. This is difficult, because there is neither firm theoretical guidance nor a general consensus as to what constitutes 'the good life' for individuals or a state of well-being for society at large. However, there is broad if not complete agreement on the desirability of certain conditions, which may be summarized under the following seven headings: high levels of income, good living environment, good physical and mental health, high levels of education, high degrees of social order (i.e. lack of social disorganization), high levels of social belonging or participation, and good recreational opportunities. These provide a working definition of the quality of life for the purpose of this study.

The second problem is the selection of data. Each of the categories suggested above requires different variables and methods of measurement, and information on some conditions which ought to be included may be impossible to obtain. At the time this study was made insufficient data were available to measure all seven criteria (for example, the income and education data from the 1970 census were not released), but some numerical approximations to the relative level of life quality in different parts of the

---

* This study is described in full in J. C. Dickinson, R. J. Gray and D. M. Smith, 'The "Quality of Life" in Gainesville, Florida: An Application of Territorial Social Indicators', *Southeastern Geographer*, 12, 1972. The project was initiated by Dr Dickinson, and the data were compiled by a group of geography students at the University of Florida under the leadership of Mr Gray.

147

Patterns in Human Geography

city could be compiled for five general conditions. They were: housing quality, home and family situation, crime as a surrogate for social disorder, the incidence of certain illnesses representative of poor health, and the number of cases under certain welfare programmes as a measure of poverty. The variables chosen to measure them are shown in Table 5.2.

Table 5.2: Criteria and Variables used to develop Social Indicators in the City of Gainesville, Florida

I *Housing*
  1 Owner-occupied units valued at less than $10,000
  2 Rented units with monthly rents less than $60·00
  3 Units without complete kitchen equipment
  4 Units without all plumbing facilities

II *Home and Family*
  5 Housing units with more than one person per room
  6 Families with children but lacking one parent

III *Crime*
  7 Public drunkenness and driving while intoxicated
  8 Petty larceny and shoplifting
  9 Burglary, breaking and entering, robbery and grand larceny
  10 Aggravated assault, rape, and murder

IV *Health*
  11 Tuberculosis
  12 Venereal disease
  13 Enteric diseases
  14 Infant mortality

V *Poverty and Welfare*
  15 Aid to families with dependent children cases
  16 Aid to the aged cases
  17 Aid to the blind and aid to the disabled cases

Sources of data: *1970 Census*, Housing Returns (Variables 1–6); City of Gainesville, Police Department – arrest files, April 1970 to April 1971 (7–10); Alachua County Health Department – incidences over various time periods (11–14); Alachua County Office, Department of Health and Rehabilitative Services, Division of Family Services, State of Florida – cases on the roles April 1971 (15–17).

Note: In every case the variable is expressed as a set of ratios of some appropriate base, e.g. total dwelling units, population, and so on.

148

The areal units of observation are Census Enumeration Districts (EDs). There are forty-six in Gainesville (code numbers 16 to 61) but special circumstances led to the omission of three of them. General ED indicators were developed for each of the five criteria adopted. This required the standardization of the variables for the purpose of amalgamation of data. A linear scale transformation was used, to generate a new set of scores for each variable on a range 0 to 100, where 0 represents the value in the ED with the lowest (i.e. most desirable) incidence and 100 represents the highest.

The transformations and the development of general social indicators from them may be illustrated with reference to housing. A portion of the original data on the four housing variables is listed in Table 5.3, with the transformed scores in Table 5.4. Each of the original variables has its own unique range, so it needs its own transformation formula; for example, the first variable has a range 0 to 78, so $X' = 0 + 1.282X$. After transformation, all the four scores may be summed for each ED, on the assumption that they contribute equally to general housing quality. The final indicator is arrived at by dividing the sum by the number of variables (i.e. 4). The housing indicator is not itself on a scale 0 to 100 because no ED scores 100 on all variables, but composite indicators arrived at in this way do have the property that any ED with a score of 0 must have the equivalent of the lowest (best) value on all contributing variables, and one with 100 must have the worst performance on them all.

Indicators for the other four general conditions have been calculated in the same way (Table 5.5). Equal weighting of individual variables in the process of combination has been violated once – in the case of variable 15; cases under the AFDC programme have been double-weighted because it is the only variable measuring families in poverty in the absence of income data. Thus the poverty and welfare indicator is derived from the sum of the transformed scores for variables 16 and 17 added to *twice* the score for 15, with the result divided by four.

The five social indicators have been combined into a single quality-of-life indicator (*QL*) by the same process as used to

149

Table 5.3: Original Housing Quality Variables for Gainesville: Portion of Data

Census ED	% Units Valued < \$10,000	% Monthly Rents < \$60	% with Incomplete Kitchen	% with Incomplete Plumbing
18	18	50	16	0
19	2	2	2	2
20	5	11	18	6
.				
.				
.				
59	59	58	26	89
60	67	85	79	344
61	45	84	30	124

Table 5.4: Transformed Housing Quality Variables and Composite Housing Indicator for Gainesville: Portion of Data

Census ED	Value (1)	Rent (2)	Kitchen (3)	Plumbing (4)	Total (Σ)	Indicator ($\Sigma \div 4$)
18	23	59	16	0	98	24·5
19	3	2	2	1	8	2·0
20	6	13	18	2	39	9·75
.						
.						
.						
59	76	69	26	25	196	49·0
60	86	100	79	96	361	90·25
61	58	99	30	35	222	55·5

generate the individual indicators. Scores on each indicator have been summed, and the result divided by five (see Table 5.5). This QL indicator has the property that an ED with the lowest possible score on all seventeen variables would rate 0, while one with the highest (worst) score on them all would rate 100. No ED occupies either of these extremes, though the actual range in values from 3 to 84 shows that the quality of life in Gainesville is subject to very considerable areal variations. In addition to the case of variable 15 mentioned above, two others (5 and 6) contribute to this final indicator with double the weight of the others; this is because

Table 5.5: Five Social Indicators and a Composite 'Quality-of-Life' Indicator (QL) for Gainesville: Portion of Data

Census ED	Housing (I)	Home (II)	Crime (III)	Health (IV)	Poverty (V)	Total (Σ)	QL ($\Sigma \div 5$)
18	25	30	0	10	8	73	14·6
19	2	18	4	7	2	33	6·6
20	10	22	7	10	6	55	11·0
.							
.							
.							
59	49	67	56	52	87	311	62·2
60	90	74	38	52	61	315	63·0
61	56	74	14	24	91	259	51·8

Note: original indicator scores rounded to nearest whole number.

under the Home and Family heading there are only two variables instead of four, and their scores are thus divided by two not four to arrive at the indicator which is amalgamated with the others to produce the *QL* score. The question of the weighting of individual variables in an exercise of this kind is difficult, of course, but in the absence of sound reasons to do otherwise equal weighting seems the sensible rule.

The territorial *QL* scores and the social conditions which contribute to them are subject to great geographical variations in Gainesville (Figure 5.1). Bad conditions tend to be highly concentrated in the EDs largely occupied by the city's black population, in the central and south eastern parts of the city, while over the northern and western parts conditions are uniformly good. Another cartographic summary is provided by Figure 5.2, which applies the pattern overlay technique (see Chapter 2, Figure 2.8). Each of the five single-indicator patterns shown in Figure 5.1 has been redrawn using five different types of shading, and the patterns superimposed: the darker the shading, the lower the quality of life. More information (i.e. more variation in levels of life quality) is shown on the overlay map than in the *QL* pattern, but this method of graphic data combination lacks the precision of a single numerical indicator.

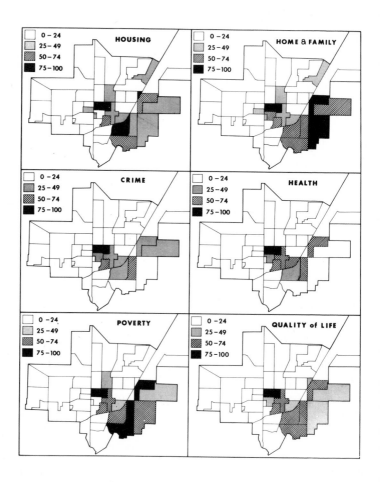

Figure 5.1   Social indicators for an American city, based on a standard
range transformation of data for census enumeration
districts. (Source: J. C. Dickinson, R. J. Gray and D. M.
Smith, 'The "Quality of Life" in Gainesville, Florida: An
Application of Territorial Social Indicators', *Southeastern
Geographer*, 12, 1972.)

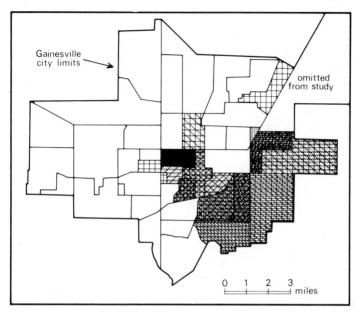

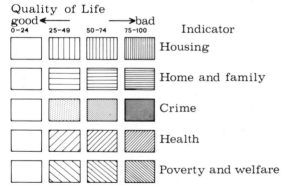

Quality of Life
good ◄──────────► bad
0-24   25-49   50-74   75-100   Indicator

Housing

Home and family

Crime

Health

Poverty and welfare

Figure 5.2   A pattern-overlay description of intra-city variations in the
'quality of life' in Gainesville, Florida. (Source: D. M.
Smith, *The Geography of Social Well-being in the
United States*, McGraw-Hill, 1973, data from
Figure 5.1.)

153

The Standard Score (Z) Transformation

Scale transformation by standardizing variable ranges has a major drawback: it is based on one of the less reliable summary measures of a set of observations. As was shown in Chapter 3, the range can be made quite unrepresentative of the general spread of values by a single extreme occurrence. In the application above this does not matter much, because most of the distributions have many occurrences at or just above zero and no real extremes at the other end of the scale, so the range is usually representative of the dispersal. But there are many circumstances in which this technique would be inappropriate, and where it is necessary to have a transformation which is not as sensitive to the effect of extremes.

The *standard score* (Z-score) transformation provides such a method. It involves standardizing different sets of observations in a way which makes two important properties of their distributions the same for all variables – the mean and the standard deviation. The means are set at zero and the standard deviation at unity. The Z-score is thus:

$$Z_i = \frac{X_i - \bar{X}}{\sigma} \tag{5.9}$$

where Z_i is the standardized score for the ith observation,

X_i is the original or raw score,

$\bar{X}$ is the mean for all values of X,

and σ is the standard deviation of X.

The Z-score has already been introduced in the context of the normal distribution, where departures from the mean are measured in standard deviation units. That the Z-score is simply another version of the linear transformation explained earlier in this chapter can be demonstrated as follows:

$$Z_i = \frac{X_i - \bar{X}}{\sigma} = \frac{X_i}{\sigma} - \frac{\bar{X}}{\sigma} = -\frac{\bar{X}}{\sigma} + \frac{1}{\sigma}X_i \tag{5.10}$$

We end up with something identical in form to the range standardization expression, with a constant of multiplication and a constant of subtraction applied to the original observations.

When converted into Z-scores, all observations with values less than the mean will be negative. If the signs seem likely to confuse, they can be eliminated simply by adding a constant greater than the largest negative value to all scores to make them positive. Similarly the decimals which appear in Z-scores irrespective of whether the raw scores had them can be removed by multiplying all values by a constant such as 10 or 100. These conversions for convenience are known as *derived scores*.

The Z-score permits comparison between sets of scores obtained from different measuring processes, in units which are independent of the original units. This transformation is used frequently in social research, not only to facilitate comparison but also for the purpose of combining information on different variables or scores on different tests.

The calculation and use of the Z-score can be illustrated very simply be reworking the attempt to compare the quality of life in four cities. Standardizing the results of the survey of dance halls, cinemas and night clubs by giving them the same mean and standard deviation, and then summing the results, provides an alternative quality-of-life score to the one previously derived by standardizing on the range 0 to 10. The calculation of Z-scores for the incidence of dance halls (X_1) is set out in Table 5.6. The Z-score transformation for all three variables gives the following results, which are summed so that the cities may be placed in order of preference:

	Z_1	Z_2	Z_3	Total	Order
A	0·00	1·48	−0·51	0·97	2
B	−1·07	−0·36	1·52	0·09	3
C	1·60	0·21	0·17	1·98	1
D	−0·53	−1·33	−1·18	−3·04	4

The order is in fact the same as in the previous transformation.

The sum of a set of Z-scores for any variable will be zero, as can be confirmed from Table 5.6 and the figures above. In amalgamating sets of Z-scores they can be weighted differentially if necessary, i.e.:

Patterns in Human Geography

$$QL_i = \sum_{j=1}^{N} w_j Z_{ij} \qquad [5.11]$$

where QL_i is some quality-of-life score for area i, w_j is the weighting for variable j, and Z_{ij} is the area's score on j.

Table 5.6: Calculation of Standard Scores (Z) for an Imaginary Variable (X)

Case	X	$X - \bar{X}$	$(X - \bar{X})^2$	$\dfrac{X - \bar{X}}{\sigma} = Z$
A	7	0	0	0·00
B	5	−2	4	−1·07
C	10	3	9	1·60
D	6	−1	1	−0·53
	$\Sigma X = 28$		$\Sigma(X - \bar{X})^2 = 14$	$\Sigma Z = 0·00$

$$\bar{X} = 7 \qquad \sigma = \sqrt{\frac{\Sigma(X - \bar{X})^2}{N}} = \sqrt{\frac{14}{4}} = 1·87$$

A real-world example of the application of the Z-score transformation to the development of social indicators can be provided by a study of eighteen American metropolitan areas. Data on ten variables are listed in Table 5.7, and Table 5.8 shows them transformed into Z-scores. The summation of the scores (weighted equally) provides a general quality-of-life indicator in which it is possible to add such diverse criteria as suicides, infant deaths, income, and air pollution. The Z-scores also make it easy to compare the performance of different cities on the ten criteria selected. According to the data used here, transformed and amalgamated into a single indicator, the 'best' city is Minneapolis and the 'worst' Los Angeles.

A further use for the table of Z-scores is as a set of quality-of-life *profiles* of the cities. Comparisons between rows help to reveal the relatively good and bad aspects of life in the individual metropolitan areas. For example, the very poor score on suicide helps to explain the position of Los Angeles at the bottom of the list and the poor performance of San Francisco, while Minneapolis does particularly well on the service mental test used as a measure

156

of educational attainment. The extremes, good and bad, are high-lighted by scores exceeding two standard deviations from the mean.

The Z-score transformation has also been used in the development of composite social indicators at the inter-state and intra-city levels in the United States (see Selected Reading to this chapter). Its range of applications in geographical research is considerable, the only major limitation being in cases where the data are highly skewed and the mean and standard deviation become poor summary measures.

Scale Transformation by Ranking

The kind of transformations described thus far convert data originally measured on a ratio scale into an interval scale. Standardization can also be accomplished by taking ratio or interval data down to an ordinal scale, to produce sets of rankings which can be directly compared in circumstances where the original scores could not. The main advantage of this is the relative ease with which it can be done, providing the number of observations is not too large for the ranking to be done quickly by eye. The disadvantage is the loss of information on ratios or intervals.

As an illustration, the original observations on the number of dance halls, cinemas and night clubs in the four imaginary cities used above may be converted into ranks. The city with the most of each facility is ranked 1 and the one with the least is ranked 4. A composite score can then be derived by simply summing the ranks for each city. In the list below these totals have been re-ranked in order of preference, giving 1 to the city with the lowest sum of ranks; the order is the same as in the other two transformations of these data:

	R_1	R_2	R_3	Total	Order
A	2	1	3	6	2
B	4	3	1	8	3
C	1	2	2	5	1
D	3	4	4	11	4

Table 5.7: Data on Ten Measures of the 'Quality of Life' in Eighteen Metropolitan Areas in the USA

City or Metropolitan Area	Adjusted per capita Income 1967	Unemployment Rate (%) 1968	Low Income Households (%) 1968	Housing Cost/year $ (family of four) 1968	Service Mental Test Rejections (%) 1968	Infant Mortality (per 1,000 live births) 1967	Suicides (per million population) 1967	Air Pollution Index 1966	Robbery Rate (per 100,000 pop.) 1968	Traffic Deaths (per million pop.) 1967
New York	3868	3·0	14·3	2727	12	227	72	4575	485	133
Los Angeles	4029	4·7	16·5	2278	7	199	224	3935	273	248
Chicago	4014	3·0	11·4	2617	11	244	82	4220	305	172
Philadelphia	3462	3·2	13·9	2222	11	248	92	4045	115	179
Detroit	3872	3·8	9·8	2208	8	227	104	3700	378	207
Boston	3371	2·5	9·3	2832	7	194	71	3890	97	156
San Francisco	4075	4·8	17·5	2578	6	193	235	2530	377	250
Washington, D.C.	3641	2·7	9·4	2406	15	207	81	3275	379	174
Pittsburgh	3441	4·4	14·8	2032	5	214	86	3900	150	190
St. Louis	3450	3·1	15·6	2315	6	240	102	3690	220	235
Cleveland	2645	3·5	12·4	2646	8	210	104	3905	186	159
Baltimore	3551	3·4	13·5	2056	10	231	81	3550	455	201
Houston	3480	3·3	17·8	1927	10	218	111	2335	232	218
Minneapolis	3788	2·4	11·9	2392	2	196	99	2570	167	205
Dallas	3729	2·3	17·1	2005	8	232	98	1780	86	253
Cincinnati	3454	2·9	16·8	2272	7	205	101	3255	75	148
Milwaukee	3656	2·9	11·0	2584	3	201	100	3015	62	171
Buffalo	3133	4·0	13·5	2498	4	223	61	2600	107	192
Average	3645	3·3	13·7	2366	8	217	106	3315	231	194

Source: M. V. Jones and M. J. Flax, *The Quality of Life in Washington, D.C.,* The Urban Institute, Washington, D.C., 1970.

A fuller example of the use of rankings for data transformation and the development of composite indicators is provided by an application to the data on the eighteen American cities listed above in Table 5.7. With the exception of the first variable (income, where high scores are 'good'), cities are ranked 1 to 18 low values to high, making low ranks 'good' and high ranks 'bad' in all cases. The summation of these ranks gives the 'best' cities low values, and these sums are themselves ranked with the 'best' city ranked 1 and the 'worst' 18 (Table 5.9). The order of the metropolitan areas produced by this method is not quite the same as in

Table 5.8: Standard Scores for Eighteen Metropolitan Areas, on Ten 'Quality of Life' Indicators

City or Metropolitan Area	Adjusted per capita Income 1967	Unemployment Rate (%) 1968	Low Income Households (%) 1968	Housing Cost/year $ (family of four) 1968	Service Mental Test Rejections (%) 1968	Infant Mortality (per 1,000 live births) 1967	Suicides (per million population) 1967	Air Pollution Index 1966	Robbery Rate (per 100,000 pop.) 1967	Traffic Deaths (per million pop.) 1967	Sum of Z-scores	Ranking on ΣZ
New York	0·86	0·44	−0·21	−1·36	−1·27	−0·56	0·72	−1·59	−1·85	1·68	−3·14	16
Los Angeles	1·49	−1·83	−0·99	0·33	0·23	1·03	−2·51	−0·74	−0·31	−1·49	−5·29	18
Chicago	1·43	0·44	0·81	−0·94	−0·97	−1·52	0·51	−1·12	−0·54	0·61	−1·33	12
Philadelphia	−0·72	0·17	−0·07	0·54	−0·97	−1·75	0·29	−0·88	0·84	0·41	−2·13	13
Detroit	0·87	−0·63	1·38	0·60	−0·07	−0·56	0·04	−0·43	−1·07	−0·36	−0·26	10
Boston	−1·08	1·10	1·55	−1·75	0·23	1·31	0·74	−0·68	0·97	1·05	3·45	3
San Francisco	1·66	−1·96	−1·34	−0·80	0·54	1·37	−2·75	1·12	−1·07	−1·55	−4·79	17
Washington, D.C.	−0·03	0·84	1·52	−0·15	−2·18	0·58	0·53	0·13	−1·08	0·55	0·70	6
Pittsburgh	−0·81	−1·43	−0·39	1·26	0·84	0·18	0·42	−0·69	0·59	0·11	0·06	9
St. Louis	−0·77	0·30	−0·67	0·19	0·54	−1·29	0·08	−0·42	0·08	−1·13	−3·09	15
Cleveland	−0·01	−0·23	0·46	−1·05	−0·07	0·41	0·04	−0·70	0·32	0·96	0·13	8
Baltimore	−0·38	−0·10	0·07	1·17	−0·67	−0·78	0·53	−0·23	−1·64	−0·19	−2·23	14
Houston	−0·65	0·04	−1·45	1·66	−0·67	−0·05	−0·11	1·38	−0·01	−0·66	−0·53	11
Minneapolis	0·55	1·24	0·63	−0·10	1·74	1·20	0·14	1·07	0·46	−0·31	6·64	1
Dallas	0·32	1·37	−1·20	1·36	−0·07	−0·84	0·17	2·11	1·05	−1·63	2·64	5
Cincinnati	−0·75	0·57	−1·10	0·36	0·23	0·69	0·10	0·16	1·13	1·27	2·67	4
Milwaukee	0·03	0·57	0·95	−0·82	1·44	0·92	0·12	0·48	1·23	0·63	5·55	2
Buffalo	−2·01	−0·90	0·07	−0·50	1·14	−0·33	0·95	1·03	0·90	0·05	0·40	7

Source: D. M. Smith, *The Geography of Social Well-being in the United States*, McGraw-Hill, 1973.

Note: The signs are such that on each variable positive is 'good' and negative 'bad'.

the Z-score summations in Table 5.8, though there is a substantial measure of agreement. The differences arise because the relationship between observations has been changed by the shift to an ordinal scale. It is a reminder that measuring the same conditions on different scales can produce different results.

Scale transformations and amalgamations of data, by ranking, Z-scores or any other method, can be used to develop indicators of change as well as geographical variations in the present state of affairs. The value of the results will, of course, depend on the criteria and variables used and the concepts from which they are

Patterns in Human Geography

Table 5.9: Rankings for Eighteen Metropolitan Areas, as on Ten 'Quality of Life' Indicators

City or Metropolitan Area	Adjusted per capita Income 1967	Unemployment Rate (%) 1968	Low Income Households (%) 1968	Housing Cost/year $ (family of four) 1968	Service Mental Test Rejections (%) 1968	Infant Mortality (per 1,000 live births) 1967	Suicides (per million population) 1967	Air Pollution Index 1966	Robbery Rate (per 100,000 pop.) 1968	Traffic Deaths (per million pop.) 1967	Sum of Ranks	Final Ranking
New York	5	7·5	11	17	17	12·5	3	18	18	1	110	15
Los Angeles	2	17	14	8	9	4	17	15	12	16	114	17
Chicago	3	7·5	5	15	15	17	6	17	13	6	104·5	10
Philadelphia	13	10	10	6	16	18	8	16	6	8	111	16
Detroit	4	14	3	5	10	12·5	14·5	11	15	13	102	9
Boston	17	3	1	18	7	2	2	12	4	3	69	3
San Francisco	1	18	17	13	5	1	18	3	14	17	107	13
Washington, D.C.	10	4	2	11	18	7	4·5	8	16	7	87·5	6
Pittsburgh	16	16	12	3	4	9	7	13	7	9	96	8
St Louis	15	9	13	9	6	16	13	10	10	15	116	18
Cleveland	9	13	7	16	11	8	14·5	14	9	4	105·5	12
Baltimore	11	12	8·5	4	14	14	4·5	9	17	11	105	11
Houston	12	11	18	1	13	10	16	2	11	14	108	14
Minneapolis	6	2	6	10	1	3	10	4	8	12	62	2
Dallas	7	1	15	2	12	15	9	1	3	18	83	5
Cincinnati	14	5·5	16	7	8	6	12	7	2	2	79·5	4
Milwaukee	8	5·5	4	14	2	5	11	6	1	5	61·5	1
Buffalo	18	15	8·5	12	3	11	1	5	5	10	88·5	7

Source of Data: See Table 5.7.

Note: rank 1 is 'best' and rank 18 is 'worst'.

derived, as well as on the way in which the data have been manipulated. Techniques for producing general territorial social indicators are by no means confined to those discussed here by way of demonstrating the process of data combination; another which has been particularly favoured in recent years is discussed in Chapter 10.

Quotients, Coefficients and Indices

In addition to the methods already described in connection with social indicators, there are a number of other ways of data transformation and combination used quite commonly. Variously referred to as 'quotients', 'coefficients' or 'indices', these have been applied most frequently in economic geography, but they also have obvious uses in the social field.

The best-known of these measures is probably the *location quotient*. It shows the extent to which each of a set of areas departs from some norm, such as regional or national employment average, with respect to its proportion of workers employed in some economic activity. Using absolute data, the location quotient (Q) for any activity in any area is given by either of the following expressions:

$$Q = \frac{X_i/Y_i}{X/Y} \qquad [5.12]$$

$$Q = \frac{X_i/X}{Y_i/Y} \qquad [5.13]$$

where X_i is employment in a given activity i in an area,

$\quad X$ is total employment in all activity in the area,

$\quad Y_i$ is national employment in activity i,

and $\quad Y$ is total employment in all activity in the nation.

The second of these two expressions, which is the most commonly used, simply represents proportion of total employment locally in a given activity divided by the national proportion. So if the base data are percentages instead of absolute data on numbers employed, the location quotient can be written simply as follows for any area j:

$$Q_j = \frac{X_j}{k} \qquad [5.14]$$

where X_j is the (variable) area percentage in the activity, and k is

161

the (constant) percentage in the nation or whatever areal base is being used. The location quotient is thus a simple linear scale transformation, in which each of the original observations as a proportion is divided by a constant.

A location quotient of 1·0 means that the activity is represented in the area in exactly the same proportion of total employment as in the nation. Less than 1·0 shows the activity to be under-represented against the norm, while over 1·0 shows that the area has more than its 'fair share'. The higher the Q value, the greater the degree of concentration of the activity in the area in question.

Sets of location quotients calculated from employment data for three British industries are shown in Table 5.10. The areal units are the ten major regions, and the base figures are national employment. As an example of the calculation, the substitution of the appropriate figures to obtain Q for metal manufacturing in the West Midlands using expression [5.11] gives:

$$Q = \frac{151/637}{1253/8920} = \frac{0·237}{0·141} = 1·69$$

Examination of the quotients in the table shows some of the things that can be learned from this transformation. In metal manufacturing the highest Q value is that for Wales, which ranks only third in total employment in this industry but has almost one third of its total regional industrial employment in metals. Similarly the highest quotient for chemicals is in the Northern region, where actual numbers employed are relatively low. The range of the quotients for any activity indicates its relative degree of regional concentration within the nation. Thus metals, with a range from 4·14 to 0·20, appears the most highly localized, followed by chemicals; engineering is the most evenly distributed, half the regions having Q within 0·10 of unity.

Areal variations in location quotient can often be illustrated effectively on maps. In Figure 5.3, Q values for the electrical machinery and transportation equipment industries are shown by major regions in Japan. The electrical industry has one region of high concentration (Kanto) and another (Kinki) with Q a little over 1; elsewhere it is under-represented. In transportation

Table 5.10: Location Quotients for Three British Industries

Region*	Metal Manufacturing Emp't (1,000 s)	Q	Engineering and Electrical Emp't (1,000 s)	Q	Chemicals Emp't (1,000 s)	Q	All Industries Emp't (1,000 s)
London and South East	35	0·27	583	1·26	123	1·17	1806
Eastern and Southern	22	0·30	312	1·20	59	0·99	1016
South Western	6	0·20	105	1·06	12	0·51	405
West Midlands	151	1·69	304	0·95	25	0·34	1253
East Midlands	47	1·07	142	0·90	18	0·50	616
Yorkshire and Humberside	124	1·93	161	0·70	45	0·85	900
North West	42	0·43	309	0·88	123	1·53	1380
Northern	61	1·85	123	1·04	55	2·04	463
Scotland	54	1·00	180	0·93	35	0·79	757
Wales	95	4·14	55	0·67	24	1·33	323
Great Britain	637	—	2275	—	520	—	8920

Source of data: Ministry of Labour, 1965. (Note: column totals subject to rounding errors.)

*Here and in Tables 6.4 and 6.5 the data refer to the 'old' standard regions; the 'new' names have been used in the cases of the Yorkshire and Midland regions.

equipment three regions have Q greater than 1·0, but in no case is this as high as the 1·84 in Kanto for the electrical industry. Of the two industries, electrical machinery manufacturing is shown to be the more highly localized.

On the face of it the location quotient seems to be quite informative as a scale transformation. It makes observations on different conditions comparable, in that their national incidences or some other base are all set at the same figure of 1·0, and the same areal departure from this norm will have the same value for Q in any activity. But it does suffer from some drawbacks. Because the scale is arranged about unity, it is compressed into 0 to 1·0 for incidences below the national norm but it can rise to any number above the norm. It has also been found extremely sensitive to the size and shape of the areal units of observation. Although relatively easy to calculate as a rough measure of how far local area values depart from some norm, Q is inferior to the Z-score trans-

163

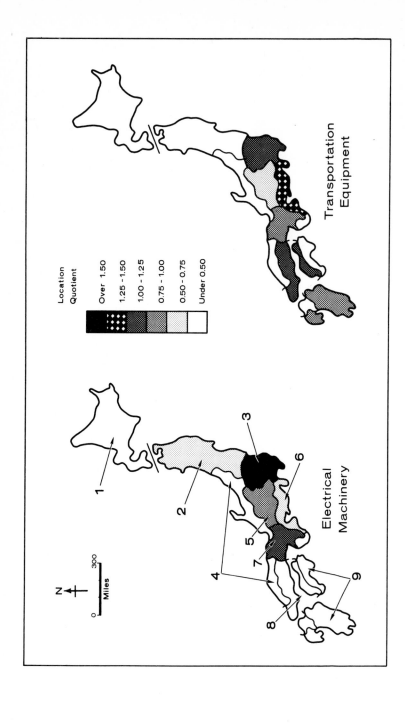

Figure 5.3 Location quotients for the electrical machinery and
transportation equipment industries in Japan, calculated
from employment data for major regions. The regions are:
1. Hokkaido; 2. Tohoku; 3. Kanto; 4. Hokuriki and Sanin;
5. Tosan; 6. Tokai; 7. Kinki; 8. Inland Sea; 9. South Kyushu,
Shikoku and Kiki. (Source of data: *Statistical Yearbook
of Japan*, 1964.)

formation in other respects. The latter can do the same thing, on
a scale determined by two important characteristics of the original
set of observations instead of just the national average. Only when
expressing occurrences in units of some norm is sufficient for
descriptive and comparative purposes should the location quotient
be used.

If data on a number of different activities or conditions in an
area are worked out as proportions of the areal total, they can be
compared collectively with the proportions in the wider region or
nation as a *profile* of the area's particular character. The more
closely the two sets of proportions coincide, the more typical or
normal the area is; the greater the difference, the more atypical or
unique. Comparisons of this kind are often performed by what is
generally termed the *Gini coefficient* or the *index of concentration*.
It is calculated as follows:

$$G = \tfrac{1}{2} \sum_{i=1}^{N} |X_i - Y_i|$$ [5.15]

where X_i and Y_i are two sets of percentage frequencies. The
vertical brackets indicate that the difference between the proportions in each activity or condition are summed irrespective of their
sign. Using raw data instead of percentages the expression is:

$$G = \tfrac{1}{2} \sum_{i=1}^{N} \left| \frac{100 X_i}{X_t} - \frac{100 Y_i}{Y_t} \right|$$ [5.16]

where X_i and Y_i are the actual occurrences of condition i and
X_t and Y_t are the totals for all conditions. The value of G will be
on a scale 0 to 100, with 0 indicating exact correspondence
between the two frequency distributions and 100 showing them
as different as possible.

There are many kinds of applications of this coefficient. One
of the most useful is as a measure of the equality of the distribution
of something between different groups in a population. For in-

165

stance, percentages of the population in certain classes defined by socio-economic characteristics might be compared with the percentage of land they own or of income they receive. Comparisons of the coefficient from area to area or year to year show the extent to which equality of distribution varies or is changing. Perfect equality is, of course, indicated by $G = 0$, where each group gets its proper proportion of whatever is being considered.

Table 5.11: Calculation of an Index of Income Equality in South Africa by Races

Date and Race	Percent of National Population X	Percent of National Income Y	Difference $|X-Y|$	Sum of Differences $\Sigma |X-Y|$	Index of Income Equality $\frac{1}{2}\Sigma |X-Y|$
1936					
Africans	68·8	19·7	49·1		
Asiatics	2·3	1·7	0·6	107·2	53·6
Coloureds	8·0	4·1	3·9		
Whites	20·9	74·5	53·6		
1946–47					
Africans	68·5	20·1	48·4		
Asiatics	2·5	1·9	0·6	106·1	53·05
Coloureds	8·2	4·2	4·0		
Whites	20·7	73·8	53·1		
1956–57					
Africans	68·0	20·6	47·4		
Asiatics	2·9	2·0	0·9	105·2	52·6
Coloureds	9·1	4·8	4·3		
Whites	19·9	72·5	52·6		
1967					
Africans	69·4	18·8	50·6		
Asiatics	2·9	2·4	0·5	110·4	55·2
Coloureds	9·5	5·4	4·1		
Whites	18·2	73·4	55·2		

Source of data: *Power, Privilege and Poverty*, Report of the Economic Commission of the Study Project on Christianity in Apartheid Society, Johannesburg, 1972, Appendix C, Table 3.

As an example, coefficients of income distribution by race in South Africa have been calculated for four different points in time (Table 5.11). Percentages of the total population classed as African (or 'Black'), Asiatic (Indians), Coloured (of mixed blood) and White are listed alongside their percentages of national income. The differences are calculated, summed, and divided by two, to give the index of income equality. The results are high on the 0 to 100 scale, indicating relatively high inequality of income, which is what would be expected given the way in which South African society is organized. A very large income redistribution would have to take place, largely from Whites to Africans, to make the two sets of percentages correspond. The differences between the index numbers calculated in Table 5.11 are very slight, showing that there has been virtually no change in the level of income equality over the years. If high income inequality can be regarded as a negative social indicator, then by this criterion there has been no real progress in South Africa over the past forty years, and the period 1956–7 to 1967 during which 'apartheid' was introduced seems to have been one of retrogression.

Another way of measuring distributions of this kind by the same general coefficient is to compare the local observed percentages with some norm such as the regional or national distribution profile. Yet another is to compare them with equality, defined as everyone in the same income bracket. The difference between these methods is illustrated in the imaginary data which follows, representing percentages of the population in each of five income categories:

Income (£)	Area % X	National % Y_1	Diff. $|X - Y_1|$	'Equality' Y_2	Diff. $|X - Y_2|$
0–500	30	15	15	0	30
500–1,000	25	20	5	0	25
1,000–1,500	20	30	10	100	80
1,500–2,000	15	20	5	0	15
2,000 +	10	15	5	0	10
$\Sigma |X - Y|$			40		160
$\frac{1}{2}\Sigma |X - Y|$			20		80

Comparison between the area's distribution and the national 'norm' produces an index of 20. Comparison with a distribution representing 'equality', with everyone in the same income category, produces an index of 80 which indicates much higher inequality. The first method allows for the existing national inequality, while the second does not.

As with the location quotient, the results of calculations of this kind can be mapped to display the geographical pattern. To provide an example, a map of the inequality of income distribution has been prepared for the city of Tampa, Florida. The index has been calculated in a similar manner to that illustrated above, with 'equality' defined as everyone in the same category. An annual family income of \$9,000–10,000 (which includes the national average) was taken as the equality level, and the index (I) was calculated as follows:

$$I_j = \sum_{i=1}^{N} X_{ij} w_i \tag{5.17}$$

where X_{ij} is the percentage in a given income category ($1, \ldots, i, \ldots, N$; $N = 15$) in one of the city census tracts ($1, \ldots, j, \ldots, 71$), and w_i is the difference between the mid-class value of income category i and that of the norm category (9,500) in thousands. Multiplication of the percentages by w weights them according to how far they are from the 'desirable' norm, thus accommodating the fact that a certain proportion in a very high or very low income category would be a greater departure from 'equality' than the same proportion in a category closer to the norm. The index I can range from 0 to approximately 2,400 in this particular case.

The results are mapped in Figure 5.4, alongside a map of per capita income transformed into Z-scores for comparison. The greatest departures from equality of distribution (i.e. high indices) correspond with high income areas, as might be expected. Deeming high inequality as 'undesirable' of course involves a value judgement, and the question of how far observed inequalities in this city or elsewhere are inequitable or unjust is beyond the scope of

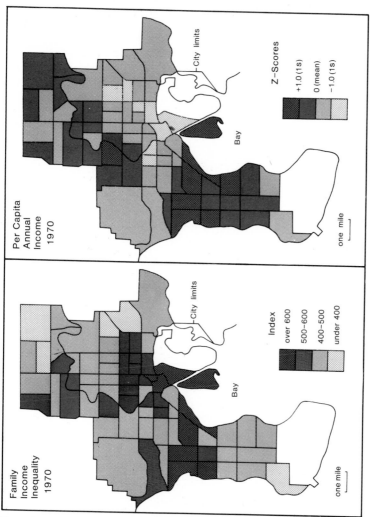

Figure 5.4   The pattern of income inequality in Tampa, Florida. The maps compare an index of income distribution measuring deviations from the 'ideal' of all in the same category ($9,000 to $10,000), with per capita income transformed into Z-scores. (Source of data: D. M. Smith and R. J. Gray, *Social Indicators for Tampa, Florida*, Urban Studies Bureau, University of Florida, 1972.)

the present discussion. However, such questions cannot be asked or answered unless inequality can be measured.

One of the most common applications of this general index or coefficient of distribution is in the measurement of industrial diversification. The percentage employment (or production) in various branches of the economy at a given time is compared with the distribution at some base year. The result is usually called the *index* (or *coefficient*) *of diversification*, though 'structural change' is a better term because all changes are not necessarily diversification.

As an example of the results which can be obtained, a comparison of the industrial structure of ninety-five areas in North West England over a twelve-year period is mapped in Figure 5.5. The index used here has a range 0 to 100, and is derived from a comparison of the percentage distribution of industrial employment between fourteen branches, using the method of calculation in expression [5.15]. The structure in certain areas changed very considerably in view of the shortness of the period under review, and these areas of rapid diversification are scattered over the map in a generally unsystematic manner.

The measurement of economic diversification can have practical significance in regional planning. The map of the North West shows that few of the large changes have taken place in the eastern fringe of the region, where there is a need for new sources of employment to replace the jobs lost in the decline of the textile industry. This is where the planners would like to see rapid diversification. But again, the results of this kind of calculation must be interpreted with care. The size of an area, in terms of its total employment if employment is the measurement criterion being used, will have a bearing on the size of the coefficient; it takes a large sectoral shift in employment to produce a large coefficient of structural change in a major city, while in a small industrial town the movement of only a few workers from one industry to another can produce a large coefficient and thus give the impression of much greater diversification.

There are other variations on the general Gini coefficient. One is the *coefficient of localization* which can be used to measure geographical distributions (see next chapter). This family of indices or coefficients provides a versatile means of summarizing frequency distributions, transforming or combining data to facilitate comparison with some norm, and the range of possible applications is wide. But as the discussion of industrial diversification showed, they must be used with caution and interpreted with care.

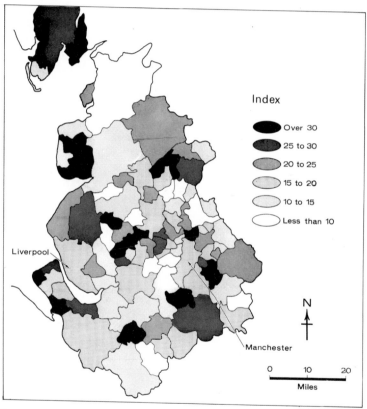

Figure 5.5   Industrial trends in North West England, 1953–65, as measured by an Index of Structural Change based on percentages employed in fourteen industrial categories. (Source: D. M. Smith, *Industrial Britain: The North West*, David & Charles, 1969.)

Back to the FBI

This chapter began with a discussion of the problems arising from the FBI's attempt to develop a composite crime index. The succeeding exploration of scale transformations and methods of combining data should have provided some ideas on how to improve what one writer on social reporting recently described as 'a statistical monstrosity'. Of the various techniques demonstrated, the Z-score transformation and summation is probably the best, in the absence of attitudinal data which would enable a weighting to be given to each type of crime on the basis of public opinion.

This standardization can be performed on the per capita rates for each crime, as calculated by the FBI, for sets of territorial units at any convenient level of aggregation. As stated earlier, some measure of local wealth would be a better base than population for calculating property crime rates, but for the purpose of demonstration here the rates to population are used in all cases. For each of the seven index crimes the Z-score transformation expresses the rate in any geographical unit as a positive or negative deviation from the mean of the rates for the whole set of areas, with one standard deviation being unity for each category. Thus the seven sets of data are weighted differently compared with their relative contributions in the FBI index, the scales for the less frequent and more serious crimes such as murder having been pulled out. The disadvantages of this method include the loss of information involved in going from a ratio scale to an interval scale, and the introduction of a numerical method less easily understood by the general public than the simple if misleading summation of per capita rates. Another problem is that the distribution of infrequent crimes like murder is likely to be highly skewed, with most places having few if any occurrences and a small number having many, a situation in which the mean and standard deviations lose some of their value as summary measures. Nevertheless, this technique would represent a great improvement on the current FBI method.

To give an example, indices have been calculated in this way for the nine major regions of the United States. The rates per 100,000 population and the FBI index are listed in Table 5.12, with the Z-scores and the new index below. The new crime index (I) is derived from:

$$I_j = \sum_{i=1}^{7} Z_{ij} \qquad [5.18]$$

where Z_{ij} is the standard score on crime category i (1, 2, ..., 7) in region j. The regions have been ranked on both indices.

On both indices the Pacific region (mainly California) is ranked 1, with the highest overall crime rate. But in all the other regions

Table 5.12: Regional Crime Rates and a General Crime Index in the United States, Using the FBI Method and the Z-Score Transformation

Region	Categories of crime								
Rate per 100,000 population	Murder	Rape	Robbery	Assault	Burglary	Larceny	Auto theft	Total Crime Index	Rank on Index
New England	3·2	11·0	97	97	1128	813	716	2868	4
Mid Atlantic	7·9	15·4	344	165	1169	870	562	3136	2
E. North Central	7·9	19·8	206	143	1035	845	448	2706	6
W. North Central	4·5	15·9	88	104	836	735	314	2098	8
South Atlantic	12·6	21·3	170	246	1109	907	332	2799	5
E. South Central	13·1	16·8	67	189	743	537	253	1821	9
W. South Central	11·0	22·2	108	208	1035	749	337	2473	7
Mountain	6·5	25·9	95	173	1208	1204	420	3135	3
Pacific	7·2	32·2	201	213	1794	1413	631	4293	1
Standard Scores (Z)									
New England	−1·47	−1·43	−0·64	−1·48	0·03	−0·32	1·17	−3·60	8
Mid Atlantic	−0·09	−0·73	2·18	−0·12	0·17	−0·10	0·73	2·04	3
E. North Central	−0·09	−0·03	0·60	−0·56	−0·23	−0·20	0·01	−0·59	6
W. North Central	−1·09	−0·65	−0·74	−1·34	−0·93	−0·62	−0·84	−6·21	9
South Atlantic	1·29	0·21	0·19	1·50	−0·03	0·04	−0·72	2·48	2
E. South Central	1·44	−0·51	−0·98	0·36	−1·27	−1·37	−1·22	−3·55	7
W. South Central	0·82	0·35	−0·51	0·74	−0·30	−0·56	−0·69	−0·15	5
Mountain	−0·50	0·94	−0·66	0·04	0·30	1·18	−0·16	1·14	4
Pacific	−0·28	1·94	0·55	0·84	2·23	1·97	1·17	8·44	1

Source of data: US Department of Justice, Federal Bureau of Investigation, *Uniform Crime Reports for the United States*, 1971. (Note: totals are subject to rounding errors.)

except East North Central there is a change of rank as between the FBI index and the new one. The largest difference is in New England, which drops from 4th on the FBI index to 8th on the Z-scores (i.e. the lowest rate of crime but one). This change is because of low regional rates for the violent crimes, which are now weighted much more heavily than in the FBI index, and a high rate for auto theft, the contribution of which has been reduced in the new index. The South Atlantic has risen from 5 to 2, because it has high rates for murder and assault and a low rate for auto theft – the reverse of the New England pattern – and the East South Central region has ceased to have the lowest rate of crime for the same reason. In general, the new index makes the level of crime in the South look worse than it does on the FBI index, because the latter under-emphasizes the violent crimes which have above-average occurrences in the South, and over-emphasizes crimes against property (in particular auto theft) which are low in this relatively poor region. The two indices clearly reveal a different regional geography of crime.

The FBI crime index is an extreme and rather notorious example of official misuse of numerical data, but it is certainly not an isolated case. Access to better statistical skills can improve the reporting of crime and other social conditions, and aid the development of composite indicators of social well-being. But it is important that members of the general public should approach the social statistics with which they are bombarded in a cautious and sceptical manner, particularly when the agency compiling and publishing them also has responsibility for controlling the condition in question and thus a vested interest in the revelation of a certain trend.

6. Measures of Geographical Patterns

Previous chapters have dealt with compiling and summarizing information, with making comparisons, and with the process of transformation and combination. Although the context has been geographical, the focus has been on information as sets of numerical observations which happen to vary from place to place, rather than directly on the spatial arrangement of things. It is now time to look at geographical patterns in a way which explicitly considers the spatial relationship of observations to each other.

This chapter reviews some common methods of describing geographical patterns numerically. It is a logical extension of what has gone before, with the principles of numerical analysis revealed in earlier chapters applied in a more directly geographical context. This will be continued in subsequent chapters, as the discussion proceeds from simple description through more abstract summarization and on to comparison, and finally to regional synthesis.

Points on a Line

The simplest geographical pattern is one of a set of points. The simplest version of this is points arranged in one dimension – along a line. Many geographical features are of this form: stations on a railway line, motorway exits, houses for sale along a street, and pipeline access points. The problem of measuring such patterns of dispersion provides a convenient introduction to the analysis of more complex patterns.

A set of points can be arranged along a line in an infinite number of ways. But three basic patterns can be recognized: regular, clustered and random. A *regular* occurrence is where the intervals between points are similar; a *clustered* arrangement is where they appear in bunches separated by gaps; a *random* pattern is one in which the spacing could have been determined by chance, or using a table of random numbers. Strictly speaking these patterns are not mutually exclusive, for clusters can occur regularly and both bunching and even spacing can arise at random. But the trichotomy of regular, clustered and random is convenient for most descriptive purposes.

How do we decide which description is appropriate? A distinction between regularity and clustering can usually be made by eye, but the difference between these and what could have arisen at random is less easy to judge. It may be important to make such a decision, however, for significant departures from a random arrangement of things suggests that some orderly process is at work. There are a number of methods of testing points on a line for randomness, and one may be illustrated briefly.

Imagine that the city police department is alarmed at the fatal accident rate on a newly opened one-kilometre stretch of urban motorway. An officer is asked to make a report. A sample of 21 accident records is selected at random for each carriageway (east to west, and west to east), and these are examined carefully for clues as to their cause. The investigator wonders whether location might have a bearing on the problem, and plots the occurrences on maps (Figure 6.1). On both carriageways there appears to be some clustering, though it is clearly more marked in the east to west direction. The officer now remembers from an old lesson in statistics that bunches can arise at random, and he decides that it might be sensible to test this before claiming that location is a relevant variable in accidental deaths on this road.

A test for randomness may be conducted as follows, using a method described by Barton and David (see Selected Readings). Assume a line of unit length with $n-1$ points. First, distances (d) between adjoining points are measured, with each end of the line regarded as a point (thus making the total distances n). Each distance is given a position order i ($i = 1, 2, \ldots, n$) from one end of the line, the first distance being 1, the second 2, and so on. Then the following statistic is calculated:

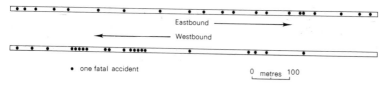

Eastbound

Westbound

• one fatal accident

0   metres   100

Figure 6.1   The location of fatal accidents on the two carriageways of
an imaginary motorway, used to demonstrate a test of
randomness of points on a line.

$$Y = \sum_{i=1}^{n} id_i \qquad [6.1]$$

When expressed in the form:

$$Y' = 1 - \frac{Y}{n} \qquad [6.2]$$

this has a normal sampling distribution if n is about 25 or more,
with a mean ($\bar{Y}'$) and standard deviation (S') derived as follows:

$$\bar{Y}' = \frac{n-1}{2n} \qquad [6.3]$$

$$S' = \sqrt{\frac{n-1}{12n^2}} \qquad [6.4]$$

These parameters are both expressed in units of the length of the
line.

   Thus any value for Y observed in a research problem can be referred to a normal distribution to estimate the probability of chance
occurrence. It can be expressed in standard normal deviates (Z)
by subtracting $\bar{Y}'$ and dividing by S'. If its departure from Y'
is great, this indicates a large departure from what could be expected at random. In using this test it is necessary to assume one
end of the line as an origin, because different Y values can be
obtained from each end. In the illustration the intervals can reasonably be ordered in the direction of traffic movement.

   The distances for the two carriageways have been measured, and
the statistic Y calculated (Table 6.1). The two values for Y' are
0·498 and 0·635 respectively in units of the length of the line

177

(1 km). The parameters of the distribution of Y' are estimated from [6.3] and [6.4] as follows:

$$\bar{Y}' = \frac{22-1}{2 \times 22} = \frac{21}{44} = 0 \cdot 477$$

$$S' = \sqrt{\frac{22-1}{12 \times 22^2}} = \sqrt{\frac{21}{5808}} = \sqrt{0 \cdot 0038} = 0 \cdot 062$$

As Y' is normally distributed, about 68 per cent of observations

Table 6.1: Testing Motorway Accidents for Randomness (Imaginary Data)

	Motorway East				Motorway West	
i	d_i (m x 10)	id_i		i	d_i (m x 10)	id_i
1	2	2		1	20	20
2	2	4		2	10	20
3	3	9		3	3	9
4	5	20		4	2	8
5	4	20		5	16	80
6	8	48		6	12	72
7	7	49		7	1	7
8	10	80		8	1	8
9	8	72		9	1	9
10	4	40		10	1	10
11	5	55		11	2	22
12	3	36		12	4	48
13	6	78		13	1	13
14	3	42		14	5	70
15	6	90		15	1	15
16	3	48		16	1	16
17	1	17		17	1	17
18	3	54		18	1	18
19	7	ι33		19	7	133
20	5	100		20	4	80
21	3	63		21	4	84
22	2	44		22	2	44

$n = 22$ $Y = \Sigma id_i = 1104$ $n = 22$ $Y = \Sigma id_i = 803$

Y in km units = $11 \cdot 04$ Y in km units = $8 \cdot 03$

$Y' = 1 - \dfrac{Y}{n} = 1 - \dfrac{11 \cdot 04}{22} = 0 \cdot 498$ $Y' = 1 - \dfrac{Y}{n} = 1 - \dfrac{8 \cdot 03}{22} = 0 \cdot 635$

will be within 0·062 of 0·477, or between 0·415 and 0·539. The limits of two standard deviations, enclosing roughly 95 per cent of all observations, are 0·353 and 0·601.

The conduct of the statistical test is as described in Chapter 4. The null hypothesis is that the spacing of accidents along the road is not different from random. The alternate hypothesis is that the arrangement is non-random. The level of confidence required to reject H_o is set at 95 per cent ($p = 0.05$), and the region of rejection is Y' beyond 1·96 (say 2·0) standard deviations of the mean, or 0·353 to 0·601. For the eastbound carriageway $Y' = 0.498$, or 0·34 in Z units, which is inside the critical range, so H_o cannot be rejected with confidence and the occurrences must be taken as random. (Y' is in fact very close to the mean value of 0·477; the spaces on this carriageway were obtained from a table of random numbers and thus appear almost perfectly random.) For the westbound carriageway $Y' = 0.635$, which is more than 0·601 ($Z = 2.52$) so H_o is rejected and H_a accepted. There is at least a 95 per cent probability that this spacing could not have arisen by chance.

Thus on one stretch of road the observed location of accidents in bunches is significant. Further investigation might reveal a causal factor, like bunches coinciding with some feature in the road or within the driver's view which affected the performance of the vehicle or distracted attention.

The technique demonstrated above enables any set of dots arranged along a line to be placed on a scale. Position on this scale measures degree of randomness, or the probability of chance occurrence. At one end of the scale is $\bar{Y}'$, or 0·477 in the illustration, representing a random pattern, and as the departure from this figure increases so does the tendency towards a regular or clustered arrangement. The values of Y' (or Z units) representing the conventional probability levels (68 per cent, 95 per cent, etc.) used in statistical analysis comprise special points of interest on the scale.

A number of other methods have been devised to measure point patterns on a line. Some are rather complicated and not easy to test for significance, while others are simple and less powerful. One of the easiest tests to apply involves looking for 'reflexive pairs' (i.e.

pairs of points which are mutual nearest neighbours), and calculating how many there are as a proportion of the total number of points. In a random arrangement this proportion will be two thirds; with a more uniform spacing it will be greater while with more grouping it will be less. In the randomly-generated accident pattern from the illustration above, 14 out of 21 points belong to reflexive pairs; exactly two thirds. For the other carriageway it is 8, or about one third, indicating a tendency towards grouping as Figure 6.1 suggests.

The Measurement of Point Patterns

The most common method of measuring point patterns in two dimensions is similar to that just described. The distance of each point to its nearest neighbour is found, and used to place the pattern on a scale indicating departure from randomness in the direction of either regularity or clustering. A number is thus assigned to the pattern with respect to the arrangement of points within it. This is a very useful operation, because many patterns in human geography can be viewed as sets of points: settlements, factories, shops, the location of crimes – indeed sets of individuals or objects distinguished by any common characteristic. The patterns adopted may be relevant to explanation, for clustering implies the operation of some force making for concentration or agglomeration, while more regular spacing might suggest that some orderly scattering process is at work.

The degree of regularity or clustering in a point pattern can be judged very approximately by eye. Figure 6.2 illustrates three imaginary situations in which 25 points are distributed over an area (for example, they might be the incidence of three types of crime in a city over some period of time). One pattern is made up of loose clusters, one shows a highly regular spacing, and in the third points are located at random. 'Random' in this context means the outcome of a locating process in which any point has the same chance as any other point of occurring at a particular place on the map, any place has the same chance of receiving a point as any

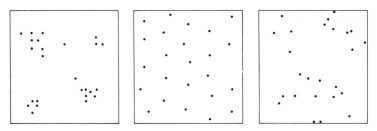

Clustered: $R_N = 0.67$ Regular: $R_N = 1.86$ Random: $R_N = 0.98$

Figure 6.2   Three imaginary location patterns measured as 'clustered', 'regular' and 'random' by nearest neighbour analysis.

other place, and the location of each point has not been influenced by that of other points. A set of points with locational coordinates generated by a table of random numbers would fit this description, and this is how the random pattern in Figure 6.2 was arrived at.

It is easy to give the label of 'clustered', 'regular' or 'random' to these three patterns, because their forms have been made rather obvious. But it may be useful to establish the degree of clustering or regularity in an objective way, for it is often difficult to distinguish less obviously clustered or regular patterns from one which could have arisen at random. This can be done by a form of *nearest neighbour analysis*, first developed in the study of plant ecology to measure the patterns of incidence of different species, and subsequently applied to the study of settlement patterns. It has become highly sophisticated mathematically, and only the simplest form of application is considered here.

Nearest neighbour analysis involves a comparison between the observed spacing of a set of points and the spacing which could be expected in a random pattern. The observed spacing is expressed as the average distance of all points from their nearest neighbouring point, which is:

$$\bar{d}_O = \frac{\sum\limits_{i=1}^{n} d_i}{n}$$

[6.5]

where $\bar{d}_O$ is the average nearest neighbour distance as observed, d_i is the distance from the ith point to its own nearest neighbour, and

n is the number of points in the pattern. The symbols n and d imply a sample; N and D can be used if the analysis is conducted over the entire population of occurrences, which is usually the case in geographical applications. The expected spacing in a random pattern, or $\bar{d}_E$, is:

$$\bar{d}_E = \tfrac{1}{2} \sqrt{\frac{A}{n}} \qquad [6.6]$$

which is sometimes alternatively written:

$$\bar{d}_E = \frac{1}{2\sqrt{n/A}} \qquad [6.7]$$

where A is the area of the territory being examined. The ratio of A to n gives a measure of density of points observed per unit of area, e.g. points per square km or mile. Expressions [6.6] and [6.7] have their origin in the fact that in a random pattern a frequency distribution of the number of points falling in each of a set of quadrats is described by the Poisson function. Some texts have different forms for these expressions, but they all say the same thing. The *nearest neighbour measure* R_N (sometimes designated simply R) is obtained by dividing the observed average nearest neighbour distance by the expected, i.e.:

$$R_N = \frac{\bar{d}_O}{\bar{d}_E} \qquad [6.8]$$

Any calculated value for R_N will fall somewhere on a continuous scale ranging from 0 to 2·1491. The smaller the values the more clustered the pattern, with $R_N = 0$ being where all occurrences are at the same place. The higher the value the more regular the pattern, with the extreme at this end of the scale indicating points distributed in an hexagonal pattern, each having six equidistant nearest neighbours. If $\bar{d}_O = \bar{d}_E$ the pattern is random and $R_N = 1\cdot0$.

As an illustration, a nearest neighbour analysis has been performed on the three patterns shown in Figure 6.2. Assume that the city area depicted is 5 miles square, so $A = 25$ (miles); n is 25. The distances are measured by ruler, and must be in the same distance units used to measure area. The calculations for the first pattern are as follows:

$$\bar{d}_O = \frac{\Sigma d}{25} = \frac{8 \cdot 4}{25} = 0 \cdot 336$$

$$\bar{d}_E = \frac{1}{2\sqrt{25/25}} = \frac{1}{2\sqrt{1}} = \frac{1}{2} = 0 \cdot 500$$

$$R_N = \frac{\bar{d}_O}{\bar{d}_E} = \frac{0 \cdot 336}{0 \cdot 500} = 0 \cdot 672$$

The nearest neighbour measure is calculated for the other two patterns in the same way. The result of 0·67 for the pattern on the left indicates clustering, but nowhere near the maximum which could have been observed at the bottom extreme of the scale. The pattern in the centre scores 1·86, which is not very far from perfect regularity as visual inspection suggests. The pattern on the right gives $R_N = 0 \cdot 98$, or very close to 'perfect' randomness, as would be expected with a pattern generated by random numbers.

An important question in this kind of analysis is how much of a departure from $R_N = 0$ is needed for it to be judged 'significant'. This can be answered by inferential statistical methods. If the set of observations are a sample or treated as such, the probability that the pattern could have arisen by chance can be established by a statistical test. The standard error (sd_E) of the expected mean nearest neighbour distance has been found to be:

$$s_{d_E} = \frac{0 \cdot 26136}{\sqrt{n(n/_A)}} \tag{6.9}$$

where n is the number of observations and A is the area. When this is related to the ratio of observed and expected nearest neighbour mean distances, a statistic c is derived such that:

$$c = \frac{\bar{d}_E - \bar{d}_O}{s_{d_E}} \tag{6.10}$$

This has a normal distribution, and is a standard normal deviate with the Z-score properties of zero mean and unit standard deviation. It can thus be used to test the probability of chance occurrence. It should be clear from [6.10] that the greater the difference

183

between the observed and expected average distances, the larger the values of the statistic c, i.e. the greater the probability that the observed pattern is non-random. A very small difference will result in a c of near zero, or the mean of the sampling distribution. This test requires that n is at least 100, and for patterns with a smaller number of points an alternative must be used. For further particulars on the testing of point patterns for randomness, reference should be made to the Selected Reading (e.g. King, 1969, Chapter 5; Clark and Evans, 1954).

The appearance of the number of points or observations in the denominator of the expression [6.10] for the c statistic is a reminder that the standard error is reduced as 'sample' size increases. An error that can be attributed to chance when a small number of observations is involved may be significant in a pattern with a larger number of points. Thus the larger the number of points, the greater the probability that the same difference between observed and expected average nearest neighbour distance is a consequence of non-random factors.

The similarity between testing geographical patterns for randomness by nearest neighbour analysis and testing points on a line should now be clear. Both place patterns on a probability scale, with respect to departures from that which could be attributed to chance.

Nearest neighbour analysis is not the only way of measuring point patterns. Another involves dividing the study area into quadrats and counting the number of points in each. It is known that in a random pattern with a relatively small number of dots per quadrat the frequency distribution of occurrences by quadrats will approximate a Poisson curve. The observed frequencies can be tested against those in a Poisson distribution by a chi-square test of goodness of fit; the closer the fit, the nearer a random pattern. However, in a pattern with many points per quadrat, a random process would tend to equalize the number of points per quadrat, and observed frequencies would then have to be tested against equality. The choice of quadrat size is thus important in this kind of analysis.

An Example of Nearest Neighbour Analysis

A real-world example may now be introduced to demonstrate further how nearest neighbour analysis can be used, and some of the problems involved. A map of employment in the British hosiery industry included earlier (Figure 2.4) indicated a tendency for concentration in an area extending from Matlock and Mansfield in the north to Hinckley and the southern fringes of the city of Leicester in the south. This part of the East Midlands has been the leading hosiery manufacturing district in Britain since the middle of the eighteenth century, and still contains about two thirds of national employment in the industry. The pattern depicted in Figure 2.4 poses two major questions: why this high degree of concentration in the East Midlands exists, and how the rather dispersed pattern within the region came about. These questions set the scene for a nearest neighbour analysis of the industry's location pattern in the early nineteenth century, at the time when the present pattern was taking shape.

In 1812 a contemporary historian published a list of places where hosiery manufacturing was carried on. The major East Midlands concentration is illustrated in Figure 6.3 in the form of a dot map. All dots are not of equal importance, for the main towns and cities are known to have had a much larger production capacity than other places, but no figures are available on this and the list of places is thus the only precise information on the location pattern at this time. A visual examination of the map suggests a certain regularity in the occurrence of hosiery-manufacturing places, with very even spacing in some parts of the region. This might be taken to imply the operation of some economic factor making for orderly arrangement of production in space. But the possibility of random distribution always exists at the local level, and the nearest neighbour method can be used to establish the pattern's exact position on the continuum from regular to random.

The observed average nearest neighbour distance is 1·38 miles. The area under review (bounded by the borders of the map) is 1,300 square miles, and there are 222 production points. The expected distance in a random pattern can thus be evaluated from expression [6.6] as follows:

$$\bar{d}_E = \tfrac{1}{2} \ \sqrt{\frac{1300}{222}} = \tfrac{1}{2}\sqrt{5\cdot8} = \tfrac{1}{2}\,2\cdot40 = 1\cdot20$$

R_N is then simply $1\cdot38 \div 1\cdot20$, which is $1\cdot15$. Though greater than unity, this figure indicates a pattern not very different from random, and certainly nowhere near highly regular. The conclusion might thus be that there are no orderly forces at work, and that within the area under review the general form of the location pattern as a whole can be largely attributed to chance or the operation of some random locational variables.

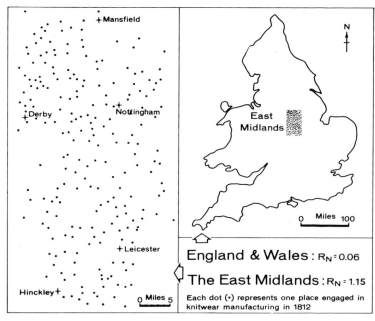

Figure 6.3   A nearest neighbour analysis of the location of the hosiery industry in England in 1812. (Source of data: J. Blackner, *History of Nottingham*, 1815.)

Is such a conclusion really justified? In view of the large number of observations, it might be worth testing the judgement of randomness by the procedure set down in the previous section. The null hypothesis is that the pattern is random, i.e. that if the observed points were a sample, the parent population would be located at random. The alternate hypothesis is that the pattern is not random. The test statistic c at the 95 per cent confidence level has to be greater than 1·96 positive or negative in order to reject the null hypothesis. The statistic is calculated as follows, from [6.9] and [6.10] above:

$$s_{d_E} = \frac{0·26136}{\sqrt{222(222/1300)}} = \frac{0·26136}{\sqrt{37·9}} = \frac{0·26136}{6·15} = 0·042$$

$$c = \frac{1·20 - 1·38}{0·042} = \frac{-0·18}{0·042} = -4·29$$

Here c is negative, because $d_O > d_E$. As the result is more than four standard deviations from the mean of the sampling distribution of c, the null hypothesis can be rejected with great confidence. The pattern must therefore be judged non-random. The 'sample' size is obviously the critical factor here; the same difference between $\bar{d}_O$ and $\bar{d}_E$ with a sample of 100 points produces $c = 1·9$, and the null hypothesis could not be rejected at this figure with $p = 0·05$.

The conclusion is, therefore, that an investigator would be justified in looking for some non-random factors in attempting to account for the pattern of hosiery manufacturing in the East Midlands in the early nineteenth century. Close examination of the map shows some areas of concentration and others which are relatively empty, and historical inquiry reveals that patterns of land ownership and competition from other economic activities were detrimental to the development of the hosiery industry in some parts of the region. This finding would not have been made if the pattern had been dismissed as random.

Just as the number of points is important in nearest neighbour analysis, so is the area used in the calculation of $\bar{d}_E$. Given the same number of points, the larger the area the smaller will be the expected nearest neighbour average distance while the observed distance will of course remain the same. This means that the value for R_N will tend to decrease with increasing area (other things remaining the same), as the denominator in expressions [6.6] and [6.7] is increased. This can be demonstrated for the hosiery industry if the calculation is extended to cover the whole of England and Wales. There are few points outside the main East Midlands concentration, and their inclusion raises $\bar{d}_O$ only slightly – to 1·4 miles. But there is a very large increase in area, to 58,000 square miles, and this increases $\bar{d}_E$ to 24·0 miles. The value for R_N now becomes 0·06, which indicates a very high degree of clustering.

Nearest neighbour analysis can thus show a pattern to be highly concentrated at a national level but, in this case, only a little more regular than random at the regional level. In fact, almost any value for R_N could be produced simply by selecting the right area, so this technique must be used with care. The area chosen for the calculation must be meaningful in relation to the problem being investigated, with points on the perimeter excluded, and the nearest neighbour analysis itself should fit logically into some wider research design. The calculation of R_N for a point pattern in an arbitrarily defined area serves no useful purpose. The quadrat sampling technique referred to earlier provides a way of overcoming the problem of size of area, but there are still some questions as to the proper size of the quadrat used to measure the frequency of points.

Centrographic Techniques

Nearest neighbour analysis is restricted in scope to the measurement of certain limited characteristics of point patterns. The techniques to be discussed next are wider in their application, being concerned with the measurement of central tendency and dispersion in areal distribution patterns in which quantities may be assigned to individual points. Centrographic techniques were being used to find the 'centre of gravity' of population distributions in the latter part of the nineteenth century. Early applications in geographical research date back more than twenty years, but it is more recent work which has revealed the wide scope of these techniques. Neft claims that measures of average position and of dispersal about the centre points constitute the basic elements in an 'integrated and internally consistent system of statistical analysis for areal distributions' in which well-known concepts of conventional statistics are shown to be applicable in spatial situations. Centrographic techniques represent a logical extension of 'linear' descriptive statistics, as outlined in Chapter 3, into the two-dimensional space of the geographer. They are sometimes referred to as 'geostatistics'.

The most frequently used measure of the average point of an areal distribution is the *arithmetic mean centre*, generally simply termed the mean centre. This is the centre of gravity or point of balance of the distribution, and is analogous to the mean in conventional statistics. To calculate this and any other centrographic measure, the location of all points in the pattern must be identified by grid coordinates. These may be the latitude and longitude of the places in question if the area is small, but they are more usually derived from a rectangular grid with any convenient origin superimposed on the study area. If the data being used are for areas and not points, the coordinates can refer to the geographical centre of each area or some other meaningful point within them. Once all occurrences have been assigned X and Y coordinates the calculation can begin.

When the measure is applied to a point pattern where the numerical value at each is unity, the mean centre is found simply by calculating the arithmetic mean of the coordinates along the X and Y axes in turn. The mean centre ($\bar{C}$) is at the point represented by the coordinates X and Y given by:

$$\bar{X} = \frac{\sum\limits_{i=1}^{N} X_i}{N} \; ; \; \bar{Y} = \frac{\sum\limits_{i=1}^{N} Y_i}{N} \qquad [6.11]$$

where X_i and Y_i are the coordinates of the individual points in the distribution pattern and N is the total number of points. The data are taken to be an entire population, for centrographic measures are not usually estimated from samples.

It is often possible to weight each point in an areal distribution in accordance with some relevant criterion measured on a ratio scale. In this case the coordinates of the mean centre are found from the average of the weights of each occurrence multiplied by its own coordinate value, with the sum divided by the sum of the weights. Thus the *weighted mean centre* ($\bar{C}_W$) is given by:

$$\bar{X}_W = \frac{\sum\limits_{i=1}^{N} (X_i W_i)}{\sum\limits_{i=1}^{N} W_i} \;;\; \bar{Y}_W = \frac{\sum\limits_{i=1}^{N} (Y_i W_i)}{\sum\limits_{i=1}^{N} W_i} \qquad [6.12]$$

where the weights are designated W (1, 2, ..., i, ..., N).

The arithmetic mean centre, weighted or otherwise, is only one of a number of possible centre points which can be found for any areal distribution. Just as in conventional statistics there is a median and a mode as well as a mean, so there is a *median centre* and *modal centre*. The median centre is particularly useful because, as in linear statistics, the median is the point at which the sum of the absolute deviations of each value is minimized. This is the point of 'minimum aggregate travel', from which a given set of points can be reached with least overall coverage of distance – a valuable fact in economic geography. It can be expressed by:

$$\bar{X}, \bar{Y}, \text{where } \sum\limits_{i=1}^{N} W_i D_i = \text{min.} \qquad [6.13]$$

where D_i is the distance of the ith point from position $\bar{X}, \bar{Y}$. In practice this can be very difficult to determine. Another useful point is the *harmonic mean centre*, which is the point of peak 'potential' in the distribution pattern, and is at:

$$\bar{X}, \bar{Y}, \text{where } \sum\limits_{i=1}^{N} \frac{W_i}{D_i} = \text{max.} \qquad [6.14]$$

The potential concept is considered further in the next chapter.

Once the mean centre has been found, it is possible to measure dispersion about that point. The most obvious method is to calculate the *average distance* of occurrences from the mean, which in the unweighted case is given by:

$$\bar{D} = \frac{\sum_{i=1}^{N} D_i}{N}$$

[6.15]

where D_i is the distance of the ith point from the mean centre. But much more commonly used is the *standard distance*, analogous to the standard deviation in conventional statistics. The expression is:

$$\bar{D}_S = \sqrt{\frac{\sum_{i=1}^{N} D_i^2}{N}}$$

[6.16]

It is usually obtained by calculating the deviations of the X coordinates from $\bar{X}$ and of the Y coordinates from $\bar{Y}$, squaring them, and finding the square root of their sum. This is done in order to avoid the tedious direct measurement of linear distances from the mean centre: it works them out from their coordinates by applying the Pythagoras theorem concerning right-angled triangles (see Figure 6.4). The distance from the mean centre $(\bar{C})$ to any point is given by the square root of the sum of the squares of the length of the other two sides of the right-angled triangle of which D_i is the hypotenuse, i.e.:

$$D_i = \sqrt{(X_i - \bar{X})^2 + (Y_i - \bar{Y})^2}$$

[6.17]

The full expression for the standard distance calculated in this way thus becomes:

$$\bar{D}_S = \sqrt{\frac{\sum_{i=1}^{N} (X_i - \bar{X})^2 + \sum_{i=1}^{N} (Y_i - \bar{Y})^2}{N}}$$

[6.18]

The *weighted standard distance* is given by multiplying each squared deviation from $\bar{X}_w$ and $\bar{Y}_w$ by the weight at the point in question,

191

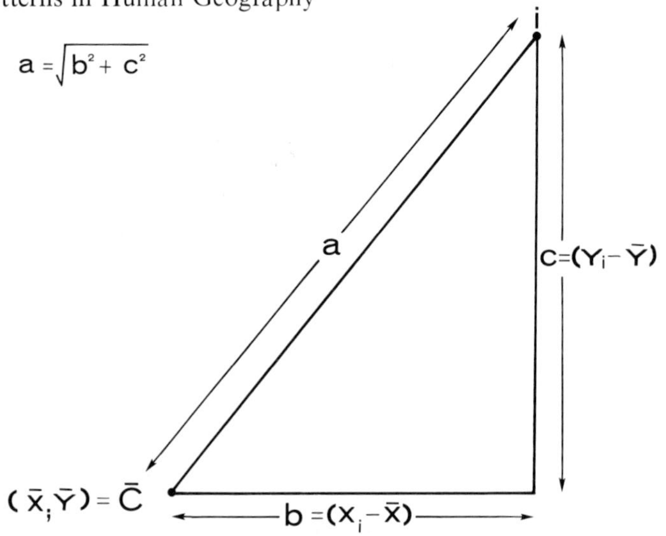

$$a = \sqrt{b^2 + c^2}$$

a

$c = (Y_i - \bar{Y})$

$(\bar{X}, \bar{Y}) = \bar{C}$

$b = (X_i - \bar{X})$

Figure 6.4   The measurement of distance in a system of Cartesian coordinates by the use of the Pythagoras theorem.

and dividing by the sum of the weights as in the weighted mean centre calculation. The formula is:

$$\bar{D}_{SW} = \sqrt{\frac{\displaystyle\sum_{i=1}^{N} W_i(X_i - \bar{X}_w)^2 + \sum_{i=1}^{N} W_i(Y_i - \bar{Y}_w)^2}{\displaystyle\sum_{i=1}^{N} W_i}} \qquad [6.19]$$

This method of calculating distance does not take into account the sphericity of the earth's surface, but it produces only small errors over quite large areas. For example, in a triangle with sides of 300 and 400 miles the error in estimating the length of the other (the hypotenuse) would be 0·06 per cent, and in a calculation covering the whole of Europe or the USA the largest error would be little more than one per cent.

The great advantage attributed to the standard distance over the average distance is that it can be used in a similar way to the standard deviation. Just as in a normal distribution in conventional statistics roughly two thirds of the occurrences will be within one standard deviation of the mean, so in a 'normal' areal distribution about two thirds of all points should be within a circle of radius $\bar{D}_S$ centred on $\bar{C}$. The general failure of areal phenomena to conform to neat bell-shaped distributions in three dimensions restricts the use which can be made of this property of the standard distance measure, but the characteristics of skewness and kurtosis can also be applied to distributions in space. To date there are very few applications of this kind to be found in geographical literature, and the average distance may be just as useful as the standard distance for most practical purposes.

An imaginary case may help to explain the calculation of the mean centre and standard distance, and the difference between the weighted and unweighted measures. There are ten occurrences of some attribute in an area five miles square (see Figure 6.5). Grid coordinates are indicated on the side of the map. In case 1, no quantitative data are assigned to the points (i.e. each is given unity), so the calculation of the mean centre and standard distance is unweighted. The results are shown in the figure. In case 2, weights are given to each point and the calculations repeated. They are set down in Table 6.2 so that they can be followed step by step. Weighting shifts the mean centre in the direction of the larger values (top left of the area) and reduces the standard distance because the total observations are now more concentrated.

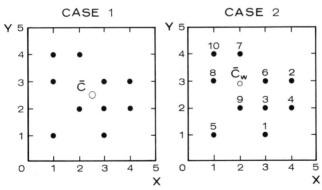

Figure 6.5   Imaginary patterns used to demonstrate the calculation of the mean centre and standard distance.

Patterns in Human Geography

Table 6.2: Calculation of Centrographic Measures (Imaginary Data)

Weighted Mean Centre $(\bar{C}_w)$

W	X	Y	XW	YW
10	1	4	10	40
8	1	3	8	24
5	1	1	5	5
7	2	4	14	28
9	2	2	18	18
6	3	3	18	18
3	3	2	9	6
1	3	1	3	1
2	4	3	8	6
4	4	2	16	8

$\Sigma W = 55$ $\Sigma XW = 109$ $\Sigma YW = 154$

$$\bar{X}_w = \frac{109}{55} = 2\cdot0; \quad \bar{Y}_w = \frac{154}{55} = 2\cdot8$$

Weighted Standard Distance $(\bar{D}_{sw})$

W	X	$X-\bar{X}_w$	$(X-\bar{X}_w)^2$	$W(X-\bar{X}_w)^2$	Y	$Y-\bar{Y}_w$	$(Y-\bar{Y}_w)^2$	$W(Y-\bar{Y}_w)^2$
10	1	-1	1	10·0	4	$+1\cdot2$	1·44	14·40
8	1	-1	1	8·0	3	$+0\cdot2$	0·04	0·32
5	1	-1	1	5·0	1	$-1\cdot8$	3·24	16·20
7	2	0	0	0·0	4	$+1\cdot2$	1·44	10·08
9	2	0	0	0·0	2	$-0\cdot8$	0·64	5·76
6	3	$+1$	1	6·0	3	$+0\cdot2$	0·04	0·24
3	3	$+1$	1	3·0	2	$-0\cdot8$	0·64	1·92
1	3	$+1$	1	1·0	1	$-1\cdot8$	3·24	3·24
2	4	$+2$	4	8·0	3	$+0\cdot2$	0·04	0·08
4	4	$+2$	4	16·0	2	$-0\cdot8$	0·64	2·56

$\Sigma W(X-\bar{X}_w)^2 = 57\cdot0$ $\Sigma W(Y-\bar{Y}_w)^2 = 54\cdot80$

$$\frac{\Sigma W(X-\bar{X}_w)^2}{\Sigma W} = \frac{57\cdot0}{55} = 1.04$$

$$\bar{D}_{sw} = \sqrt{1\cdot04 + 1\cdot00} = 1\cdot43 \text{ (miles)}$$

$$\frac{\Sigma W(Y-\bar{Y}_w)^2}{\Sigma W} = \frac{54\cdot8}{55} = 1\cdot00$$

Applications of Centrographic Measures

The application of centrographic techniques to the measurement of location patterns has been largely confined to the mean centre and standard distance. A number of examples have been selected to demonstrate what can be accomplished. The first is simply a tabulation of the mean centre and standard distance for selected major industry groups in the United States (Table 6.3). In almost all cases the mean centre is found well within the major manufacturing belt; half of them are in the state of Indiana. The major exception is for lumber and wood products, where the Pacific coast concentration pulls the mean centre to the north-west corner of Arkansas. The figures for standard distance reflect the relative degree of dispersal of the industries within the United States; of those listed, the lumber industry is most dispersed. But care must be taken in interpreting these measures. For example, two clusters some distance apart can have a quite unrepresentative mean centre located between them, and hence a large standard distance; such is the case with the timber industry. Mapping the pattern in

Table 6.3: Mean Centre and Standard Distance of Employment by States in Selected US Industries

Industry	Mean Centre (degrees)		Standard Distance (miles)
	lat.	long.	
Food and kindred products	40	91	390
Apparel and related products	40	83	350
Lumber and wood products	40	95	490
Furniture and fixtures	39	87	360
Printing and publishing	41	86	380
Chemicals and allied products	39	86	330
Stone, clay and gravel products	41	88	360
Primary metal industries	41	85	290
Fabricated metal products	40	88	280
Machinery, except electrical	40	86	360

Source of data: US *Census of Manufacturing*, 1963.

question can help to avoid erroneous impressions gained from summary measures alone.

Centrographic measures are most revealing when comparisons are made between different patterns, for the calculation of a single value for $\bar{C}$ or $\bar{D}_S$ has little meaning in isolation. One of the most common uses of the mean centre is in making comparisons over time, and the mapping of shifts provides an effective method of illustrating changing locational tendencies. A well-known example is the westward shift of the population of the United States, which the Census Bureau maps by mean centre. Population movement has been accompanied by a westward shift of industry, and mapping this by different criteria provides an interesting example of the application of this technique (Figure 6.6). The map shows a

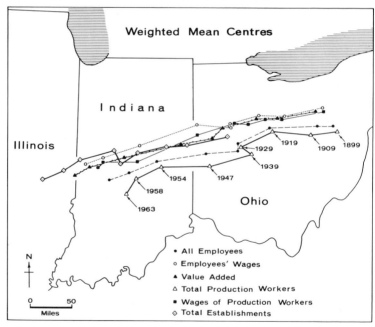

Figure 6.6   Shifts in the mean centre of manufacturing industry in the United States, 1899–1963, as measured by different criteria. (Source of data: US *Census of Manufacturing*, 1963.)

general tendency for the mean centre (weighted) to move steadily in a direction slightly south of due west, or towards California, but there are a number of other features worth commenting on. First, the paths for all employees and for total production workers are somewhat to the south of the others, reflecting in part the labour intensity of industry in the south. By contrast the path of the mean centre for employees' wages is almost always to the north of the others, reflecting the relatively higher rates of pay in the north. The path for total establishments starts well to the west of the others, and finishes still ahead of the rest, indicating that when plants are weighted by any of the five other criteria the mean centre is pulled to the east where the average size of plant has been larger. In most cases the period 1929 to 1939, which included the depression, was one in which the westward march was slowed down or halted, and for total production workers and wages for manufacturing workers there was a distinct shift back to the east. Many other points could be made, but these are sufficient to show that the measurement of shifts in the mean centre by different criteria can raise problems of interpretation as well as describing what has taken place.

Two applications of the shifting centre technique to specific industries may be considered briefly, to demonstrate further the versatility of this kind of analysis. The first (Figure 6.7) shows the movement of the mean centre of the paper industry in the southern region of the United States, plotted at five-year intervals, and indicates the difference between the weighted and unweighted measures. The track for $\bar{C}$ shows a steady movement to the southwest after 1910, fairly rapid at first but slowing down in more recent years. But when mills are weighted by capacity the mean centre is shown to move markedly eastwards between 1935 and 1940, at the time when new mills were being set up in the south to exploit the large timber reserves there. Since then $\bar{C}_W$ has moved only slightly.

The second example relates to the British lace industry. Shifts in the weighted mean centre, as measured by the number of manufacturers in business, are plotted over a period of almost 100 years (Figure 6.8). This industry has been highly localized in and around

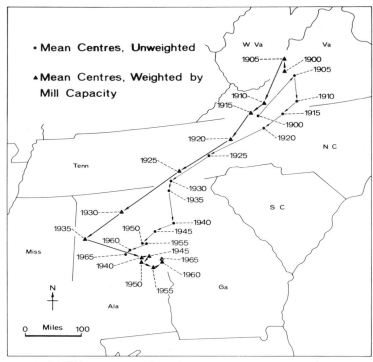

Figure 6.7   Shifts in the weighted and unweighted mean centres of the
paper industry in the south-eastern United States, 1900–
1965. (Source: K. Runyon, *The Pulp and Paper Industry
in the United States*, unpublished MA thesis, Southern
Illinois University, 1967.)

the city of Nottingham since it was mechanized, but important
local locational changes have taken place. From about 1870 to the
start of the 1914–18 war the lace industry expanded rapidly, accompanied by a movement of firms out of Nottingham and into small
towns and villages to the west in search of cheaper labour and land
for factory sites. The map shows the westwards movement of the
mean centre between 1876 and 1912, with the only slowing down of
this trend occurring in the 1890s when the industry's rate of growth
slackened and the number of firms in business fell temporarily.
After the First World War the lace trade collapsed as fashions

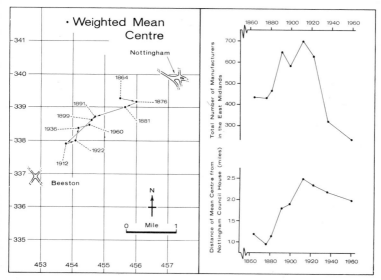

Figure 6.8   Changes in the location of the machine lace industry in
the Nottingham district, 1864–1960, as measured by
shifts in the mean centre of manufacturers. (Source of
data: *Kelly's Directories*, 1864–1960.)

changed and demand fell, and the number of firms was reduced
dramatically. There was an immediate reversal of the westward
shift of the mean centre, as the survival rate for Nottingham manufacturers was much higher than for the newer ones tempted out of
the city during boom conditions. A comparison between the two
graphs in Figure 6.8 shows the close relationship between dispersal
of manufacturers as measured by distance of the mean centre from
Nottingham, and the size of the lace industry as measured by the
number of manufacturers in business.

These examples certainly do not exhaust the possible applications of centrographic techniques to measurement problems in
human geography. The mean centre has even been suggested as a
means of finding the best location for a factory, given information
on sources and destinations of shipments in and out, and the
weights to be moved. This method of finding the point of minimum
weight/distance movement is described in a booklet produced for

199

the Small Business Administration in the United States (see J. H. Thompson, *Methods of Plant Site Selection Available to Small Manufacturing Firms*, University of West Virginia, 1961, 31–4). Unfortunately the mean centre is not the correct solution to this problem. The *median* centre is the point of minimum aggregate travel, and it has been found that the mean centre can give highly erroneous results and identify a location which is far from optimal with respect to the distance minimizing objective. How many small businesses followed the advice in the book, and with what results, is not known.

The Gini Coefficient and Lorenz Curve

Nearest neighbour analysis and centrographic techniques both provide measures of the degree of concentration in geographical patterns. Another possible approach to the same problem is provided by the family of Gini coefficients or indices of concentration described in the previous chapter. They have been used quite frequently in economic geography on data relating to areas, and involve the comparison of percentage frequencies. The results can be displayed graphically by a device known as the *Lorenz Curve*.

The general form of the most commonly used version of the *coefficient of concentration* (C) is identical with expression [5.15]:

$$C = \tfrac{1}{2} \sum_{i=1}^{N} |X_i - Y_i| \qquad [6.20]$$

where X_i and Y_i represent frequencies of the occurrence of two variables in a set of areas $(1, 2, ..., i, ..., N)$ expressed as percentages of the total occurrences. The alternative expression for use on raw data is equivalent to [5.16]:

$$C = \tfrac{1}{2} \sum_{i=1}^{N} \left| \frac{100X_i}{X_t} - \frac{100Y_i}{Y_t} \right| \qquad [6.21]$$

where X_i and Y_i are the actual numbers of occurrences instead of percentages and X_t and Y_t are the totals in all N areas, e.g. the national or regional totals. As in the versions explained in the previous chapter, the vertical brackets indicate the 'modulus' or absolute values of the expression within, i.e. the difference irrespective of whether it is positive or negative. Instead of taking half the sum of the differences ignoring the sign, the sum of either the positive or the negative differences can be used, as they will be the same. The result of the calculation of C can be anything from 0 to 100, though it is sometimes divided by 100 to give a range 0 to $1 \cdot 0$. A coefficient of 0 indicates exact correspondence between the one areal distribution and the other (some norm) – in other words no concentration or localization. The higher the figure, the greater the concentration, just as in the Gini coefficients in the last chapter. Expression [6.21] is sometimes written without the hundreds inside the brackets, and if the calculation is done this way there is no need to divide C by 100 to place it on the 0 to $1 \cdot 0$ range.

The particular measure described above is generally known as the *coefficient of localization*. It operates on the same basic data as the location quotient described in the previous chapter, but manipulates it in a different way. Whereas the location quotient is a transformation which produces a new column of figures showing how each areal unit compares with some wider average with respect to the incidence of the condition in question, the localization coefficient produces a single measure of the extent to which the condition or activity is concentrated areally by comparison with some other distribution (generally the areal allocation of all activity).

As an example, the coefficient of localization has been calculated for the three British industries for which the location quotients were worked out in Chapter 5 (see Table 5.10). One of the calculations is set out for demonstration in Table 6.4. The results, on the scale 0 to $1 \cdot 0$, are $0 \cdot 35$ for metals, indicating a moderate degree of localization, $0 \cdot 18$ for chemicals, and a very low $0 \cdot 08$ for engineering, indicating close correspondence with the regional allocation of all manufacturing employment. These confirm the general impression gained from the location quotients.

An effective way of summarizing and comparing the localization of different activities is by the use of the *localization curve* – a simple graph based on the *Lorenz* principle. To draw the graph for

201

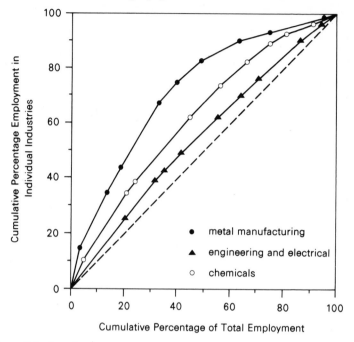

Figure 6.9   Localization curves for three British industries, calculated
from employment figures by regions. (Sources of data:
Ministry of Labour, 1965.)

any activity, the regions or areal subdivisions have to be ranked
according to their location quotients, or fX divided by fY. This is
shown for the British metals industry in Table 6.5. Then the
cumulative percentages for the activity are plotted against cumulative percentages for all activity, or whatever distribution is
considered the norm. The kind of result obtained is illustrated in
Figure 6.9, where localization curves are plotted for the three
British industries referred to above. The straight line corner to
corner indicates perfect correspondence between the cumulative
percentages for one industry and all industry. The greater the departure of the curve from this diagonal, the greater the degree of
localization. The coefficient of localization in fact measures the
area beneath the curve.

Table 6.4: Calculation of a Coefficient of Concentration for the British
Metal Manufacturing Industry (X) with Reference to Total
Industrial Employment (Y)

Standard Region	fX(%)	fY(%)	fX−fY +	fX−fY −
London and South East	5·5	20·3		14·8
Eastern and Southern	3·4	11·4		8·0
South Western	0·9	4·5		3·6
West Midlands	23·7	14·0	9·7	
East Midlands	7·4	6·9	0·5	
Yorkshire and Humberside	19·5	10·1	9·4	
North West	6·6	15·5		8·9
Northern	9·6	5·2	4·4	
Scotland	8·5	8·5		
Wales	14·9	3·6	11·3	
Totals	100·0	100·0	35·3	35·3

$$C = \frac{1}{2} \sum_{i=1}^{N} |fX-fY| = \frac{70\cdot6}{2} = 35\cdot3$$

Source of data: Ministry of Labour, 1965.

Table 6.5: Data for the Regional Distribution of the British Metal
Manufacturing Industry Arranged for Drawing a
Localization Curve

Region	$\frac{fX}{fY}$	cumulative %f X	cumulative %f Y
Wales	4·14	14·9	3·6
Yorkshire and Humberside	1·93	34·4	13·7
Northern	1·85	44·0	18·9
West Midlands	1·69	67·7	32·9
East Midlands	1·07	75·1	39·8
Scotland	1·00	83·6	48·3
North West	0·43	90·2	63·8
Eastern and Southern	0·30	93·6	75·2
London and South East	0·27	99·1	95·5
South Western	0·20	100·0	100·0

Source of data: Tables 5.10 and 6.4.

Despite the popularity of this simple coefficient for describing location patterns in economic geography, it does have its deficiencies. Like the similar coefficients described in Chapter 5, it is sensitive to the size and shape of the areal units of observation, and the result can change substantially with different levels of areal aggregation. Another problem is that these measures are not true *statistics*, in the sense that there is a sampling distribution of their values against which the result in a particular case can be tested for significance. This is not a great impediment to the use of the coefficient of concentration or localization, for it is highly unlikely that they would be applied to data other than entire populations. However, they are at best rather rough and ready measures of a pattern – useful for obtaining a quick impression of concentration, but not very powerful descriptive devices.

7. Areal Distributions as Surfaces

As measures of distribution patterns, nearest neighbour analysis, centrographic techniques and concentration coefficients can provide very useful summaries in certain circumstances. But they reveal little about the detailed form of a particular pattern. The study of areal distributions as three-dimensional surfaces opens the way for a number of other possible approaches which have considerable conceptual importance as well as providing valuable measurement tools.

The idea of depicting geographical patterns in three dimensions is an old one. Climatic conditions have long been seen this way through isotherm, isobar and isohyet maps, while the land itself is a three-dimensional surface. Patterns of human existence may at first seem more difficult to view in this manner, but there is no reason why such things as population density, industrial production costs, or even human happiness should not be thought of as varying continuously over distance like temperature or rainfall. If the physical climate can be looked at in this way, so can the social or economic 'climate'.

Before proceeding, the use of the term 'areal distribution' in the title of this chapter should be explained. A distinction is sometimes made between a pattern or arrangement of incidents on the surface of the earth, on the one hand, and a distribution of their frequency in a set of areas plotted as a two-dimensional histogram, on the other. An areal distribution may be thought of as a set of magnitudes assigned to areal units, with the values 'plotted' against the two additional dimensions of geographical space. Just as curves may be drawn to summarize distributions in the conventional two dimensions of magnitude and frequency, so surfaces can summarize distributions in the three dimensions of magnitude and geographical space.

Introducing Geographical Surfaces

Many patterns in human geography can be thought of as sets of discrete points. They may have numbers assigned to them, and they may for convenience be aggregated for certain areas. Whatever the exact circumstance, the transformation of discrete data into a continuous surface requires that certain methods be followed. The best way to introduce the problem is through a simple illustration (Figure 7.1).

Figure 7.1a depicts an imaginary section of territory ten miles square as if viewed from an elevated position but not in true perspective. A social problem exists (e.g. a type of crime) with 125 occurrences as indicated by the dots. In attempting to examine this pattern as a surface, the first step is to aggregate the individual occurrences by areas, and to do this a grid is established dividing the territory into 25 quadrats, each of four square miles. The total number of occurrences in each square is shown in Figure 7.1b. A very simple way of depicting this distribution in three dimensions would be to draw columns proportional in height to the number of crimes in each square (Figure 7.1d) to produce, in effect, a spatial equivalent of the histogram used to depict distributions in conventional statistical analysis (see Chapter 3). But this method produces an irregular surface which displays the data quite effectively but which is impossible to portray as a map or to summarize by a numerical measure. Another method is to assign the numerical value in each area to some appropriate point, in this case the centre of each square, and consider these to have an elevation in the third dimension according to a scale relating to the number of occurrences (Figure 7.1c). This third dimension is designated Z (not to be confused with the Z-score transformation). To depict such a three-dimensional scatter of points as a continuous surface, it is now necessary to make some assumption concerning the values at intermediate places, usually that the gradient between values at neighbouring control points is linear. Figure 7.1e shows the points connected to their neighbours by straight lines to give a visual impression of the assumed surface, which can be identified by

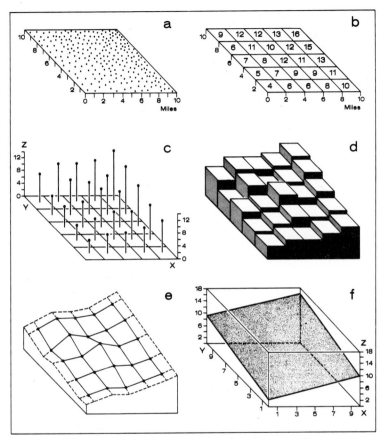

Figure 7.1   The transformation of an imaginary location pattern into a surface.

isopleths on a map. As a final stage a simple plane surface has been fitted to the distribution (Figure 7.1f), having the property of most nearly summarizing the general trend of the data across distance, within the constraints imposed by the linear form of the plane. This *trend surface* can be described by a simple equation, the derivation of which is explained in the next section of this chapter.

This illustration demonstrates what it means to transform a set of discrete geographical observations into a continuous surface.

207

Technically the portrayal of such surfaces is not a simple matter, though recent advances in computer graphics have made the construction of three-dimensional diagrams much easier than it once was (e.g. Figure 2.12). The isopleth map is used much more frequently for visual display, and as this has already been discussed in Chapter 2, with examples, no further attention is required here. The rest of this chapter is devoted to two special aspects of the analysis of geographical patterns which figure prominently in recent literature: trend surfaces and the concept of 'potential'.

Trend Surface Analysis

Conventional isopleth maps can depict areal distributions as three-dimensional surfaces with considerable accuracy. But often it is useful to be able to suppress some of the detail, and to summarize the situation by extracting general trends in the pattern of observations as they vary over distance. This can be accomplished by the fitting of trend surfaces to the distribution. Trend surface analysis has been used extensively by geologists and mining engineers to estimate the form and slope of beds of rock from the discrete observations provided by borings, and Haggett and others have demonstrated its application to a range of problems in human geography (see the Selected Reading to this chapter). The basic features of trend surface analysis are considered in some detail here because, as well as explaining this interesting range of descriptive techniques, it provides an introduction to the principles of correlation and regression analysis dealt with more fully in Chapter 8.

The initial problem to be considered is the fitting of a plane, or *linear* surface, to a three-dimensional situation of the kind illustrated in Figure 7.1. But first it may help to review the simpler two-dimensional case, in order to introduce the idea of changes in a variable (Z) as a function of distance. In Figure 7.2a and 7.2b the data from the imaginary case featured above (Figure 7.1) are plotted independently against distance along the X and Y axes.

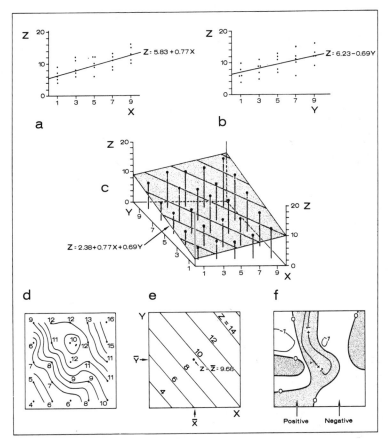

Figure 7.2   Trend surface analysis applied to an imaginary areal
distribution: a. the trend of Z in the X distance dimension;
b. the trend of Z in the Y dimension; c. plane fitted to the
Z values; d. the original data; e. the linear surface; f.
residuals from the surface.

The numerical values (Z dimension) relating to the number of
crimes have been attributed to the centre point of each quadrat, and
show distinct trends in both distance dimensions. These trends can
be summarized by fitting *regression lines*, which have the property
of minimizing the sum of the squares of the deviations of the

observations from the line. This has the same general form as the linear equation introduced in Chapter 5 [5.4], i.e.:

$$Z = a + bX \qquad [7.1]$$

where Z is the variable under study and X (or Y) is the distance variable. The symbol a is a constant representing the intercept of the regression line with the vertical axis of the graph, and b is a constant indicating the slope of the line. It will be convenient to think of Z as the 'dependent' variable, because the magnitude of Z is being viewed as attributable to or dependent on position in geographical space. The distance dimension is the 'independent' variable. The constants in [7.1] are found from the following:

$$b = \frac{\Sigma(XZ) - N(\bar{X}\bar{Z})}{\Sigma(X^2) - N(\bar{X})^2} \qquad [7.2]$$

$$a = \bar{Z} - b\bar{X} \qquad [7.3]$$

The data and calculations necessary to fit regression lines and a linear surface to the incidence of our imaginary crime are set out in Table 7.1. The adjusted sums in the bottom row are not required at this stage, but will be used later; they are obtained by subtracting from the actual sums adjustment items (the mean multiplied by the number of observations N) and show the value at the head of the column in deviations from the mean. Variables expressed in this way simplify calculations by reducing the size of the numbers to be handled without altering the final result, which is helpful if an electric calculator is being used. They are usually denoted by lower-case letters (x, y, z) instead of capitals.

The fitting of the regression line may now be illustrated. To find the b parameter for Z along the X axis, evaluate [7.2] using the appropriate figures from Table 7.1:

$$b = \frac{1364 - 1210}{825 - 625} = \frac{154}{200} = 0.77$$

To find a from [7.3]:

$$a = 9.68 - (0.77 \times 5) = 9.68 - 3.85 = 5.83$$

Table 7.1: Derivation of Values Required for the Calculation of a Plane Surface

i	Z	X	Y	X^2	XY	XZ	Y^2	YZ	Z^2
1	4	1	1	1	1	4	1	4	16
2	5	1	3	1	3	5	9	15	25
3	7	1	5	1	5	7	25	35	49
4	6	1	7	1	7	6	49	42	36
5	9	1	9	1	9	9	81	81	81
6	6	3	1	9	3	18	1	6	36
7	7	3	3	9	9	21	9	21	49
8	8	3	5	9	15	24	25	40	64
9	11	3	7	9	21	33	49	77	121
10	12	3	9	9	27	36	81	108	144
11	6	5	1	25	5	30	1	6	36
12	9	5	3	25	15	45	9	27	81
13	12	5	5	25	25	60	25	60	144
14	10	5	7	25	35	50	49	70	100
15	12	5	9	25	45	60	81	108	144
16	8	7	1	49	7	56	1	8	64
17	9	7	3	49	21	63	9	27	81
18	11	7	5	49	35	77	25	55	121
19	12	7	7	49	49	84	49	84	144
20	13	7	9	49	63	91	81	117	169
21	10	9	1	81	9	90	1	10	100
22	11	9	3	81	27	99	9	33	121
23	13	9	5	81	45	117	25	65	169
24	15	9	7	81	63	135	49	105	225
25	16	9	9	81	81	144	81	144	256
Sums (Σ)	242	125	125	825	625	1364	825	1348	2576
Means ($^-$)	9·68	5·0	5·0						
Adjustment items (A)				$N(\bar{X})^2$	$N\bar{X}\bar{Y}$	$N\bar{X}\bar{Z}$	$N(\bar{Y})^2$	$N\bar{Y}\bar{Z}$	$N(\bar{Z})^2$
				625	625	1210	625	1210	2343
Adjusted sums ($\Sigma - A$)				Σx^2	Σxy	Σxz	Σy^2	Σyz	Σz^2
				200	0	154	200	138	233

So the regression equation to estimate Z from X, i.e. expression [7.1], is:

$$Z = 5 \cdot 83 + 0 \cdot 77X$$

The intercept of the Z axis where $X = 0$ is 5·83, and to draw the line on the graph where Z is plotted against X one more value of Z is needed. Calculating Z where $X = 10$ gives $Z = 5 \cdot 83 + (0 \cdot 77 \times 10)$, which is 13·53. The regression line can now be drawn joining the two predicted values of Z. The regression line for Z and Y is:

$$Z = 6 \cdot 23 + 0 \cdot 69Y$$

and this can be drawn on the appropriate graph which in Figure 7.2 is depicted at right angles to the graph of Z and X.

How close these lines fit the scatter of points on the graphs can be judged from the *product moment correlation coefficient* (r). The formula for this can be written in a number of different ways, but the most convenient in the present context is:

$$r = \frac{\Sigma(XZ) - N(\bar{X}\bar{Z})}{\sqrt{[\Sigma(X^2) - N(\bar{X})^2] \times [\Sigma(Z^2) - N(\bar{Z})^2]}} \qquad [7.4]$$

This coefficient varies on the range $+1 \cdot 0$ to $-1 \cdot 0$, the former indicating a perfect positive linear relationship while the latter indicates a perfect inverse relationship between the two variables. Evaluating [7.4] for X and Z, using the values from Table 7.1:

$$r = \frac{1364 - 1210}{\sqrt{(825 - 625)(2576 - 2342)}} = \frac{154}{\sqrt{46600}} = 0 \cdot 72$$

For Y and Z, $r = 0 \cdot 65$. Both correlation coefficients show that there is a positive relationship between Z and distance from the origin of the graph. But the relationship is by no means perfectly linear, as visual inspection verifies.

The proportion of the variance in Z accounted for by the independent variable is found by squaring the correlation coefficient, to give the *coefficient of determination* (r^2). For the relationship between Z and $X, r^2 = 0 \cdot 52$, indicating 52 per cent of the variance 'explained', while for Z against Y it is 0·42, or 42 per cent. So in both cases substantial shares of the variation in Z cannot be attributed to the distance variable. If these relationships are considered carefully with the aid of the graphs, it should be obvious that when Z is plotted against X or Y alone, the vertical scatter of the Z values is partly attributable to the other variable Y or X because Z changes simultaneously in both dimensions. So if the two distance variables could be taken together they should be able to account for more of the variation in the Z values than X or Y alone.

How can variations in Z be related to changes in X and Y at the same time? In other words, how can the combined effect of two independent variables be expressed in a predictive equation? This brings the discussion back to the three-dimensional surface, for what is required is in fact to fit a plane as closely as possible to the scatter of points as they are suspended in space in Figure 7.1c (see Figure 7.2c). The equation for this plane will then summarize the effect of the two distance dimensions on the Z values.

The best fit plane surface will be represented by a *multiple regression model* of the form:

$$Z = a + bX + cY$$

where Z is the dependent variable or value to be predicted, X and Y are the independent variables or predictors, and a, b and c are constants. The constants are found by solving the following:

$$\left. \begin{array}{l} \Sigma xz = \Sigma(x^2)b + \Sigma(xy)c \\ \Sigma yz = \Sigma(y^2)c + \Sigma(xy)b \end{array} \right\} \qquad [7.6]$$

$$a = \bar{Z} - b\bar{X} - c\bar{Y} \qquad [7.7]$$

The lower-case letters used to denote the three variables in [7.6] indicate that they are measured as deviations from the mean – the adjustment explained above. The two expressions bracketed in [7.6] indicate that they are simultaneous equations, but as one value in each of them here will be zero (to leave only one unknown) the rather cumbersome method which generally has to be used to solve them is bypassed in this case. Substituting the appropriate values from [7.6] gives:

$$\text{to find } b: 154 = 200b + 0c = \frac{154}{200} = 0 \cdot 77$$

$$\text{to find } c: 138 = 200c + 0b = \frac{138}{200} = 0 \cdot 69$$

These two constants are identical with those calculated for the simple regression equations above, because X and Y are statistically independent and uncorrelated; however this is very seldom the case in more usual multiple regression analyses (as described in Chapter 8).

To find the value of a, evaluate [7.7] as follows:

$$a = 9 \cdot 68 - (0 \cdot 77 \times 5 \cdot 0) - (0 \cdot 69 \times 5 \cdot 0)$$
$$= 9 \cdot 68 - 3 \cdot 85 - 3 \cdot 45$$
$$= 2 \cdot 38$$

So the final equation for the best fit plane or linear surface is:

$$Z = 2 \cdot 38 + 0 \cdot 77X + 0 \cdot 69Y$$

The next step is to depict the plane graphically. To draw it in a three-dimensional diagram of the kind shown in Figures 7.1f and 7.2c, it is necessary to calculate from the above equation the Z value at each of the four corners, i.e.:

$$\text{where } X = 0, \ Y = 0 \quad : Z = 2 \cdot 38 + 0 + 0 = 2 \cdot 38$$
$$X = 10, \ Y = 0 \quad : Z = 2 \cdot 38 + 7 \cdot 7 + 0 = 10 \cdot 08$$
$$X = 0, \ Y = 10 \quad : Z = 2 \cdot 38 + 0 + 6 \cdot 9 = 9 \cdot 28$$
$$X = 10, \ Y = 10 \quad : Z = 2 \cdot 38 + 7 \cdot 7 + 6 \cdot 9 = 16 \cdot 98$$

These values can then be joined together to depict the plane, as in Figure 7.2.

The linear surface can also be depicted in a conventional isopleth map. The isopleths will be lines intersecting the axes at equal intervals, and their position is calculated from the regression equation. To find where, say, the isopleth of value 6 intersects the edges of the map, the points on the X and Y axes are found as follows:

where $Z = 6$ and $X = 0$: $6 = 2\cdot38 + 0 + 0\cdot69\,Y$

$$0\cdot69\,Y = 3\cdot62$$
$$Y = 3\cdot62 \div 0\cdot69 = 5\cdot2$$

where $Z = 6$ and $Y = 0$: $6 = 2\cdot38 + 0\cdot77 + 0$

$$0\cdot77X = 3\cdot62$$
$$X = 3\cdot62 \div 0\cdot77 = 4\cdot7$$

These values have been used to construct Figure 7.2d showing isopleths at intervals of 2 units.

A useful check on the accuracy of the plane surface is provided by the fact that one point on a regression line will be the mean of the two variables. On the plane the three means $\bar{X}$, $\bar{Y}$ and $\bar{Z}$ will thus occur at the same point. At the intersection of $X = 5$ and $Y = 5$ the value of Z on the plane should be $\bar{Z}$, or $9\cdot68$. Figure 7.2d shows that this is so.

The closeness of the fit of the plane to the original data can be measured by the *coefficient of multiple correlation* (R), which is:

$$R = \frac{b(\Sigma xz) + c(\Sigma yz)}{\Sigma(z^2)} \qquad [7.8]$$

Substituting the b and c parameters found above and the other required values as listed in Table 7.1:

$$R = \frac{(0\cdot77 \times 154) + (0\cdot69 \times 138)}{233} = \frac{214}{233} = 0\cdot92$$

The coefficient of multiple correlation is noticeably higher than the r values for X ($0\cdot72$) and Y ($0\cdot65$) calculated above. But the variance accounted for ($R^2 = 0\cdot846$) is less than the sum of the variance accounted for by X and Y independently ($0\cdot52 + 0\cdot42 = 0\cdot94$), because some of it is common to both the independent variables.

Another measure of how closely the plane fits the actual Z values is the *standard error* (S_Z). This is given by:

$$S_Z = \sqrt{\frac{\Sigma(z^2) - [b(\Sigma xz) + c(\Sigma yz)]}{N - M}} \qquad [7.9]$$

215

where N is the number of occurrences and M is the number of constants (3) in the predictive equation. $N - M$ is the degrees of freedom. Evaluating this expression:

$$S_Z = \sqrt{\frac{233 - [(0.77 \times 154) + (0.69 \times 138)]}{25 - 3}}$$

$$= \sqrt{\frac{19}{22}} = \sqrt{0.86} = 0.93$$

So the standard error of the estimated Z values from the actual Z is less than 1·0, which seems small relative to the size of the original observations.

Because trend surface analysis is a version of well-developed methods for multiple correlation and regression, it can be subjected to the same tests if the question of significance arises. This is important, for the data used to compute the surface may be a sample of an infinite number of possible observations on a spatially continuous variable, and the possibility of the observations taken not being representative should always be kept in mind. By regarding the data as a random sample and using statistical tests, the probability of chance occurrence can be judged and limits of confidence set (see next chapter).

The equation for the linear plane identified above can be used to estimate the value of each of the original observations. All that is required is to put the appropriate X and Y values into the equation. The difference or error between the observed and estimated Z is the *residual*: that which is not predicted or accounted for by the linear variation of Z in the two distance dimensions. The calculation of estimates for Z and the resulting residuals is set down in Table 7·2, and Figure 7.2 contains a map of the residuals (positive and negative).

The broad changes in Z with distance, as indicated by a trend surface, are sometimes termed the *regional component* of areal variation, as distinct from the *local component* represented by the residuals. The regional component is what Krumbein has described as 'that part of an observed value which is relatively stable and changes systematically if at all from point to point on the map', while the local component is 'a relatively unstable part of the

Table 7.2: Calculation of Predicted Z Values and Residuals from a Linear Trend Surface

i	X	Y	a	bX	cY	Z_{obs}	Z_{est}	Z_{res}
1	1	1	2·38	0·77	0·69	4	3·84	0·16
2	1	3	2·38	0·77	2·07	5	5·22	−0·22
3	1	5	2·38	0·77	3·45	7	6·60	0·40
4	1	7	2·38	0·77	4·83	6	7·98	−1·98
5	1	9	2·38	0·77	6·21	9	9·36	−0·36
6	3	1	2·38	2·31	0·69	6	5·38	0·62
7	3	3	2·38	2·31	2·07	7	6·76	0·24
8	3	5	2·38	2·31	3·45	8	8·14	−0·14
9	3	7	2·38	2·31	4·83	11	9·52	1·48
10	3	9	2·38	2·31	6·21	12	10·90	1·10
11	5	1	2·38	3·85	0·69	6	6·92	−0·92
12	5	3	2·38	3·85	2·07	9	8·30	0·70
13	5	5	2·38	3·85	3·45	12	9·68	2·32
14	5	7	2·38	3·85	4·83	10	11·06	−1·06
15	5	9	2·38	3·85	6·21	12	12·44	−0·44
16	7	1	2·38	5·39	0·69	8	8·46	−0·46
17	7	3	2·38	5·39	2·07	9	9·84	−0·84
18	7	5	2·38	5·39	3·45	11	11·22	−0·22
19	7	7	2·38	5·39	4·83	12	12·60	−0·60
20	7	9	2·38	5·39	6·21	13	13·98	−0·98
21	9	1	2·38	6·93	0·69	10	10·00	0·00
22	9	3	2·38	6·93	2·07	11	11·38	−0·38
23	9	5	2·38	6·93	3·45	13	12·76	0·24
24	9	7	2·38	6·93	4·83	15	14·14	0·86
25	9	9	2·38	6·93	6·21	16	15·52	0·48

Estimating equation: $Z = 2·38 + 0·77X + 0·69Y$.

observed value that varies in a more or less irregular manner over the area. It contains no significant gradients and represents a series of non-systematic (positive or negative) departures from the smooth regional form.' The computation of a plane of best fit, and the mapping of residuals from it, may enable a researcher to distinguish between the broad systematic way in which a variable changes with distance, and the more local changes which may require a different explanation. However, it is important that systematic departures from the surface are tested for and eliminated before the residuals are interpreted as a 'local component', and this may well require a more complex surface than a plane (see section on non-linear surfaces below).

As a general descriptive model of areal variation, the trend surface may be expressed as follows:

$$Z_{ij} = t(X_i, Y_j) + e_{ij} \qquad [7.10]$$

where Z_{ij} is the observed value of some variable Z at grid locations X_i and Y_j,

    t is the general trend or 'regional' variation,

and e_{ij} is the residual error, or local component of variation.

If the surface is a good fit, the local component should be no more than a small random error normally distributed about the surface.

Examples of Trend Surface Analysis

Two examples of the fitting of linear trend surfaces to real-world situations may now be described. Both concern industrial costs – something which can legitimately be thought of as virtually a continuous spatial variable with some possible magnitude at any selected location. Both examples are set in the United States.

The first pattern for analysis is that of variation in wage rates. The basic figures for gross hourly earnings of production workers in manufacturing are mapped by states in Figure 7.3a, indicating a general tendency for wages to increase from south to north and from east to west. Exactly how close is the relationship between a state's geographical position and its average wage rate, and which states depart most from the general trend? This can be answered in the first instance by fitting a linear surface to the data. For convenience, the centre points of the states are taken as control points. The plane of best fit was found to be:

$$Z = 250 - 0.68X + 1.24Y$$

where the wage rates are in cents and the distances are in units of the arbitrary grid in Figure 7.3. The plane is drawn as an isopleth map with intervals of 10 cents in Figure 7.3b. It dips in a direction

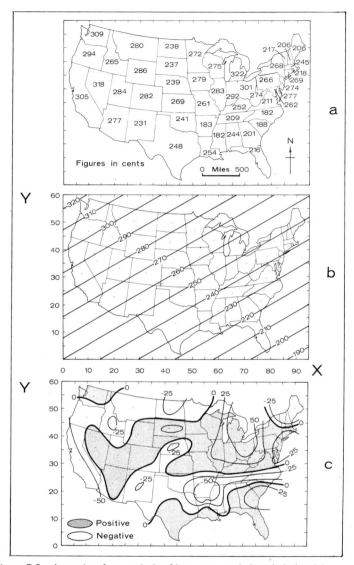

Figure 7.3   A trend surface analysis of inter-state variations in industrial
             wage rates in the United States. (Source of data: average
             hourly earnings of production workers in manufacturing,
             from US Department of Labor.)

slightly south of south east, showing that the general tendency is for wages to increase from the Gulf Coast states in the direction of the northern part of the mountain and Pacific coast regions. A further graphic portrayal of the surface is shown in Figure 7.4, a three-dimensional diagram of the kind used previously in Figures 7.1f and 7.2c.

The closeness of fit is shown by a coefficient of multiple correlation (R) of 0·593. Thus the surface accounts for about 35 per cent of the areal variation in wage rates, measured by R^2. By using the equation for the plane residuals have been calculated, and these are mapped in Figure 7.3c to show the extent to which the surface fails to predict the wage figures. In some states, such as Minnesota, Washington and Florida, the prediction is correct to within a few cents, i.e. the true values are almost exactly on the surface. But in others, such as California, Michigan and Arkansas, the prediction has an error of over 50 cents. The isopleths in Figure 7.3c suggest that the residuals follow a distinct geographical pattern (i.e. they are not random or 'unsystematic'), with a ridge from New York to the Rockies flanked by two troughs. This suggests that if the surface could somehow be curved, a more accurate description of the original pattern would be possible.

The second example applies to total production costs in a particular industry. As part of a study of cost variations in a branch of the electronics industry, a leading firm of American plant location consultants* compiled data on the cost of labour, freight (transportation of materials and finished product), occupancy (i.e. land and buildings), utilities and taxes, for over 100 different locations throughout the United States. The total for all these items provided a fairly accurate estimate of the geographically variable element of total cost. During an analysis of this information, it was decided to test the hypothesis that total cost could be accurately predicted by location alone. The figures appeared to indicate a general tendency for costs to fall in a fairly regular fashion from north to south, and trend surface analysis provided a means of

* The Fantus Company, Chicago. The author is grateful to Mr Ronald Reiffler of Fantus for making available the data used here, and to Mr Robert Klingensmith who performed the analysis.

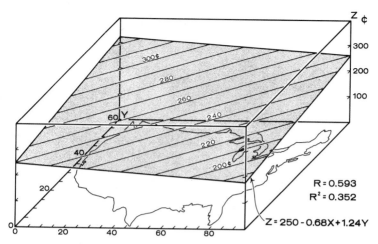

Figure 7.4 A three-dimensional representation of a linear trend surface fitted to state data on industrial wage rates in the United States, from Figure 7.3. (Designed by Tso-Hwa Lee.)

establishing the exact nature of the pattern of change with distance.

The linear surface is illustrated in Figure 7.5. The slope is almost due north-south; the azimuth or angle is actually 165 degrees, only a 15 degree departure from a north-south line. But the surface accounts for only a relatively small share of the cost variation between locations, with $R^2 = 0.139$ or about 14 per cent variance explained. Thus the initial hypothesis of regular and predictable variation could not be substantiated by the linear model. The second map in Figure 7.5 shows the residuals from the surface, revealing that most of the peaks of high positive deviation from the general trend are in the major manufacturing belt, and that the Gulf coast also has higher costs than predicted by the surface. With the exception of the area extending across the northern part of the Rockies and the plains, the major areas of negative residuals are also the areas of lowest costs as identified in the original data. However, the weakness in the fit of the surface makes speculation about the residuals of little value, for if the surface accounts for only 14 per cent of the variance the residuals will closely replicate the original data. A perfectly horizontal linear surface, which accounts for nothing, leaves the residuals accounting for everything.

221

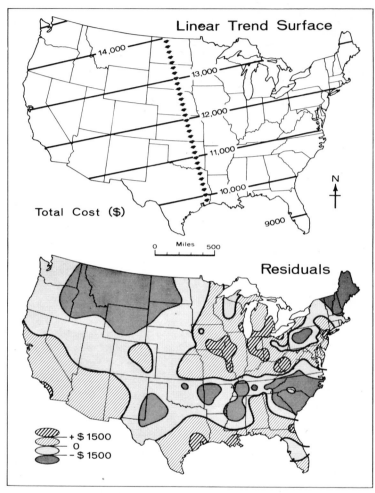

Figure 7.5   A trend surface analysis of the cost of production in a
branch of the electronics industry in the United States.
(Source of data: for full explanation, see D. M. Smith,
Industrial Location: An Economic Geographical Analysis,
John Wiley, 1971, Chapter 18.)

Non-Linear Surfaces

Regularity in the pattern of residuals raises the possibility that a 'higher-order' surface of a non-linear type might be a better fit to the original data than a plane. For example, Figure 7.3c shows a distinct ridge of positive residuals with a trough of negative residuals to the right, which suggests that if the surface could be bent up in the area over the ridge and down over the trough a better fit could be achieved. There are a number of possible approaches to this problem.

The simplest kind of non-linear surface is the *quadratio*, which has a ridge or trough tilted as in the plane – a sensible form to attempt on the wage data above. It is defined by:

$$Z = a + bx + cY + dX^2 + eXY + fY^2 \qquad [7.11]$$

where the lower-case letters indicate constants. The next highest order is the *cubic* surface, in which the pattern can be depicted as a dome or basin, and the curvature can change twice on any cross section. The equation is:

$$Z = a + bX + cY + dX^2 + eXY + fY^2 + gX^3 + hX^2Y + iXY^2 + jY^3$$
$$[7 \cdot 12]$$

As the *quartic, quintic*, and even higher order surfaces are reached, the form becomes successively more complex, as does the equation. These surfaces, like the plane, are normally calculated by computer, using a programme which prints maps of the surface and the residuals from it.

An example of computer-generated curvilinear surfaces may be offered as a special application of automated cartography as introduced in Chapter 2. With the recent public concern over atmospheric pollution, there is a renewed interest in the weather as an important aspect of man's everyday environment, and this example is taken from a study of urban climatology. Rainfall figures were obtained for 50 stations in greater Johannesburg, South Africa, to find what variation exists in the city and its suburbs. It was discovered that almost half of the variability could be accounted for by the quartic surface. This is illustrated in Figure 7.6. On the computer print-out reproduced directly here, the dots roughly define the 750 mm isohyet. The areas marked by letters have a lower rainfall than 750 mm, and the areas with numerals have more than this. The isohyet interval is 25 mm.

As successively higher order non-linear surfaces are computed, the proportion of variance accounted for increases. This is illustrated in Table 7.3, where some of the results of a trend surface analysis of inter-state variations in selected social conditions in the United States are listed. The figures show that some conditions are rather well described by trend surfaces, especially the state murder rate and the average monthly payments on the Aid to Families with Dependent Children (AFDC) programme. In other cases the fits are much weaker however, especially in the larceny rate. Why some of these conditions should display such regularity in spatial variation while others do not is a complex question concerning the underlying social and economic processes at work; trend surface analysis can describe the patterns but it cannot explain them.

This kind of analysis obviously requires access to a computer and the appropriate program, and these are not always available. However, some simpler methods of fitting non-linear surfaces have been devised, one of which is Krumbein's *expected-value method*. This is easy to calculate, and is worth illustrating as a quick way of drawing a smooth surface which adequately summarizes the general trend in an areal distribution without an equation. It can only be used where the control points or data collection units form a regular grid, which restricts its application in human geography unless samples can be taken in this way. The first step involves setting down the observations (Z values) in the form of a matrix. Then an 'expected value' is calculated for each cell, or control point, from the averages for the row and column to which it belongs. The expression is:

$$Z_{exp} = I + J - T \qquad [7.13]$$

where I is the average of the original Z values in the row to which

```
TREND SURFACE ANALYSIS OF JOHANNESBURG RAINFALL.

CONTOURED FOURTH DEGREE SURFACE

PLOTTING LIMITS
MAXIMUM X #      14.63256R      MINIMUM X #     -1R.367432
MAXIMUM Y #      14.373530      MINIMUM Y #     -14.676470

X-SCALE IS HORIZONTAL
X-VALUE # -1R.37 ( 0.3333 X XSCALE VALUE<

Y-SCALE IS VERTICAL

CONTOUR INTERVAL #              25.00
REFERENCE CONTOUR #.....< #     730.00
```

Figure 7.6   An example of a computer-generated map of a trend
surface: a quartic surface fitted to rainfall data in a city.
(Source: J. R. N. Wilcocks, *Rainfall Variations in Greater
Johannesburg*, unpublished BSc thesis, University of the
Witwatersrand, 1970.)

225

Table 7.3: Trend Surface Analyses of Inter-State Variations in Selected Social Conditions in the United States

Variable	Percentage of Variance Explained ($R^2 \times 100$)		
	Linear	Quadratic	Cubic
Per capita annual income ($) 1968	16·4	31·2	47·1
Houses dilapidated, etc., (%) 1960	15·5	33·5	60·6
Public assistance recipients (% popn) 1964	15·2	19·5	41·1
Average monthly AFDC payments ($) 1968	46·3	52·4	66·1
Physicians per 10,000 popn 1967	15·5	33·4	60·6
Dentists per 10,000 popn 1967	34·2	46·5	54·9
Median school years completed 1960	34·0	46·0	58·1
Persons aged 25 or over at college (%) 1960	3·3	24·1	44·1
Murders per 100,000 popn 1967	55·5	69·3	71·3
Rapes per 100,000 popn 1967	24·0	28·4	37·4
Larceny per 100,000 popn 1967	3·8	12·ʊ	17·7

Source of data: *Statistical Abstract of the United States.*

the cell belongs, J is the average for the column, and T is the average for all cells.

As an illustration, this method has been applied to the imaginary crime data used in the initial demonstration of the linear surface in section 7.2 (Table 7.4). The results are illustrated in Figure 7.7, which shows a set of curved isopleths somewhat similar to those of the linear surface in Figure 7.2. A comparison between the residuals from the expected-value method and those from the earlier one confirms that the non-linear surface has captured a little more of the variance, for the residuals in Figure 7.7 tend to be smaller.

As a practical example, median income in part of northern Texas has been subjected to this kind of trend surface analysis. The area chosen contains 32 counties which conform to an almost perfectly regular grid. The actual median income by counties is shown in Figure 7.8a, and the calculated Z_{exp} values are placed beside control points representing the centre of each county in Figure 7.8b. The third map (Figure 7.8c) shows the surface as interpolated from the expected values, the smooth form indicating that only the broad regional trend in the data has been taken into account. The map of residuals (Figure 7.8d) shows that only isolated peaks deviate to any considerable extent from the expected-value surface, and their spatial occurrence suggests that they can be interpreted very largely as local random deviations from the general trend of incomes rising from the south east to the north west.

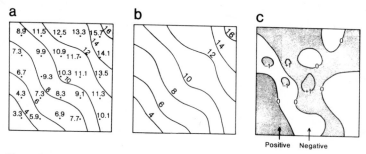

Figure 7.7   An illustration of a non-linear surface and residuals, calculated by the Krumbein 'expected value' method from imaginary data (see Figure 7.1).

58	59	61	51
61	63	44	52
56	55	60	44
67	46	34	35
48	37	37	42
47	43	34	30
54	37	32	35
40	52	42	39

a $ 100

65	60	54	52
63	58	52	50
61	56	50	48
53	48	42	40
49	44	38	36
46	41	35	33
47	42	36	34
51	46	40	38

b $ 100

c $ d $

Figure 7.8   A non-linear surface fitted by the expected value method to geographical variations in median income in north-eastern Texas, 1960: a. original county data ($100s); b. the 'expected values' ($100s); c. the trend surface; d. residuals from the surface. (Source of data: *City and County Data Book*, 1965.)

Table 7.4: Computation of Trend Surface and Residuals by the 'Expected Value' Method

Observed Z values (Z_{obs})

Cell	$X = 1$	$X = 3$	$X = 5$	$X = 7$	$X = 9$	Row Sums	Row Means (I)
$Y = 9$	9	12	12	13	16	62	12·4
$Y = 7$	6	11	10	12	15	54	10·8
$Y = 5$	7	8	12	11	13	51	10·2
$Y = 3$	5	7	9	9	11	41	8·2
$Y = 1$	4	6	6	8	10	34	6·8
Col. Sums	31	44	49	53	65	242	
Col. Means (J)	6·2	8·8	9·8	10·6	13·0		$T = 9·68$

Expected Z values (Z_{exp})

Cell	$X = 1$	$X = 3$	$X = 5$	$X = 7$	$X = 9$
$Y = 9$	8·9	11·5	12·5	13·3	15·7
$Y = 7$	7·3	9·9	10·9	11·7	14·1
$Y = 5$	6·7	9·3	10·3	11·1	13·5
$Y = 3$	4·7	7·3	8·3	9·1	11·5
$Y = 1$	3·3	5·9	6·9	7·7	10·1

Residuals ($Z_{obs} - Z_{exp}$)

Cell	$X = 1$	$X = 3$	$X = 5$	$X = 7$	$X = 9$
$Y = 9$	+0·1	+0·5	−0·5	−0·3	+0·3
$Y = 7$	−1·3	+1·1	−0·9	+0·3	+0·9
$Y = 5$	+0·3	−1·3	+1·7	−0·1	−0·5
$Y = 3$	+0·3	−0·3	+0·7	−0·1	−0·5
$Y = 1$	+0·7	+0·1	−0·9	+0·3	−0·1

Trend surface analysis in its various forms offers a wide range of possible applications in the field of human geography, most of which have yet to be even partly explored. It can be used as a quantitative tool to describe areal distributions, as a test of models which suggest that patterns should have a specific trend, as a device to predict or infer values at a point where no data are available, and as a search procedure through which the identification of significant patterns of residuals may lead to further research problems. But trend surface analysis also has its limitations and dangers. Many areal distributions in human geography are not regular enough to have anything more than a very small proportion of their variance accounted for by one of the lower order surfaces, as was shown in the application to social conditions in the USA above, and advancing to higher order surfaces often seems simply to replace one kind of complexity by another. Fitting, say, a cubic or quartic surface to a location pattern may be an impressive technical achievement, and if the fit is good it can provide an accurate if cumbersome numerical description of the pattern. But it is unlikely to have any great theoretical significance. A full evaluation of the use of trend surfaces in human geography must await the results of many more careful applications and analyses.

Potential Surfaces

Simple isopleth maps and trend surfaces are not the only ways in which a set of discrete observations can be transformed into a spatially continuous variable. Another method used quite frequently is based on the notion of *potential*, which applies the gravitational concept of a body exerting an 'influence' on another body to areally distributed economic and social phenomena. The influence at any point with reference to another point is proportional to the mass exerting the influence and inversely proportional to the distance between the points. The sum of all influences at any point is termed the 'potential'. Closely related to the potential concept is the *gravity model* used to describe patterns of human interaction over distance (see Chapter 9).

The advantage of the potential concept over other methods of deriving surfaces is that by measuring at a large number of points the 'influence' of every other point, a set of discrete observations can be turned into a truly continuous spatial variable. There is some possible value for any point in space, determined by the magnitudes at all other points for which data are available on the initial condition representing influence.

The influence, or potential (V), exerted on any point i by another point j is given by:

$$_iV_j = \frac{P_j}{D_{ij}{}^b}$$ [7.14]

where P_j is the mass at point j measuring influence (i.e. number of people, number of shops, volume of possible sales, etc.) and D_{ij} is the distance between points i and j measured in miles, tens of miles, hours of travel time, cost, or whatever other units seem appropriate as a measure of true distance. Distance may be raised to a power, designated by the constant b in the equation, if this helps to describe the actual influence of the one point on the other more exactly. The total potential exerted at any point is the sum of the influence of all other points, i.e.:

$$_iV = a \sum_{j=1}^{N} \frac{P_j}{D_{ij}{}^b}$$ [7.15]

where the summation is over all N points $(1, 2, ..., j, ..., N)$. The inclusion of the symbol a representing the 'constant of proportionality' helps to describe empirical relationships exactly, as will be explained further in the treatment of the gravity model in Chapter 9. Ignoring this and the distance exponent (i.e. assuming it to be one), then if the calculation was of 'population potential' the population at each place (P_j) is divided by distance to the place i (D_{ij}), and the results are summed to give the potential value at i.

A simple illustration will help to demonstrate the calculation. An imaginary region is divided into six areas, and data (e.g. number of people), are collected for each. The problem is to calculate the population potential at a point i, which is the geographical centre of one of the areas. The situation is shown in Figure 7.9, where the mass data (population) are written beside the centre point of each areal unit and the distances (miles) are indicated along the lines from i to each other point. Area boundaries are shown by the discontinuous lines. The a and b constants are assumed to be unity. The influence exerted at i by point (i.e. area) i

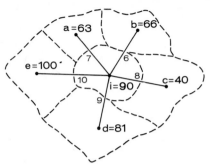

Figure 7.9   An imaginary case to illustrate the calculation of potential.

is calculated by assuming that the 90 people there are at an average distance of 3 miles from the centre point, thus giving a value of 3 for D_{ii}. The calculation is now as follows:

Place	P_j	D_{ij}	P_j/D_{ij}
a	63	7	9
b	66	6	11
c	40	8	5
d	81	9	9
e	100	10	10
i	90	3	30
Total			74 = potential

So the population potential at point i is 74 *persons per mile* – the units being determined by the units used in the mass and distance measures.

When the potential has been worked out in this way for all points, its spatial variation can be mapped using isopleths or *equipotential lines*. The result is a *potential surface*. The more points for which data are used, the more detailed will the surface be. Potential is expressed in units of mass per unit of distance, e.g. persons per mile (as above), income (£) per 100 miles, or tens of pigs per kilometre. An alternative is to express each value as a proportion of the potential at the highest point on the surface, to avoid these strange descriptions.

A number of important technical questions arise in the calculation of potential. The first is that of the influence of a point (or area) on itself, which cannot be zero. As the mass figures are almost invariably calculated for some territory of areal extent, a convenient average distance is generally used as in the simple illustration above. The second question concerns the distance exponent. This is often assumed to be unity, but there are occasions where it might be necessary to take the square of the distances, for example, to describe accurately a real world situation where the influence of the more distant points may be less than untransformed linear distance would indicate. The estimation of the distance exponent to best fit a given set of observations is explained in connection with the gravity model of human interaction in Chapter 9. Discussion of the third problem – the constant of proportionality – is also reserved for Chapter 9.

Once a potential surface has been identified, what are the uses to which it can be put? Its most important property is that the potential at any point is a measure of access to the total population, or whatever the mass figures represent. Thus if it is assumed that the mass is some measure of the market for a product at given places, and that this sales expectation falls off with increasing distance from the point of production, then the result of expression [7.15] for alternative locations can be interpreted as the *market potential*. The point of maximum potential is where production could be undertaken with maximum volume of sales, given the assumption about the behaviour of the market implicit in the division of expected sales by distance from the plant. This may be a reasonable assumption if the cost of supplying a point increases with distance from the factory, and if this is reflected in the price charged. Further discussion of the market potential concept is beyond the scope of this book, but it is quite useful in economic geography.

The point of maximum potential has other interesting properties. It is the *harmonic mean centre* of an areal distribution, which often coincides with the *modal centre* – two of the centrographic measures of average position described in the previous chapter. The potential pattern for population and income has been identified and mapped for a number of countries, and has been found to reflect quite closely other important patterns of social and economic geography. This is discussed more fully in some of the references in the Selected Reading to this chapter.

An actual example of a potential surface, relating to the lumber and wood products industry in the United States, is presented in Figure 7.10. The P data are the number of employees by states, and the D values are linear distances between the centre point of each state. This could be regarded as a market potential map, e.g. for the supply of machinery for this industry, if the number of employees was a fair measure of the likely volume of sales in any state. The unusual isopleth intervals arise from the fact that the original of this map was generated by computer, with the range in the 48 values divided into equal segments to create the class intervals, as described in Chapter 2. The pattern itself is of interest because there are two areas of high potential, in the South and the Pacific north west respectively, coinciding with the two major national concentrations of this industry.

Considerable claims have been made as to the value of the potential surface as a general descriptive device in human geography. After a spate of applications in the 1950s and 1960s interest seems to have subsided, however, as the mainstream of quantitative analysis moved in other directions. In its special forms as models of market potential and of human interaction, the potential surface has been shown useful, not only in geographical study but also for locational analysis in planning. But, like trend surface analysis, the potential concept is best seen as just one of a number of descriptive devices available to the human geographer. Although helpful in certain circumstances, their general value remains to be fully demonstrated by a revealed capacity to shed light on the reality of human existence.

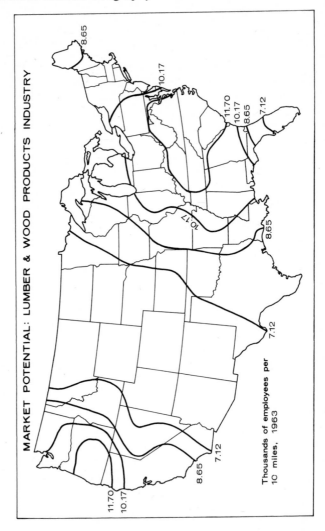

Figure 7.10   A market potential surface for the United States lumber and wood products industry. (Source of data: US *Census of Manufacturing*, 1963.)

8. Association between Patterns

The similarity or association between geographical patterns can be established in many ways. Some have already been suggested in the previous two chapters, for applying the same descriptive measure to different patterns obviously provides some basis for comparison. Thus a comparison between the nearest neighbour measures for two patterns, between their mean centres and standard distances or between the equations for their trend surfaces, would all give some idea of similarity. And the extent of the difference observed can usually be tested for significance.

This chapter addresses a somewhat different aspect of comparison – the extent to which patterns are associated with one another. *Association* implies a systematic or regular change in one variable as the other changes. An alternative term for this is *covariation* or varying together; another is *correlation*.

Correlation techniques are among the most widely used methods of numerical analysis in geography. An immediate distinction must be made between the use of these techniques to describe the areal association between different conditions, and their use to infer causal relationships. The distinction is between the discovery of relationships which enable one condition to be accurately predicted by another, and the setting of relationships within some theoretical framework which can elevate the prediction to an explanation. It is often easier to predict than to explain, for prediction is possible on the basis of observed or empirical associations the reasons for which may not be known. Explanation requires an understanding of the functional nature of the relationship – of why one condition is necessarily associated with another and not simply observed together. We may be able to predict the effect of aspirin on a headache or hangover, but unless we are doctors or chemists we are unlikely to be able to explain it.

As the focus of this book is on descriptive analysis, the emphasis in this chapter is on measuring observed associations. Only passing reference will be made to the problem of establishing causal relationships. As in a number of previous chapters, all that can be offered here is a taste of the range of techniques available; those wishing to savour them more fully should consult the specialized works and examples of applications listed in the Selected Reading to this chapter.

When 'Association' is not Association

The meaning of association as used here may be clarified by considering a common calculation which purports to measure geographical association but in fact does not. It is known as the *coefficient of geographical association*, and has been used quite often in economic geography. It is simply a version of the general Gini coefficient of concentration introduced in Chapter 5 and illustrated as a measure of geographical patterns in Chapter 6. Given information on the occurrence of two conditions in a set of areas, the coefficient of geographical association (C_g) is as follows:

$$C_g = \frac{1}{2} \sum_{i=1}^{N} \left| \frac{X_i}{X_t} - \frac{Y_i}{Y_t} \right| \qquad [8.1]$$

where X_i and Y_i are the areal occurrences of the two conditions and X_t and Y_t are the total occurrences in all areas. The numerators are sometimes multiplied by 100, as in expression [6.21] for the coefficient of concentration in Chapter 6, so that the subtraction is between percentages; the coefficient is then on a range 0 to 100 instead of the 0 to 1·0 given by expression [8.1]. A low coefficient is supposed to indicate high association between the two sets of observations expressed as per unit or per cent frequencies, with $C_g = 0$ indicating exact correspondence. A high coefficient shows low association.

An example of the calculation of this measure is set out in Table 8.1. Figures for two different methods of measuring the quantity of manufacturing industry by major regions in the United

Table 8.1: Calculation of the Coefficient of Geographical Association
(C_g) between Two Different Measures of Manufacturing in
the United States

Region	Employees (1000s) X	Value Added ($M) Y	$\frac{100X_i}{X_t}$	$\frac{100Y_i}{Y_t}$	$\left\lvert\frac{100X_i}{X_t}-\frac{100Y_i}{Y_t}\right\rvert$
New England	1,379	13,589	8·5	7·0	1·5
Middle Atlantic	3,811	43,560	23·5	22·7	0·8
East North Central	4,264	56,327	26·2	29·3	3·1
West North Central	975	11,809	6·0	6·1	0·1
South Atlantic	2,068	21,134	12·7	11·0	1·7
East South Central	874	9,383	5·4	4·9	0·5
West South Central	838	10,942	5·2	5·7	0·5
Mountain	279	3,472	1·7	1·8	0·1
Pacific	1,746	22,112	10·8	11·5	0·7
US Total	16,234	192,328	100·0	100·0	9·0

$$C_g = \frac{1}{2} \sum_{i=1}^{9} \left\lvert \frac{100X_i}{X_t} - \frac{100Y_i}{Y_t} \right\rvert = \frac{9·0}{2} = 4·5$$

Source of data: US *Census of Manufacturing*, 1963.

States are listed, and it is required to show how closely they correspond. The base data are transformed into percentages, and the resulting coefficient is 4·5 on the 0 to 100 scale. This indicates close 'association', and the two sets of percentages are in fact very much the same.

But suppose that the distributions had been of a different form. The figures below show two percentage frequencies for an imaginary set of four regions, and the differences between them:

Region	$100X_i/X_t$	$100Y_i/Y_t$	$\lvert 100X_i/X_t - 100Y_i/Y_t \rvert$
North	10	40	30
South	20	30	10
East	30	20	10
West	40	10	30
	100	100	80

237

Half the sum of the differences irrespective of sign is 40 so $C_g = 40$ on the 0 to 100 scale, suggesting weak association. But the two sets of figures are in reality very closely associated. One is the 'mirror image' of the other, and X can be predicted perfectly by Y from the linear equation $X = 50 - Y$. In other words, there is a perfect negative association or correlation. Changes in one condition are systematically associated with changes in the other.

So despite its name, the coefficient of geographical association does not measure association in the true sense. It is not a correlation technique. It simply measures what proportion of one variable would have to be reallocated between areas in order to make it correspond with the distribution of the other variable. Although it can give an approximation to a coefficient of correlation of the kind discussed later in this chapter if the two sets of observations correspond closely, the coefficient of geographical association can also produce results which differ considerably from those of more conventional correlation techniques. There are thus very few circumstances in which C_g would be preferred to the methods outlined in the remainder of this chapter.

Comparing Nominal Classifications

The appropriate method for testing geographical patterns for association or correlation depends firstly on the nature of the data. Nominal, ordinal, and interval or ratio measurements all require different methods.

The capacity to test the association or independence of areal classifications based on nominal measurement is important in human geography, where the use of higher-order data may be impracticable. Even if quantities cannot be assigned to occurrences of attributes in a set of areas, their presence or absence can usually be established. Correlation between patterns of occurrences can then be measured by the chi-square test described in Chapter 4. Because the problem now involves two or more sets of observations or samples neither of which may legitimately be regarded as an expectation, the procedure differs somewhat from the one independent sample case described earlier. But the basic principle of comparing sets of frequencies is the same.

Imagine a set of observations on whether each of a set of N areas has or has not each of two or more attributes. The first step is to set out the data (i.e. the observed frequencies) in tabular form, in what is known as a *contingency table*. If there are two attributes, the data are arranged in a 2×2 contingency table of the kind shown below:

Attribute A

		Yes	No
	Yes		
Attribute B			
	No		

Here any observation can be classified in any one of four ways, and N is the number of observations in all classes. The contingency table may be of any size. For example, if a set of farms was classified according to four farming regions and six soil types, this would require a 4×6 table. The general form of the contingency table with k columns and r rows is as illustrated in Table 8.2.

The question arising now is this: are the two (or more) classifications of the areas associated, or are they independent of one another? If they are independent, then we could expect to find the proportion of areas in any column the same for every row. This can be demonstrated from the following data, which classify ten imaginary areas according to whether they are prosperous or not (yes = 1, no = 0) and whether they are northern or not (yes = 1, no = 0):

Area	1	2	3	4	5	6	7	8	9	10
Prosperous?	1	1	0	0	0	1	1	0	0	0
Northern?	1	1	1	1	1	0	0	0	0	0

There is obviously no correspondence between these two attributes. Half (five out of ten) of the areas are northern, half of the four prosperous areas are northern, and half of the six non-prosperous

Table 8.2: *General Form of the Contingency Table Used to Arrange Data for Testing the Independence of Nominal Classifications*

Classes	A_1	A_2	A_3	$\ldots A_j$	$\ldots A_k$	Row totals
B_1 B_2 B_3 $\vdots$ B_i $\vdots$ B_r						
Column totals						N

areas are northern. Two fifths (four out of ten) of the areas are prosperous, two of the five northern areas are prosperous, and two of the five non-northern areas are prosperous. In short, the two areal classifications are independent of each other. The contingency table in this case is as follows:

Prosperous

class	Yes (1)	No (0)	sums
Northern Yes (1)	2	3	5
No (0)	2	3	5
sums	4	6	$10 = N$

Now consider the probability of any area falling into any cell ij of the table, designated p_{ij}. The probability of being in any row i $(p_{i.})$ is obviously related to the proportion of all observations in this row, e.g. if five out of ten areas are northern the probability of any one chosen at random being northern is five tenths or one in two. Similarly the probability of an area being in any column j $(p_{.j})$ is related to the proportion of all observations falling into that column. If the two classifications are independent the following will be true:

$$p_{ij} = p_{i.} \, p_{.j}, \text{ for all } ij \qquad [8.2]$$

In other words, the content of any cell will be proportional to the product of the appropriate row and column probabilities. If they are not independent and some association exists between the classifications, then:

$$p_{ij} \neq p_{i.} \, p_{.j}, \text{ for at least one pair } ij \qquad [8.3]$$

In the imaginary case it can be verified from the 2×2 table above that $p_{ij} = p_{i.} \, p_{.j}$ by multiplying any row sum and column sum divided by N (10), to give the actual frequency in the cell in question.

The statement of no dependence [8.2] is a null hypothesis, which can be subject to statistical testing. The statement of what must be true if H_o is found not to be true, i.e. H_a, is [8.3] above. Testing involves calculating the values for p_{ij} if H_o is true, in other words the frequencies in each cell if the two distributions are independent. This is then compared with the observed frequencies, and the difference is tested by the chi-square statistic to establish the level of probability that the difference can be attributed to chance or sampling error. If the observed frequencies are not significantly different from those which would arise if the two attributes occurred independently, then they are judged independent.

For any cell in a contingency table the expected frequency required for this test is found by multiplying the sum of its row by the sum of its column and dividing by the total number of occurrences. The general expression is thus:

$$E_{ij} = \frac{\sum\limits_{i=1}^{r} O_i \times \sum\limits_{j=1}^{k} O_j}{N} \qquad [8.4]$$

where O indicates the observed frequencies in a table with r rows and k columns. The table of all the expected values E_{ij} represents the frequencies with which the observations would fall into each cell if the attributes occurred independent of one another. The null hypothesis that they do in fact occur independently is tested by calculating chi-square as follows:

$$\chi^2 = \sum_{i=1}^{r} \sum_{j=1}^{k} \frac{(O_{ij} - E_{ij})^2}{E_{ij}} \qquad [8.5]$$

where i is the ith of the rows and j is the jth of the columns. This expression simply describes the summation of the squares of the observed frequencies minus the expected, divided by the expected, for all cells in the $r \times k$ matrix. The degrees of freedom involved in the test are in general $(r-1) \times (k-1)$, which in the 2×2 table is one.

If the chi-square test shows that two (or more) attributes do not occur independently, the degree of association between them can be measured by the *contingency coefficient*. This is found from:

$$C = \sqrt{\frac{\chi^2}{N + \chi^2}} \qquad [8.6]$$

The coefficient (C) will be zero where there is no association, and will get closer to 1·0 as the degree of dependence increases. But, unlike other coefficients of correlation, it never reaches 1·0; in the 2×2 case its maximum value is 0·707. There are other drawbacks to the use of the contingency coefficient, but it does have the great advantage over other techniques of being applicable to nominal data.

An example of the use of this chi-square method may now be described. In an investigation of areal levels of prosperity in Southern Illinois it is required to establish whether counties with low incomes are significantly concentrated in the southern half of the region, i.e. whether income correlates with location. Low incomes are defined as those below $4,200. The southern half of the region is taken to be the southern seventeen of the thirty-four counties, or south of boundary I as marked in Figure 8.1. Each county can thus be classified as 'high' or 'low' in terms of its per capita income, and as 'north' or 'south' by location, to produce the following contingency table:

		Income		sum of
		high	low	rows
Location	north	12	5	17
	south	7	10	17
sum of columns		19	15	34

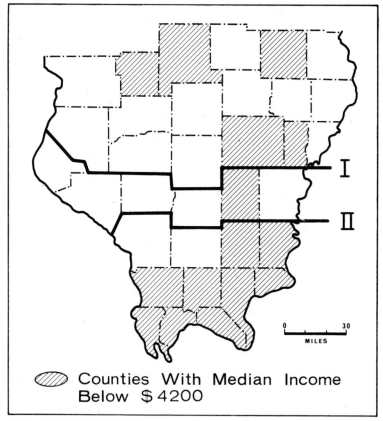

Figure 8.1   The framework for a chi-square test of the correlation
between income and location in Southern Illinois counties.

If there is no association between a low income and a southern
location, low counties could be expected to fall into the northern
or southern categories in the same proportion as all counties, i.e.
17 to 17, or half and half. Therefore the expected frequency in the
north/low cell is 7·5, or half the total number of low income
counties (15). This is what expression [8.4] above gives:

$$E = \frac{\Sigma \text{ row} \times \Sigma \text{ column}}{N} = \frac{17 \times 15}{34} = 7\cdot5$$

The full table of E calculated in this way is:

	high	low	sums
north	9·5	7·5	17
south	9·5	7·5	17
sums	19	15	34

The test required may now be set out in the formal manner introduced in Chapter 4:

H_o: $p_{ij} = p_{i.} p_{.j}$, for all ij (i.e. the two areal classifications are independent)

H_a: $p_{ij} \neq p_{i.} p_{.j}$, for at least one pair ij (i.e. the two classifications are to some extent dependent)

test statistic: χ^2 as defined in [8.5] above, $df = 1$
significance level: 95 per cent, or $p = 0.05$
rejection region: $\chi^2 > 3.84$ (from tables).

To calculate the differences between observed and expected frequencies required by the test statistic's equation, the data may be set out as follows:

cell	O	E	$O-E$	$(O-E)^2$
north high	12	9·5	2·5	6·25
north low	5	7·5	−2·5	6·25
south high	7	9·5	−2·5	6·25
south low	10	7·5	2·5	6·25

Now the value of χ^2 can be found from [8.5] above:

$$\chi^2 = \frac{6·25}{9·5} + \frac{6·25}{7·5} + \frac{6·25}{9·5} + \frac{6·25}{7·5}$$
$$= 0·658 + 0·833 + 0·658 + 0·833$$
$$= 2·982$$

As this is less than 3·84, the null hypothesis cannot be rejected. The test shows that the observed frequencies are not significantly different from the expected at 95 per cent confidence. In other words, the observed distribution of low income counties between north and south could have occurred by chance at least one time in twenty, so the two attributes of prosperity and location must be regarded as independent of one another.

As this finding would suggest, the contingency coefficient is low:

$$C = \sqrt{\frac{\chi^2}{N+\chi^2}} = \sqrt{\frac{2\cdot982}{34+2\cdot982}} = \sqrt{0\cdot081} = 0\cdot285$$

This reinforces the impression of a weak association between low income and southern location.

But a closer look at Figure 8.1 shows that low income counties are in fact concentrated in the southern extremity of the region, and this raises the question of whether the arbitrary splitting in half of the thirty-four counties as represented by boundary I is really a meaningful division of Southern Illinois in the present research context. What if the boundary is shifted to II, to make the southern eleven counties 'south' and the rest 'north'? This changes the observed and expected frequencies, to produce the following:

	high		low		sums
north	O 17	13 E	O 6	10 E	23
south	O 2	6 E	O 9	5 E	11
sums	19		15		34

The calculation of $(O-E)^2 \div E$ now gives:

$$\chi^2 = 1\cdot25 + 1\cdot60 + 2\cdot67 + 3\cdot20$$
$$= 8\cdot72$$

Testing the same hypothesis as before, H_o can now be rejected. This new value for χ^2 is in fact significant at the 99 per cent level, so H_a can now be accepted with great confidence. There is a close association between low income and southern position by the new definition of 'southern'. The value for the contingency coefficient

(0·452) indicates the improved correlation. This example shows how much depends on the way in which the problem is framed before the statistics come into play.

If there are only a small number of cases the usual calculation of chi-square over-estimates its true value and can thus lead to rejection of H_o when it should be accepted. This problem can be overcome in the 2 × 2 table by *Yates's correction*, which involves subtracting 0·5 from each of the four absolute values of $(O-E)$ before squaring. In the case above where $\chi^2 = 8·72$ this is reduced to 6·66 by applying the correction – still high enough to reject the null hypothesis but now only just over the critical value (6·64) at the 99 per cent confidence level.

An alternative to the contingency coefficient for measuring the correspondence between classifications is provided by the *phi coefficient* (ϕ), which is given by:

$$\phi = \sqrt{\frac{\chi^2}{N(m-1)}} \qquad [8.7]$$

where m is the number of rows or columns, whichever is smaller. The result is on a scale from 0 to 1·0, with zero implying perfect independence and unity perfect dependence or association. As the value for χ^2 increases, so does ϕ. In the case above where $\chi^2 = 6·66$, phi is 0·44 (or 0·52 using chi-square before the Yates's correction), while in the earlier case where $\chi^2 = 2·98$ the result is $\phi = 0·29$. In the 2 × 2 table phi can be calculated without chi-square, subtracting the product of the top right and bottom left cells from that of the other two and dividing the result by the square root of the product of the row and column totals. In the Southern Illinois case above using boundary II this is:

$$\phi = \frac{(17 \times 9)-(6 \times 2)}{\sqrt{19 \times 15 \times 23 \times 11}} = \frac{141}{269} = 0·52$$

which is the same result as given by expression [8.7] from chi-square before applying Yates's correction.

Rank Correlation

There are circumstances in which the best information available on the geographical occurrence of two attributes may be on an ordinal scale. Such data contain more information than a nominal classification, but not enough to enable correlation techniques designed for interval or ratio data to be used. However, there are two methods of correlation specifically for ordinal data. Both are easy to calculate, and useful when ordinal data are the most detailed available or when figures on the actual magnitudes seem of doubtful accuracy in themselves but probably good enough to rank observations. Rank correlations can also be helpful if data are readily available in rank form and a quick measure of correlation is required, for they can estimate the product moment correlation coefficient generally used on interval or ratio data quite closely.

Spearman's rank correlation coefficient is the measure most often used. The first step is to rank each set of observations, high to low or low to high. Equal observations should be given the average of their possible ranks, e.g. 6·5 if the 6th and 7th occurrences are tied. Then Spearman's coefficient (r_S) is calculated from:

$$r_S = 1 - \frac{6 \sum\limits_{i=1}^{N} D_i^2}{N^3 - N}$$

[8.8]

where D_i is the difference between the two ranks for any observation i, and N is the total number of observations in the population (n if sample data are used). The value of r_S ranges from $+1\cdot0$ to $-1\cdot0$. A large positive value indicates a strong positive correlation; a large negative value indicates the opposite; a coefficient near 0 indicates lack of correlation or a random relationship between the two sets of ranks. The coefficient may be tested for significance by the Student's t statistic if the number of observations is 10 or more. Minimum values for r_S at $p = 0\cdot05$ and $0\cdot01$ are tabulated in Siegel's *Nonparametric Statistics* (p. 284) for N between 10 and 30.

An example may be used to demonstrate Spearman's rank correlation. Suppose that the investigator of income in Southern Illinois from the previous section wishes to explain further the level of income in the southernmost eleven counties. He wants to test the hypothesis that median income can be accounted for by the average value of farm products sold per farm. He can get published data for both variables, but he has lived in the region long enough to suspect that the inhabitants are less than truthful in making their returns of income and farm sales to the representatives of officialdom. He thus doubts the accuracy of the published data as they stand, but considers them reliable enough to rank the counties. The null hypothesis is that the rankings of the two variables are independent of one another. The alternate hypothesis is that they are to some extent dependent, or correlated. The test statistic is r_S, and with 11 observations H_o can be rejected at the 95 per cent confidence level if r_S is greater than 0·56 positive or negative.

The data required to calculate r_S are set down in Table 8.3. Inserting the sum of D^2 and N in expression [8.8] above:

$$r_S = 1 - \frac{6 \times 262}{11^3 - 11} = 1 - \frac{1572}{1320} = 1 - 1·19 = -0·19$$

Thus there is a weak negative association between the two sets of ranks. The statistic r_S is too small to be significant at 95 per cent confidence, so the null hypothesis cannot be rejected and no support is given to the hypothesis that average farm sales account for county income levels. The investigator now tries another hypothesis: that income can be explained by the proportion of workers in manufacturing and white-collar jobs. The ordinal scale of measurement is again preferred, and the data for a Spearman rank correlation are set out in summary form in Table 8.3. Evaluating r_S:

$$r_S = 1 - \frac{6 \times 48}{11^3 - 11} = 1 - \frac{288}{1320} = 1 - 0·22 = 0·78$$

This result shows a strong positive correlation, which can be accepted as significant at $p = 0·05$ and also at 0·01 (where the

Table 8.3: Data for the Calculation of Spearman's Rank Correlation
Coefficient Between Median Income and Average Annual
Farm Sales in Eleven Southern Illinois Counties

County	Median Income ($)	Annual Farm Sales ($)	Rankings		D	D^2
	X	Y	X	Y	$X-Y$	
Alexander	3,146	10,182	6	2	4	16
Gallatin	2,711	18,900	11	1	10	100
Hardin	3,136	2,673	7	11	−4	16
Jackson	4,671	7,245	1	4	−3	9
Johnson	3,097	3,856	8	8	0	0
Massac	4,095	5,085	3	7	−4	16
Pope	2,787	3,617	10	9	1	1
Pulaski	2,789	8,113	9	3	6	36
Saline	3,502	6,973	5	5	0	0
Union	4,043	6,042	4	6	−2	4
Williamson	4,465	2,905	2	10	−8	64

$\Sigma D = 0 \quad \Sigma D^2 = 262$

Source of data: *City and County Data Book.*

critical value for the test statistic is 0·73). The second hypothesis
thus appears to be much sounder than the earlier one.

It should be noted that the tests of significance in this example
are not strictly necessary or meaningful, as the data are not a
sample. However, as in the case of some other statistics used
commonly in geography, the confidence levels provide some
indication of the importance which can be attached to a rank
correlation coefficient in circumstances where the arbitrary areal
subdivision introduces some element of error in the data.

The second method of rank-order correlation is by the use of
the statistic τ (Greek tau), called *Kendall's tau*. It is less often used
in geography than Spearman's r_S, but in some circumstances it is
a more legitimate measure. Whereas Spearman's method places
relatively great weight on the larger rank differences because they
are squared, the Kendall method concentrates on *changes* in rank.
If one observational unit has a higher rank than a second observa-

tion on one variable while the second is higher than the first on the other variable, an 'inversion' is said to occur. Kendall's tau compares the actual number of inversions with the maximum possible number. The higher the actual compared with the possible, i.e. the more changes in rank, the weaker the correlation. The formula for the coefficient tau is:

$$\tau = 1 - \frac{2n_{inv}}{N(N-1)/2} \qquad [8.9]$$

where n_{inv} is the number of inversions observed and N is the number of observations or pairs of ranks. The denominator gives the number of possible inversions for that number of observations. The statistic tau operates on exactly the same kind of data as Spearman's r_S. The random sampling distribution is normal if $N = 10$ or more.

Table 8.4: Data for Rank Correlation Between Median Income and Employment in Certain Occupations in Eleven Southern Illinois Counties

County	Rankings			
	Median Income ($)	% Manufacturing and White-collar Workers	D	D^2
	X	Y	$X-Y$	
Alexander	6	4	2	4
Gallatin	11	10	1	1
Hardin	7	11	-4	16
Jackson	1	2	-1	1
Johnson	8	8	0	0
Massac	3	3	0	0
Pope	10	9	1	1
Pulaski	9	5	4	16
Saline	5	7	-2	4
Union	4	6	-2	4
Williamson	2	1	1	1
			$\Sigma D = 0$	$\Sigma D^2 = 48$

Source of data: City and County Data Book.

250

There are two methods of working out the actual number of inversions. Both will be demonstrated on the data for Southern Illinois from Table 8.4. First, the observations must be written in rank order on any one of the variables – median income is used here (see Table 8.5). One method involves drawing lines connecting the observation with the same rank on both variables, i.e. rank 1 on income with rank 1 on the other variable, 2 with 2, and so on, as shown by the lines in Table 8.5. The number of intersections of lines when this process has been completed is the number of inversions, 10 in this case. The second method is to take the second set of ranks and for each rank in turn count the number of smaller ranks below it in the column. For example the first rank is 2, which has one smaller rank below (i.e. rank 1). These are listed in the table, and their sum (10) is the number of inversions. Putting the number 10 in expression [8.9]:

$$\tau = 1 - \frac{2 \times 10}{11 \times 10/2} = 1 - \frac{20}{55} = 1 - 0\cdot36 = 0\cdot64$$

Table 8.5: The Calculation of Kendall's Tau on Ranks for the Occurrence of Two Variables in Southern Illinois

County	Median Income	% Manufacturing and White-collar Workers	Number of Smaller Ranks below*
Jackson	1	2	1
Williamson	2	1	0
Massac	3	3	0
Union	4	6	2
Saline	5	7	2
Alexander	6	4	0
Hardin	7	11	4
Johnson	8	8	1
Pulaski	9	5	0
Pope	10	9	0
Gallatin	11	10	0
			$\Sigma = 10$

* See text for explanation.

This result is somewhat lower than the 0·78 given by Spearman's method. The reason is that although there are quite a lot of rank changes to reduce the value of tau, only two are of more than two places which makes the D^2 in the calculation of r_S quite small. A case where there were only two rank changes but very large ones would give a high value for tau but a lower one for r_S. However, in most cases the results will not lead to conflicting conclusions concerning whether association exists or not.

Regression Analysis and the Product Moment Correlation Coefficient

Simple regression and the associated correlation technique are probably the most popular of all statistical methods. They are often used to test hypotheses concerning cause and effect, and simple linear regression is a basic element in many predictive models. The product moment coefficient, known also as *Pearson's r*, is certainly the most widely used measure of correlation. Regression and correlation analysis require data on an interval or ratio scale, though in special circumstances lower-order data can be used for one variable. The major difference between these techniques and those already considered in this chapter is that while the others tell us whether association exists at a given level of confidence, and what its strength is, regression analysis tells us about the nature of the relationship. It describes how one variable behaves in relation to the other.

The basics of regression and correlation analysis have already been introduced in the context of trend surfaces (see Chapter 7). All that is required here is a brief recapitulation with some warnings, before examples are offered to demonstrate these techniques in human geography.

The first step in regression and correlation analysis should be to plot the values for the two sets of data on a graph, of the kind shown in Figure 8.2. By convention, Y is the *dependent* variable, or the hypothesized 'effect', and is plotted on the vertical axis. X is the *independent* variable or hypothesized 'cause', plotted on the

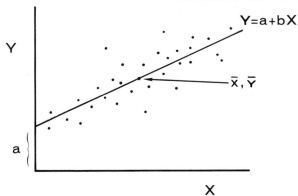

Figure 8.2   The general form of a regression line.

horizontal axis. This graph can give an initial indication of the relationship between the two variables – positive or negative, strong or weak.

The nature of the relationship is stated in the regression equation. This describes a line drawn through the scatter of dots on the graph such that the sum of the squares of the vertical deviations of the dependent variable from it are minimized. The general form of the equation is:

$$Y = a + bX + e \qquad [8.10]$$

where the constant a indicates the position of the intercept on the Y axis, b indicates the slope of the regression line, and e in an error term representing that which is not accounted for by the linear relationship. The value of a will be negative if it cuts the Y axis below the origin of the graph at zero, and b will be negative if the line slopes down from left to right to show Y decreasing as X increases. The two constants can be found from expressions identical to [7.2] and [7.3] in the previous chapter except that Y is now the dependent variable instead of Z. However it is often more convenient to use the data transformed into deviations from the mean instead of raw scores, in which case:

$$b = \frac{\Sigma xy}{\Sigma x^2} \qquad [8.11]$$

253

where the lower-case x and y indicate deviations from the mean as in Chapter 7. The other formula remains the same:

$$a = \bar{Y} - b\bar{X} \qquad [8.12]$$

When these expressions have been evaluated, the regression line can be drawn by calculating Y for any two values of X. In fact, only one is needed because the intercept of the vertical axis is known, and this one point can be provided by the means of X and Y both of which are on the regression line. Illustrations were included in the discussion of the fitting of the linear surface in the previous chapter and there are examples below.

From the regression equation, a prediction of Y can be made from any value of X. Unless the relationship between the two variables is perfectly linear, individual occurrences of Y will depart from Y as predicted, in most if not all cases. These deviations are the vertical distances between observed Y and the regression line, and are known as *residuals from regression*. They can be positive or negative. They are, of course, analogous to the residuals from a trend surface. Residuals are calculated from the general expression:

$$Y_{res} = Y_{obs} - Y_{est} \qquad [8.13]$$

where Y_{obs} is the observed value and Y_{est} is that predicted or estimated from the regression equation. Residuals may be expressed in a number of ways, the most common being the actual value given by [8.13] and the value as a proportion of the original observation, i.e. $(Y_{obs} - Y_{est}) \div Y_{obs}$. In geographical applications the addition of one or more independent variables is suggested if the residuals appear to vary systematically when mapped, for they should be random errors.

The *product moment correlation coefficient*, or coefficient of linear correlation, measures the degree to which a change in direction and magnitude of one variable is associated with comparable changes in the other. The notation of the formula varies, depending on whether raw scores or transformed scores are used. A raw score formula appeared as expression [7.4] in the previous chapter. The modified formula using adjusted values from the variable means is:

$$r = \frac{\Sigma xy}{\sqrt{\Sigma x^2 \ \Sigma y^2}}$$ [8.14]

where $x = X - \bar{X}$ and $y = Y - \bar{Y}$ for each observation. The value of r^2 gives the proportion of variance in Y accounted for by the linear relationship with X.

The calculations required in simple linear correlation and regression analysis have already been described in Chapter 7, but a further example may help at this point. In Table 8.6 the necessary data for measuring the relationship between infant mortality and aboriginal share of the population are set out for fourteen divisions of Queensland, Australia. Using the raw score formula [7.4] from the previous chapter, the correlation coefficient is found from the values in the table as follows:

$$
\begin{aligned}
r &= \frac{\Sigma(XY) - N(\bar{X}\bar{Y})}{\sqrt{[\Sigma(X^2) - N(\bar{X})^2] \times [\Sigma(Y^2) - N(\bar{Y})^2]}} \\[2mm]
&= \frac{42581 - 14(70\cdot6 \times 26\cdot1)}{\sqrt{[199338 - (14 \times 4984)] \times [12687 - (14 \times 681)]}} \\[2mm]
&= \frac{42581 - 25797}{\sqrt{129562 \times 3153}} \\[2mm]
&= \frac{16784}{20211} = 0\cdot8303
\end{aligned}
$$

This figure indicates a strong positive association between infant mortality and aboriginal population.

The constants in the regression equation are found from expressions [7.2] and [7.3] as follows:

$$b = \frac{\Sigma(XY) - N(\bar{X}\bar{Y})}{\Sigma(X^2) - N(\bar{X})^2} = \frac{16784}{129562} = 0\cdot13$$

$$a = \bar{Y} - b\bar{X} = 26\cdot1 - (0\cdot13 \times 70\cdot6) = 16\cdot9$$

So the equation is: $Y = 16\cdot9 + 0\cdot13X$.

The regression line is drawn in Figure 8.3, where the individual observations are plotted. The estimated values for X on the line are listed in Table 8.6, along with the residuals representing the vertical distances between the dots and the line on the graph.

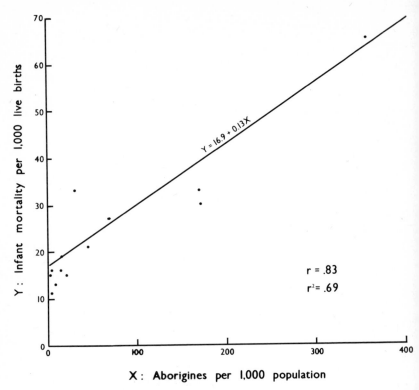

Figure 8.3 A regression line measuring the relationship between infant mortality and aboriginal share of the population in Queensland, Australia. (Source of data: Table 8.6.)

The largest departures from the regression estimates are in the South-Western and Central-Western divisions; otherwise no residuals exceed 10 and half the values for Y_{est} are within 3 of observed Y.

The coefficient r can be tested for significance against the Student's t distribution. The statistic is found from:

$$t = \frac{r\sqrt{N-2}}{\sqrt{1-r^2}} \qquad [8.15]$$

The test may be set out formally as in the manner already explained earlier in this book, with the null hypothesis of no association or correlation between the variables (i.e. $r = 0$) and a critical value for

256

Table 8.6: Data on Infant Mortality per 1,000 Live Births (Y) and
Aboriginals per 1,000 Population (X) in Queensland,
Demonstrating Correlation and Regression Analysis

Statistical Division	Y	X	Y²	X²	XY	Y_{est}	Y_{res}
Brisbane	15	3	225	9	45	17·29	−2·29
Moreton	13	9	169	81	117	18·07	−5·07
Maryborough	15	22	225	484	330	19·76	−4·76
Downs	16	4	256	16	64	17·42	−1·42
Roma	21	45	441	2025	945	22·75	−1·75
South-Western	51	73	2601	5329	3723	26·29	24·61
Rockhampton	19	15	361	225	285	18·85	0·15
Central-Western	33	31	1089	961	1023	20·93	12·09
Far-Western	30	173	900	29929	5190	39·39	−9·39
Mackay	11	5	121	25	55	17·55	−6·55
Townsville	16	14	256	196	224	18·72	−2·72
Cairns	27	69	729	4761	1863	25·87	1·13
Peninsula	65	356	4225	126736	23140	63·18	1·82
North-Western	33	169	1089	28561	5577	38·87	−5·87
sums	365	988	12687	199338	42581		
means	26·1	70·6					

N = 14

Source of data: Statistics of Queensland 1970–71 and Queensland Year
Book 1971–2.

t at the required confidence level indicating the range beyond
which H_o would be rejected and the H_a of some correlation
accepted. However, the test is made easier by tabulations of
minimum r values at different confidence levels and with different
numbers of observations, thus bypassing the calculation of t.
These figures will be found in sets of statistical tables, and as an
appendix to many statistics textbooks.

Once the correlation coefficient is known the *standard error* of
the estimate of Y can be calculated very simply. It is given by:

$$e_Y = \sigma_Y \sqrt{1 - r^2}$$
[8.16]

where e_Y denotes the standard error of the regression estimate of

257

Y, σ_Y is the standard deviation of Y, and r^2 is the coefficient of determination. The standard error is the standard deviation of the residuals from regression about the predicted values of Y. With the errors normally distributed, which random errors should be, 68 per cent of the actual values of Y will be within one standard error ($+$ or $-$) of the predicted value, 95 per cent will be within two standard errors, and so on. *Confidence limits* denoting standard errors are sometimes drawn parallel to the regression line when the relationship between two variables is displayed graphically. An example appears in the next section of this chapter.

A useful variation on the product moment correlation technique is the *point biserial correlation coefficient* (r_{pb}). This can be used if one variable is measured on an interval or ratio scale and the other on a dichotomous scale. The procedure is simply to assign arbitrary numbers to the nominal data, generally $1 =$ has and $0 =$ has not. Then the product moment calculation is followed. As an example, data on infant mortality in Queensland and the geographical position of districts are set out for the calculation of r_{pb} in Table 8.7. The Y are as in Table 8.6, while the X data are 1 if the district is one of the seven in the south-eastern part of the state and 0 if it is not. The anticipated association is between low infant mortality and south-eastern position, i.e. a negative correlation. Following the calculation for r from expression [7.4] as above:

$$r_{pb} = \frac{110 - 14(0{\cdot}5 \times 26{\cdot}1)}{\sqrt{(7 - 3{\cdot}5) \times 3153}}$$

$$= \frac{110 - 182{\cdot}7}{\sqrt{3{\cdot}5 \times 3153}}$$

$$= \frac{-72{\cdot}7}{105} = -0{\cdot}692$$

So the association is fairly strong, and in the expected direction; infant mortality is markedly lower in the more settled south east than in the northern and interior parts of Queensland.

As with other statistical methods, a number of important assumptions are involved in the use of simple correlation and regression. The values of the two variables should be measured

Table 8.7: Data on Infant Mortality per 1,000 Live Births (Y) and
South-Eastern Location (X) in Queensland, for Calculation
of Point Biserial Correlation

Division	Y	X	Y^2	X^2	XY
Brisbane	15	1	225	1	15
Moreton	13	1	169	1	13
Maryborough	15	1	225	1	15
Downs	16	1	256	1	16
Roma	21	1	441	1	21
South-Western	51	0	2601	0	0
Rockhampton	19	1	361	1	19
Central-Western	33	0	1089	0	0
Far-Western	30	0	900	0	0
Mackay	11	1	121	1	11
Townsville	16	0	256	0	0
Cairns	27	0	729	0	0
Peninsula	65	0	4225	0	0
North-Western	33	0	1089	0	0
sums	365	7	12687	7	110
N = 14 means	26·1	0·5			

Source of data: see Table 8.6.

Note: in variable X, 1 = south-eastern, 0 = not south-eastern.

without error, and the relationship between them is assumed
linear. Strictly speaking, for any value of X the residuals of Y
should have zero mean, and their variances should be constant –
the assumption of 'homoscedasticity' or equal scatter. The values
of the residuals should be independent of one another, otherwise
'autocorrelation' is present; this is a serious problem in spatial
analysis where the contiguity of areal units of observation makes
dependence between their observations quite likely. The variable
Y should be normally distributed, and so should X in certain
circumstances such as when a t test is used. Failure of the data
to satisfy the assumptions can lead to errors in the calculation of
r or the regression parameters. Just how important the particular
assumptions are depends on the nature of the application, and
specialist guidance should be sought on this (e.g. Poole and

259

O'Farrell, 1971; see Selected Reading). In general the assumptions are more important when inferential questions arise.

Once again, it is necessary to draw attention to the problems of applying standard statistical procedures to areally distributed data. It has been demonstrated that varying the size of the areal units used to compile the data can substantially affect the result when calculating r, and this problem has been examined quite extensively in geographical literature dealing with quantitative methods (see Selected Reading to this chapter). Robinson has suggested a method of weighting the values in correlation analysis involving areal units, and others have put forward an inferential approach to the problem based on knowledge of the probability of specific r values being attributable to random factors. It seems sensible to view the system of area units upon which the data are based as one of an infinite number of possible arrangements, as was suggested in Chapter 3, and if the actual system can be viewed as a chance occurrence – just as a random sample of observations would be – it is possible to regard calculated r values as being correct within margins of error which can be worked out by the usual methods. There is also the problem common to all kinds of ecological correlation – that of applying findings based on a group of observations amalgamated by geographical area to the behaviour of individual human beings.

The difficulties of spatial correlation are revealed with particular effect by the fact that there may appear to be different relationships between the same conditions at different levels of areal aggregation. This can be demonstrated briefly by the relationship between wealth and property crimes in the USA. At the state level there is a fairly high positive correlation, i.e. more crime in the wealthier states; $r = 0.63$ between per capita annual income and property crimes per 100,000 people. At the city level the relationship is positive but much weaker: $r = 0.12$ between per capita income and burglary rates for Standard Metropolitan Statistical Areas with populations over 250,000, and for larceny $r = 0.26$. But within the city the relationship appears to be reversed, with crime rates highest in low income areas. For example at the census enumeration district level in Gainesville, Florida, the proportion of families on welfare (an indicator of poverty) correlates 0·82 with the burglary rate and 0·56 with larceny. Thus the nearer we get to the individual, the more property crime seems a response to poverty rather than an accompaniment of affluence.

Correlation and regression analysis in human geography must thus be approached with caution. Further guidance for research applications will be found in specialized texts, such as those indicated in the Selected Reading. Especially recommended are the standard work by Ezekiel and Fox and the discussion of geographical applications in King's advanced textbook. In using these techniques all but very small problems are generally run on a computer, which in addition to its speed eliminates the very considerable possibility of human error which exists if the mathematics is performed manually or on a calculating machine.

Applications of Simple Correlation and Regression

Two applications of simple correlation and regression analysis may now be described briefly, to demonstrate the techniques more fully. The term 'simple' is used here to distinguish the association of one variable with one other from 'multiple' correlation and regression as explained in the last section of this chapter.

The first study examines the relationship between the size of a city and the level of living of its inhabitants. The geographical context is the United States, with observations on 109 major cities (i.e. Standard Metropolitan Statistical Areas) with populations of over 250,000 at the end of the 1960s. The dependent variable (Y) is the living standard of the city populations, measured by a general social indicator derived by 'factor analysis' (see Chapter 10) of numerical information on about thirty different criteria of social well-being. It identifies the average situation of the inhabitants of each city, with particular emphasis on wealth and income but also reflecting health, education and housing conditions. This measure may be referred to as the Affluence Indicator, and is expressed as a set of standard scores (Z). The independent variable of city size (X) is simply total population.

The hypothesis that there is a positive association between affluence and city size can be tested by a product moment correlation coefficient. The result is $r = 0.538$, and although the high degree of skewness in the population data (X) makes a statistical test hazardous, a significant t test at the 99 per cent confidence level would justify acceptance of the hypothesized association (i.e. it can hardly be attributed to chance). However, the observed relationship is not very close. The coefficient of determination r^2 is only 0.289, which means that less than one third of the inter-metropolitan variance in affluence can be accounted for statistically by city population.

The nature of the relationship is shown in Figure 8.4. This confirms the impression of a positive relationship but one which is not closely linear. In fact, at the lower end of the scale it is evident that there are very considerable variations in performance on the Affluence Indicator for cities of similar size. Regression analysis produced the following equation for the prediction of the affluence level from city size:

$$Y = -0.383 + 0.365X$$

where population (X) is in millions and affluence (Y) is in standard (Z) scores. The regression line is drawn in Figure 8.4, where it can be verified that the intercept of the vertical axis is at $Y = -0.383$, and that the line goes up by 0.365 for each million along the horizontal axis.

The vertical distance between the individual affluence scores and the regression line are the residuals. The standard error of the estimate of Y, as calculated from expression [8.15], is 0.85, and confidence limits of plus and minus one standard error are shown in Figure 8.4. Because the relationship between the variables is not closely linear, the standard error is rather large, as the figure shows. With normally distributed errors, 68 per cent of all the observations should be between the $+1$ and -1 lines; the actual number is 73 out of 109, or 66 per cent. Only three observations have predicted values which differ from the actual Y by more than two standard errors.

Although a significant association has been found and described

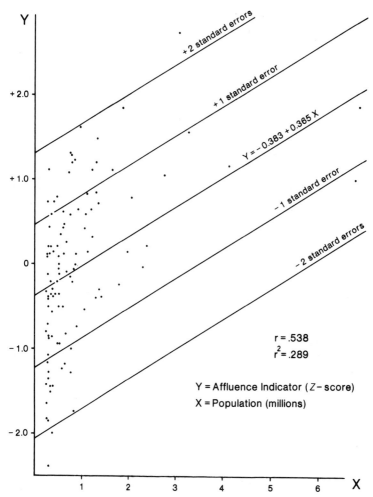

Figure 8.4   The relationship between affluence and city size in
American metropolitan areas with populations over
250,000, showing a regression line and confidence limits.
(Source of data: see D. M. Smith, *The Geography of
Social Well-being in the United States*, McGraw-Hill,
1973, Chapter 8, for an explanation of the derivation of
the Affluence Indicator.)

263

by an equation, it cannot be claimed that this analysis has taken us very far in the direction of understanding the relationship between city size and affluence. The distinction between prediction and explanation is relevant again here; population can predict the affluence score, within the fairly broad limits which have been established, but we do not necessarily know why the one increases with the other. And we certainly do not know why the relationship is exactly as identified in the regression equation. Another obvious fact is that population size alone cannot account for city affluence levels, even as simply a statistical prediction, and that other variables must be involved. We will return to this problem later in the chapter, to see how a better prediction of affluence might be arrived at.

The second example is concerned with the relationship between infant mortality and level of economic development in 25 European nations. Infant deaths (Y) are expressed per 1,000 live births and economic development (X) is measured by GNP per capita (Table 8.8). As X increases Y decreases quite regularly, the linear correlation coefficient (r) being -0.804.

Table 8.8: Data for Correlation and Regression Analysis of Infant Mortality and Level of Economic Development in Europe

Nation	Infant Deaths /1,000 Live Births Y	GNP per capita ($US \times 10$) X	$\log X$	Nation	Infant Deaths /1,000 Live Births Y	GNP per capita ($US \times 10$) X	$\log X$
Albania	87	36	1·56	Italy	36	110	2·04
Austria	28	128	2·11	Luxembourg	24	197	2·29
Belgium	24	180	2·26	Netherlands	14	155	2·19
Bulgaria	31	82	1·91	Norway	16	189	2·28
Czechoslovakia	25	156	2·19	Poland	42	97	1·99
Denmark	19	212	2·33	Portugal	65	40	1·60
Finland	18	179	2·24	Rumania	44	77	1·89
France	22	192	2·28	Spain	37	56	1·75
Germany (East)	24	126	2·10	Sweden	13	254	2·40
Germany (West)	24	190	2·28	Switzerland	18	233	2·37
Greece	34	68	1·83	UK	20	181	2·25
Hungary	39	109	2·04	Yugoslavia	71	45	1·65
Ireland	25	98	1·99				

Source of data: *World Handbook of Political and Social Indicators* (2nd edn), Yale University Press, 1972 (figures *c.* 1965).

Regression analysis gives the following equation for the linear relationship between the two variables:

$$Y = 63\cdot4 - 0\cdot23X$$

The line is plotted in Figure 8.5, sloping down to the right because the relationship is negative, and a fairly close fit to the scatter of dots is revealed. The residuals are mapped in Figure 8.6. The pattern fails to show any obvious spatial regularity or geographical grouping which might suggest additional causal factors. Tests of association between positive or negative residuals and the dichotomous variables of communist or non-communist government, above or below average number of doctors per capita and above or below average protein in national diet also failed to reveal anything of significance (chi-square tests at $p = 0\cdot05$).

On the basis of all this we might conclude the analysis, satisfied that an interesting empirical relationship had been established and that there was little further to be learned. However, an examination of the graph (Figure 8.5) suggests that the linear trend identified may not be the most accurate description, for some pattern can be discerned in the residuals. The regression equation underpredicts infant mortality at the lower and upper ends of the GNP scale and over-predicts in the middle. Thus a *curvilinear* relationship is suggested, for infant mortality falls rapidly at first as GNP increases but tends to even off around 20 when the richer nations are reached.

Curvilinear correlation and regression analysis can be attempted by any appropriate transformation of either of the variables. In this case an effective method is to convert the data on GNP per capita into logarithms (Table 8.8). Putting log X instead of X into the formula for the correlation coefficient produces the result $r = -0\cdot853$, and an explained variance (r^2) of $0\cdot728$ compared with $0\cdot646$ from the linear relationship. The regression equation can also be reworked using the log X values, to give:

$$Y = 157\cdot8 - 60\cdot6 \log X$$

Calculating the estimates of Y from this expression and plotting them on a graph now produces a curve (Figure 8.7) which is a

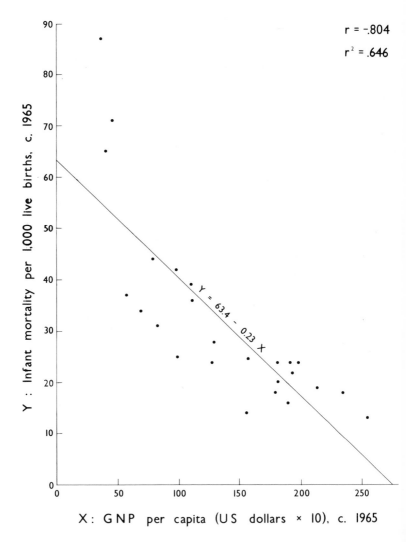

Figure 8.5   The linear relationship between infant mortality and level
of economic development (GNP per capita) in Europe.
(Source of data: Table 8.8.)

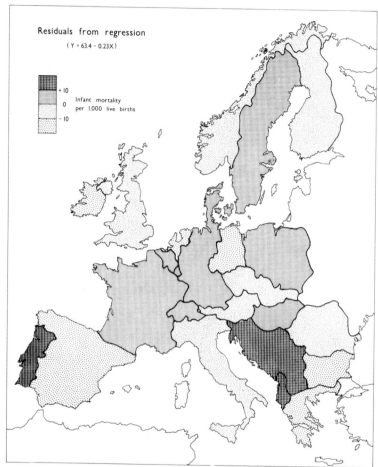

Figure 8.6   Residuals from a linear regression analysis of the relationship between infant mortality and level of economic development in Europe. (Source of data: Table 8.8.)

better fit to the data than the line in Figure 8.5. The curve can itself be transformed into a line simply by replacing the horizontal scale of actual GNP values by their logs (Figure 8.8). The relationship depicted is thus log-linear, or very nearly so.

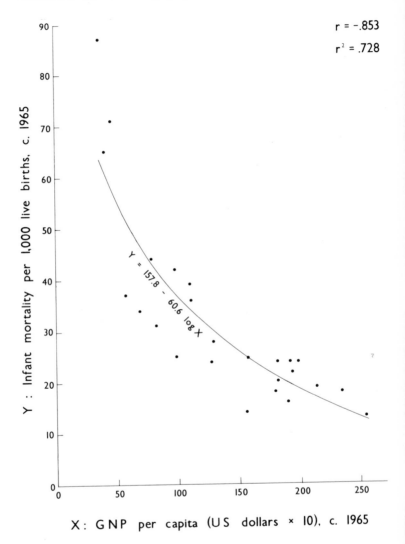

Figure 8.7   A curvilinear regression analysis achieved by transforming
the independent variable into logarithms. (Source of data:
Table 8.8.)

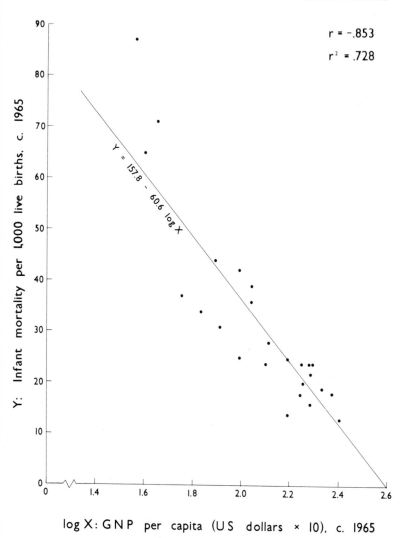

Figure 8.8   A regression curve transformed into a line by using a
logarithmic scale on the *X* axis. (Source of data: Table 8.8.)

269

This example emphasizes the importance of the nature of the relationship when correlation and regression analysis is used. Many 'input–output' relationships within a society or economy are similar to that between GNP and infant mortality, with increasing wealth or investment having progressively less additional benefit in terms of raising output or reducing a social problem. To work on non-linear relationships without an appropriate transformation thus risks misinterpretation of the process involved as well as underestimating the strength of the association and predicting less accurately than might otherwise be possible. An initial examination of a plot of the data can help to avoid this.

The Correlation Matrix

The examples above were concerned with the relationship between only two variables. Using a computer the simple correlation between very many pairs of variables can be calculated in seconds, to provide data which can pose explanatory problems and suggest possible causal links as well as describing the strength of empirical associations. Examples may be considered briefly.

The first example comes from the case in Chapter 5 where social indicators and a composite 'quality-of-life' score were derived for sub-areas of the city of Gainesville. The patterns of geographical variation in the results (Figure 5.1) suggest close associations, and this visual impression can be verified by calculating the correlation between all six sets of scores taken in turn as pairs. They are listed in the form of an *intercorrelation matrix* in Table 8.9. Only half of this is filled in, because the missing part would be identical to the figures shown. The general impression from the table is of fairly close positive correspondence between all five indicators, and close agreement with the general quality-of-life score (QL). Even without speculating on possible causal relationships, certain observations seem quite interesting. For example, the poverty and welfare indicator correlates at least 0·73 with all the others and with QL. The lowest correlation, of 0·50 between housing quality and health, perhaps reflects the fact that in the United States even

Table 8.9: Correlation Coefficients (r) among Five Social Indicators and a Composite 'Quality of Life' Score in Gainesville, Florida

	Housing	Home	Crime	Health	Poverty	QL
Housing	1·00	0·81	0·59	0·50	0·87	0·83
Home and Family		1·00	0·67	0·63	0·87	0·92
Crime			1·00	0·88	0·73	0·85
Health				1·00	0·79	0·84
Poverty and Welfare					1·00	0·94
'Quality of Life'						1·00

Source: J. C. Dickinson, R. J. Gray and D. M. Smith, 'The "Quality of Life" in Gainesville, Florida', *Southeastern Geographer*, 12, 1972.

Table 8.10: Correlation (r) among State Social Indicators in the USA

Criteria		I	II	III	IV	V	VI	S
I	Income, Wealth and Employment	1·00						
II	Environment (Housing)	0·91	1·00					
III	Health	0·76	0·85	1·00				
IV	Education	0·82	0·85	0·85	1·00			
V	Social Disorganization	−0·30	−0·24	−0·20	−0·12	1·00		
VI	Alienation and Participation	0·67	0·67	0·75	0·79	0·11	1·00	
	General Social Well-Being (S)	0·88	0·90	0·88	0·92	0·05	0·87	1·00

Source: D. M. Smith, *The Geography of Social Well-being in the United States*, McGraw-Hill, 1973.

relatively poor housing is above the level at which housing alone is severely detrimental to health.

As a second example, a similar table of correlations between social indicators calculated by states is presented (Table 8.10). The indicators here have been arrived at by summing standard scores on a number of different variables, in the manner described

Table 8.11: Correlation (r) Between State Social Indicators and Other Selected Variables in the USA

Variable		I	II	III	IV	V	VI	S
					State Social Indicators			
1.	Distance, west–east	0·04	−0·14	−0·36	−0·20	0·34	−0·13	−0·07
2.	Distance, south–north	0·56	0·47	0·49	0·63	0·32	0·68	0·71
3.	Population/sq. mile 1969	0·45	0·36	0·17	0·21	−0·02	0·20	0·32
4.	Population change (%) 1960–69	0·12	0·15	0·10	0·00	−0·54	−0·29	−0·09
5.	Urban Population (%) 1960	0·17	0·21	0·18	0·15	−0·38	0·10	0·09
6.	Non-white population (%) 1960	−0·62	−0·61	−0·72	−0·78	−0·12	−0·83	−0·81
7.	Humphrey vote (%) 1968	0·58	0·43	0·46	0·51	0·07	0·61	0·60
8.	Nixon vote (%) 1968	0·02	0·07	0·08	0·08	−0·21	0·07	0·01
9.	Wallace vote (%) 1968	−0·68	−0·61	−0·67	−0·78	0·03	−0·77	−0·77

Source: D. M. Smith, *The Geography of Social Well-being in the United States*, McGraw-Hill, 1973.

Note: The indicators are as in Table 8.10.

in Chapter 5. The basic data are state observations on forty-seven variables, which will reappear in another context in Chapter 10. The intercorrelation matrix has been filled in the opposite way to that in Table 8.9, to show that both are legitimate. The most interesting fact emerging from these correlations is the apparent independence of one indicator (V) as it varies in magnitude between the states, compared with the close association between the others. This strongly suggests two independent dimensions of social well-being at the inter-state level, one broadly measuring income, environment, health, education and belonging to society, while the other measures social disorganization. This finding is explored further in Chapter 10 in a demonstration of some other techniques.

A different type of correlation matrix is shown in Table 8.10. Here the six state social indicators and the general social well-being score from above are correlated against nine other variables. Although there may be some sound reasons for hypothesizing causal relations here, this table is best viewed as the result of an exercise in simple curiosity. At 95 per cent confidence all seven social indicators are significantly correlated with south–north distance (i.e. the latitude of the state centre points), and this variable alone accounts for half (i.e. $r^2 = 0·52$) of the variance in the general indicator S. Social Order (V), which measures largely the incidence of social pathologies, correlates very significantly (99 per cent) with population change, though in a negative direction; social disorganization is often hypothesized as associated with rapid population turnover. Contrary to what might have been anticipated, the proportion of non-whites in the population is not (at 95 per cent) significantly associated with social disorganization at the state level, though poor performance on the other indicators is highly correlated with high non-white population.

Interesting relationships exist between non-white population, social well-being, and the 1968 vote for George Wallace (the racist-turned-populist Presidential candidate). The sign of the coefficients shows that low social well-being is strongly associated with high votes for Wallace and with high proportions of non-whites. The possible causal links are not clear, however, even with such close associations. If the non-white factor is designated B, social well-being as S, and the Wallace vote as W, and if $\rightarrow$ is used to represent 'causes' or 'leads to', then one possibility would be:

$$B \longrightarrow S \longrightarrow W$$

i.e. the existence of many blacks in the population leads to low social well-being (because blacks are discriminated against) and this leads to high support for Wallace. But alternatively it might be:

$$B \longrightarrow W$$
$$\downarrow$$
$$S$$

i.e. because there are many blacks Wallace gets many votes (from threatened whites) and because there are many blacks social well-being is low. Or it could be that some other unidentified factor accounts for the high correlation between variables which are not causally linked to the extent that the close empirical associations might be taken to imply. Again, observing a high correlation is one thing; explaining it is quite another.

Simple correlation analysis is clearly a useful descriptive device, identifying levels of association between conditions and raising some provocative questions. It achieves its greatest power, however, when it tests some cause-and-effect hypothesis, built from theory and careful observation within a research framework which logically makes the statistical test a verification of a process supposedly at work within a society. As the discussion above will have indicated, this is much more difficult than simply running a series of correlations in the hope that they might reveal something 'significant'.

Multiple Correlation and Regression

If it is necessary to examine the relationship between more than one independent variable and a single dependent variable, *multiple* correlation and regression analysis can be used. The general model is:

$$Y = a + b_1 X_1 + b_2 X_2 + \cdots + b_N X_N + e \qquad [8.17]$$

where a is the constant of intercept as in simple regression, b (1, 2, ..., N) are the constants for the independent variables X (1, 2, ..., N), and e is the error term.

The basics of multiple regression and correlation in a case with two independent variables were outlined in the linear trend surface demonstration in the previous chapter. This showed how the variance in the dependent variable could be partly attributed to variation with respect to each of two dimensions, both uniquely accounting for some of the variance individually and also accounting for some jointly or in common. Multiple regression with more than two independent variables is simply an extension of this principle into any number of dimensions.

The calculation of the constants in the equation and the coefficient of multiple correlation (R) was illustrated in Chapter 7 in the two independent variables case. With more variables added the mathematics becomes rather complicated, and no further explanation is offered here. Practical problems of multiple correlation and regression are almost invariably solved on a computer, and an understanding of the mechanics of this, though helpful,

274

is not essential to appreciate the application of the technique. (Full particulars will be found in Ezekiel and Fox, 1959, and King, 1969; see Selected Reading.) The treatment which follows is purely demonstrative.

For an example of multiple correlation and regression we return to the case of the metropolitan Affluence Indicator above. It will be recalled that the single independent variable of population size could account for only about 30 per cent of the variance in the affluence scores. How much better might they be predicted by the addition of more variables? Six have been selected, relating respectively to population density, population change, migrational change, non-white population, employment in manufacturing, and changes in industrial employment. In each case there is some theoretical expectation of a positive association with affluence, except in the case of non-white population where it should be negative.

The simple correlation coefficients with the Affluence Indicator are listed in Table 8.12. It is possible to establish the association between the seven independent variables together and the dependent variable, by putting them all into a multiple correlation analysis at the same time. The result is $R = 0.746$. The coefficient of determination of $R^2 = 0.557$ indicates that almost 56 per cent of the variance in the city affluence scores is accounted for by the

Table 8.12: Correlation Coefficients (r) Between an Affluence Indicator and Selected Independent Variables, for 109 Metropolitan Areas in the United States

Variable	r
X_1 Total population (millions) 1967	0·538
X_2 Population per square mile 1966	0·335
X_3 Population change (per cent) 1960–66	0·152
X_4 Net population migration (per cent of total) 1960–66	0·235
X_5 Non-white population (per cent of total) 1960	−0·366
X_6 Employment in manufacturing (per cent of total) 1968	0·054
X_7 Change in manufacturing employment (per cent) 1958–63	0·067

Source: D. M. Smith, The Geography of Social Well-being in the United States, McGraw-Hill, 1973.

Patterns in Human Geography

seven variables, or almost double what population size alone could 'explain'.

A common alternative approach to this type of analysis is to perform the correlation in a 'stepwise' manner. Instead of putting all the independent variables in initially they are entered one at a time, the first being the one with the highest simple correlation with the dependent variable, the next being the one accounting for the most of the remaining variance, and so on until they are all entered. The procedure can be automatically terminated at any step when the addition of subsequent variables contributes no significant increase to the variance accounted for.

Table 8.13 shows the results of a stepwise multiple correlation analysis of the present problem. After total population, the next variable to enter is non-whites, adding 17·1 per cent to the explained variance. Next population migration adds another 5.4 per cent, and so on. At each step the standard error of the estimate of Y is reduced, showing the growing accuracy of the predictive model. The table indicates that two variables (manufacturing employment and population change) each add only minutely to the increase in R^2, almost all the variance accounted for by these two already having been contributed by others. In association with the other variables, they have virtually no unique contribution to the 'explanation' of city affluence levels.

Table 8.13: A Stepwise Multiple Correlation Analysis on an Affluence Indicator for 109 Metropolitan Areas in the United States

Step	Variable Entered	R	R^2	Increase in R^2	Standard Error
1	X_1	0·538	0·298		0·85
2	X_5	0·678	0·460	0·171	0·76
3	X_4	0·717	0·514	0·054	0·72
4	X_7	0·735	0·540	0·026	0·70
5	X_2	0·745	0·555	0·015	0·69
6	X_6	0·746	0·557	0·002	0·69
7	X_3	0·746	0·557	0·000	0·69

Note: The independent variables (X) are as in Table 8.12.

276

One reason why the explained variance may not be reduced much after the initial steps in an analysis of this kind is high inter-correlation between some independent variables. This is the problem of 'multicollinearity'. Ideally the independent variables in multiple correlation and regression should be statistically independent (like the two distance dimensions in trend surface analysis), and the technique is in fact based on this assumption. In the present example most pairs of variables have low correlations (i.e. $r < 0.3$) though there are a few high ones: population migration has $r = 0.95$ with population change and 0.77 with changes in manufacturing employment, while the latter has 0.81 with migration. This helps to explain why some variables have so little to add once others have been entered into the model.

At each step the addition of a new variable requires the re-calculation of the regression equation, as the relationship between the dependent variable and each of the independent variables changes. This is illustrated in Table 8.14, where the coefficients in each of the five steps are shown. The final regression equation with five independent variables is thus:

$$Y = 11.1 + 33X_1 - 0.51X_5 + 0.53X_4 - 1.01X_7 + 0.01X_2$$

where Y is the affluence score (Z) multiplied by 100. This equation can now predict the values of the affluence scores to a standard error of 0.69 (Z-scores) compared with the 0.85 in the simple regression with population size. As examples, New York has an

Table 8.14: A Stepwise Regression Analysis on an Affluence Indicator (Y) for 109 Metropolitan Areas in the United States

Step	Constant (a)	Coefficients (b)				
		X_1	X_5	X_4	X_7	X_2
1	−38.3	36				
2	7.8	39	−0.74			
3	5.1	39	−0.49	0.28		
4	18.9	36	−0.52	0.53	−1.04	
5	11.1	33	−0.51	0.53	−1.01	0.01

Note: The independent variables (X) are as in Table 8.12. The dependent variable (Y) is expressed as Z × 100.

actual score of 3·24 and a predicted Y of 3·92, Chicago 1·01 and 1·71, and Los Angeles 1·92 and 2·13.

Before concluding, a warning about the possible misuse of multiple correlation and regression is required. Access to a computer makes the technique easy to apply, and in the process the assumptions underlying correlation and regression analysis generally (outlined earlier in the chapter) are sometimes overlooked. A not uncommon practice in recent years has been to run simple and multiple correlations rather indiscriminately on a mass of data in the hope of revealing some hitherto unsuspected relationships. This so-called 'shotgun' approach is generally frowned upon by statisticians, who remind us that correlation is designed to test specific hypotheses. To use it as a search procedure, attempting to find close empirical associations by trial and error, runs the risk of accepting entirely spurious correlations as indicative of cause and effect. The distinction between prediction and explanation has been made so often that it requires no repetition at this point. All that might be added is the advice to regard with suspicion massive correlation analyses in which the theoretical justification for the choice of variables is not stated, and to seek support other than high correlation coefficients for any 'explanations' claimed in this kind of application.

9. Networks and Movement

So far this book has been concerned mainly with patterns of human existence expressed in areal differentiation. The data have been sets of observations describing the incidence of conditions as they vary from place to place or area to area, and as they are associated with one another. But human activity also occurs *through* or *across* geographical space. Individual places are physically connected, and areas are functionally integrated into wider wholes, within networks of communication. Movement takes place through these networks, in the form of people travelling, goods being shipped, messages passing and ideas spreading. As these networks and movements adopt distinctive patterns in space, focusing on some places and in certain directions while avoiding others, territory is organized in a distinctive manner. The way man thus imposes himself on the landscape dynamically is an important aspect of human geography.

Many of the general techniques of measurement discussed in the first five chapters of this book are just as applicable to the description of networks and patterns of movement as they are to areal distributions. In Chapter 1 it was shown that connectivity between places can be displayed in matrix form, and Chapter 2 illustrated the idea of the cartographic representation of flows. The measurement of central tendency and dispersion in a set of observations described in Chapter 3 can be applied to movement, as can the frequency distribution; for example the volume of traffic along different routes or at different times could be described by these methods. Similar applications readily come to mind for the comparative measures and techniques for data transformation and combination set down in Chapters 4 and 5. Additional illustrations should not be necessary to demonstrate this.

Patterns in Human Geography

It is in the description of spatial arrangement that patterns of networks and movement begin to pose their own special measurement problems, for the methods of describing areal distributions in Chapters 6 and 7 are not appropriate. This chapter offers a brief review of some alternative techniques designed specifically to measure characteristics of networks and volumes of movement, and to identify some of the features of spatial organization which result.

As in previous chapters, the distinction between pure description and the elucidation of possible causal processes is not always clearcut. This is particularly true in the case of patterns of movement, which can be effectively described in terms of some of the likely causal factors. Although the focus remains descriptive, the possibility of functional relationships both describing a set of observations and accounting for their magnitudes in a causal sense is clearly worth noting. This is ideally the essence of correlation and regression analysis, a special application of which will appear in this chapter. To find a mode of description which can accurately predict reality in terms of other variables is a first step towards explanation and understanding, which is the ultimate objective of scientific description.

The Nature of Networks

Networks may be visible or invisible, tangible or intangible. They may comprise roads or railway lines directly observed, or they may be airline connections or telegraph links identified primarily by reference to some printed schedule or other secondary source. But whatever their physical nature, networks may be described in the same manner, involving transformation into a *graph*. The network can further be portrayed as a connectivity matrix, and various summary measures can be calculated.

A simple imaginary case can demonstrate the numerical description of a network. Suppose that there are two different networks of communications between the same set of places, as in Figure 9.1a: the upper map could be of roads, and the lower one telephone

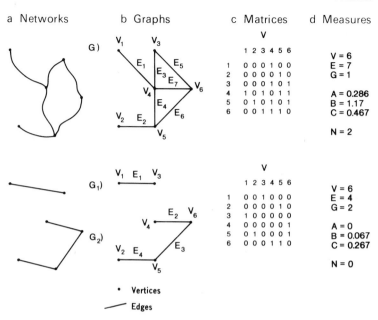

a Networks   b Graphs   c Matrices   d Measures

Figure 9.1   Measuring characteristics of networks via graphs and matrices.

or telex links. In Figure 9.1b both are transformed into topological diagrams or graphs, which simply indicate the existence of the routes without reference to their true length or direction. This is the first stage in the process of simplification of reality. There are three important elements to any network or graph: its nodes or *vertices* (V), its routes or *edges* (E), and its *sub-graphs* (G) or independent and unconnected parts. These are all identified by symbols in Figure 9.1b. The first network has six vertices (V_1, ..., V_6) and seven edges (E_1, ..., E_7), and as all are parts of a continuous system of links there is only one sub-graph. The second network has the same number of vertices as the one above but only four edges, and because there is now no connection between V_1 and V_3 and any of the other points the network is composed of two independent sub-graphs (G_1, G_2). Thus there are some important differences between the two networks.

281

Next, the two situations are set down in matrix form. The procedure is exactly as illustrated in Chapter 1 (see Figure 1.3): the numeral 1 identifies nodes or vertices which have direct connections, and 0 those which do not. The more ones and the less zeros in the matrix, the more interconnection within the network.

This observation suggests a basis for a summary measure of connectivity. If every node had a direct connection with every other, there would be a matrix with 1 in every cell, except in the major diagonal because nodes are not linked with themselves. The total number of connections would be $V^2 - V$, where V is the number of nodes. But in the matrix each link is shown twice (e.g. the edge between V_5 and V_6 is shown in row 5 and column 6, and also in row 6 and column 5), so the total should be halved to give $\frac{1}{2}(V^2 - V)$ connections. Relating the actual number to this figure gives the following index of connectivity (C):

$$C = \frac{E}{\frac{1}{2}(V^2 - V)} \qquad [9.1]$$

where E is the number of edges or connections in the observed pattern or network. This measure is sometimes denoted by the Greek letter gamma (γ), and is generally referred to as the *gamma index*.

Applying this to the top network in Figure 9.1:

$$C = \frac{7}{\frac{1}{2}(36 - 6)} = \frac{7}{15} = 0\cdot467$$

For the second network it is $0\cdot267$. The values of this index are on a range 0 to $1\cdot0$, with 0 representing no edges or connections and $1\cdot0$ representing the maximum number, i.e. direct connections between all nodes.

Another simple measure is provided by what is known as the *cyclomatic number* (N). This is the number of circuits in the network, and is given by:

$$N = E - V + G \qquad [9.2]$$

where E is the number of edges, V the number of vertices and G

the number of sub-graphs. For the top network in Figure 9.1 the cyclomatic number is:

$$N = 7 - 6 + 1 = 2$$

There are two circuits: V_2 to V_4 to V_6, and V_4 to V_5 to V_6. For the other network N is $4 - 6 + 2 = 0$. The cyclomatic number increases with the completeness of the connections and the complexity of the network.

A further measure is provided by relating the actual number of circuits to the maximum possible within the system. This is termed the *alpha index* because it is often designated by the Greek letter alpha (α), and is as follows:

$$A = \frac{E - V + G}{2V - 5} \qquad [9.3]$$

Like the gamma index, it varies on a scale 0 to 1·0, or from no circuits to the maximum number which is $2V - 5$. Calculating this for the two patterns in Figure 9.1 gives A values of 0·286 for the top pattern and 0 for the less complete network with no circuits.

It should be noted at this point that the expressions for both the alpha and gamma indices set down here relate to *planar* graphs. These are networks in two dimensions, where every line intersection is a node. *Non-planar* graphs describe three-dimensional cases where one line can jump over another with no connection, as in some motorway and airway routes for example. Modifications of expressions [9.2] and [9.3] are needed for non-planar graphs, as follows:

$$C = \frac{E}{3(V - 2)} \qquad [9.4]$$

$$A = \frac{E - V + G}{\frac{1}{2}(V^2 - V) - (V - 1)} \qquad [9.5]$$

One more network measure remains – the *beta index* (from Greek β), which is calculated by:

$$B = \frac{E}{V} \qquad [9.6]$$

283

This is the simplest of all the indexes, but it has some very useful properties. Disconnected graphs and those in the form of 'trees' with branches but no circuit all have a B value of less than 1·0. Exactly 1·0 describes a network with one circuit. As the network structure becomes more complex, with an increasing number of edges in relation to vertices, so the beta index goes up, to reach a maximum of 3·0 for planar graphs and infinity for non-planar graphs. The values for B in the two graphs in Figure 9.1 are 1·17 for the more complex one at the top and 0·67 for the other.

The various measures illustrated above may now be applied to a real transport network: that of the island of Madagascar (the Malagasy Republic). Figure 9.2 shows the major road network and its nodes, on a conventional map and as a graph. The A and N measures are zero as there are no circuits, and the B and C indices indicate a very low degree of connectivity on the 0 to 1·0 scale. With one main artery and the coastal towns connected by branches, the network is in fact typical of underdeveloped nations and of areas with rugged relief. If a new road were constructed, for example to complete the present discontinuous coastal circuit, the measures would increase considerably. There would be 9 new edges, which would raise the cyclomatic number (N) to 9 and the alpha index to 0·27. The B index would become 1·4 and C would be 0·15.

In general, the degree of connectivity in transport networks increases with the level of economic development. This has been demonstrated in detail by Kansky, in his monograph *Structure of Transportation Networks*, which first brought to the attention of geographers most of the measures described above. Calculating the B index for a sample of national railway systems, Kansky found that $B = 1·4$ (approximately) in France, Hungary and Czechoslovakia – all industrialized nations. Figures of 1·1 to 1·2 were obtained for Yugoslavia and Bulgaria, and 1·0 (approx.) described the networks of such nations as Turkey and Iraq. At the bottom of the scale with $B = 0·9$ were Ghana, Bolivia and other relatively underdeveloped nations.

As individual nations progress through successively more advanced stages of development, so the connectivity of the network

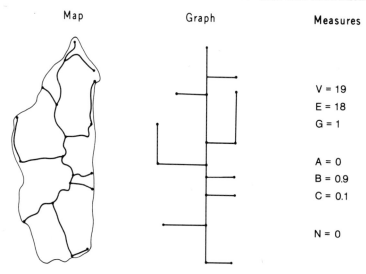

Map   Graph   Measures

V = 19
E = 18
G = 1

A = 0
B = 0.9
C = 0.1

N = 0

Figure 9.2   The major road network of Madagascar, with graph measures.

increases. In Ghana, for example, the *B* measure for the road system has been observed to increase from 0·6 in 1910 to about 0·9 in 1927 and almost 1·3 in 1959.

A major deficiency in all these network indices is that they disregard both the actual distances and the quality of communications. As these are important characteristics, it is desirable to have a way of measuring them. One method sometimes used is the *accessibility index*, which simply measures the sum of the distances from any selected place (V_i) to all others. The larger the result, the less accessible the place. These indices can themselves be summed for all vertices in the network, to give what is usually termed the *dispersal index*. Taken as it stands or divided by the total number of vertices, this provides a measure of overall accessibility within the network, for the smaller the index the more accessible places are to each other. In both cases, network distances can be converted into time-distance, cost-distance, or any other units which will reflect relevant qualitative characteristics of transport and communications.

Patterns in Human Geography

Spatial Interaction and Movement

The characteristics of a network describe the system of communications which man has created. How he actually uses it is a quite different question. Some routes may be heavily used while some are almost ignored; some may generate many trips or messages, while others generate very few. To describe all this requires information on spatial interaction and movement, and some special methods of measurement.

The flow of goods, people, ideas, and so on can be depicted in both map and matrix form, as was explained in Chapters 1 and 2. But what general measures may be devised to summarize the essential nature of these patterns? The most commonly used are those which relate interaction to two important characteristics of the network: the attraction or generating power of the nodes, and the length or friction of the routes between them. The operational framework is the *gravity model*.

The general principle of the gravity model has been introduced already, in the discussion of the potential concept in Chapter 7. There it was explained that the 'influence' or potential of any point in space on another can be expected to be proportional to the attractive power of the first point and inversely proportional to the intervening distance measured in the units most appropriate to express friction. This is the basis of the most general model of spatial interaction, which may be written $I = f(P, D)$ or more specifically:

$$_iI_j = f \ \frac{P_i}{D_{ij}} \qquad [9.7]$$

where $_iI_j$ is the volume of interaction or flow to a point i from another point j,

P_i is some measure of the attractive power of point i,

D_{ij} is some measure of the distance between points i and j,

and f means 'some function of'.

The subject of interest may be anything which can be thought of

286

as moving from one point to another. The measure of attraction or pull (P) may refer to the size of the place, its status as a shopping centre, its quality of life, or whatever is appropriate in the particular research context. Distance may be measured in conventional units such as miles, or in units of time, of cost, and so on. This model thus offers an effective way of describing patterns of movement in terms of the impulse to move and the opposing friction of distance. The problems posed to the investigator are the accurate measurement of the variables involved and the estimation of the constants (or parameters) which define the functional relationship.

The application of the simplest form of this model may be demonstrated with imaginary data. Suppose that observations are made on the number of people travelling to snop at a certain city i from ten near-by places (1, 2, . . ., j, . . ., 10), with the results set down in Table 9.1. Distances from each j to i are also tabulated. If the known movements (I) are plotted on a graph against the respective distances, a regular relationship is suggested. The number of people coming to the city falls away with distance in an apparently regular and predictable manner. The general form of the curve shown has in fact been found to fit real patterns of human interaction closely. The imaginary numbers used here have been chosen so as to be perfectly predictable from D; Table 9.1 lists the reciprocals of the distances, and it can be seen that if they

Table 9.1: Imaginary Data Representing Persons Travelling to Shop, Used in Demonstrating the Gravity Model

j	$_iI_j$	D_{ij}	$\dfrac{1}{D_{ij}}$	$_iI'_j$
1	500	2	0·500	250
2	333	3	0·333	111
3	167	6	0·167	28
4	250	4	0·250	63
5	200	5	0·200	40
6	100	10	0·100	10
7	1000	1	1·000	1000
8	125	8	0·125	16
9	111	9	0·111	12
10	143	7	0·143	20

are each multiplied by 1,000 they become the I values. In other words, if expression [9.7] was rewritten as follows:

$$_iI_j = \frac{1000}{D_{ij}}, \quad \text{or} \quad _iI_j = 1000 \, \frac{1}{D_{ij}}$$

this would describe the situation perfectly. The use of the constant 1,000 or 1 in place of P_i in the original expression is legitimate, because the city can be thought of as exerting the same attraction on any of the ten places.

The second version of the predicting equation above is more useful than the first. As the numeral 1,000 is the same for each of the ten places in this calculation, it may be replaced by the symbol a representing a constant, to generalize the expression as follows:

$$_iI_j = a \, \frac{1}{D_{ij}} \tag{9.8}$$

Interaction may thus be described by the product of the reciprocal of distance and a constant.

But is simple linear distance, in miles, cost, or any other units, adequate as a measure of the effect of this variable? It is satisfactory in the imaginary case just considered, but suppose that the number of shoppers had actually been as listed under $_iI'_j$ in Table 9.1 instead of as originally. These figures show a much more rapid falling off with increasing distance from the city (see Figure 9.3). They have been generated by taking the reciprocal of the *square* of the distance from the city, i.e. they are perfectly predictable from the equation:

$$_iI'_j = 1000 \, \frac{1}{D_{ij}^{\,2}}$$

So in order to be able to describe the pattern of interaction in situations where the friction of distance varies, linear distance may have to be raised to some power. This distance exponent is the second of the two parameters needed to make the model complete. It can now be written generally as:

$$_iI_j = a \, \frac{1}{D_{ij}^{\,b}} \tag{9.9}$$

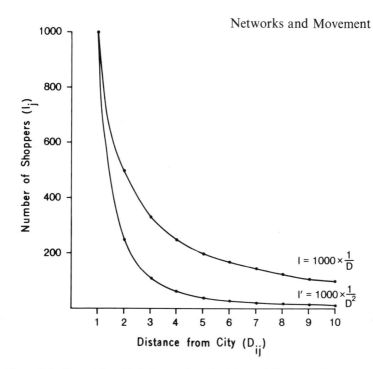

Figure 9.3 The relationship between shopping trips and distances of a set of origins from an imaginary city.

The greater the friction of distance and the more rapidly interaction falls off, the higher the value of the parameter b.

In using this expression to describe a particular set of movements, it is necessary to find the actual values for a and b which provide the best fit to the data. (The fit will seldom if ever be perfect, as in the imaginary case above.) Estimating the parameters is facilitated by a reformulation of the model. By simple algebra, expression [9.9] may be rewritten as follows:

$$_iI_j = a \times D_{ij}^{-b} \qquad [9.10]$$

By taking the logarithm of each side, it can be turned into the following:

$$\log {_iI_j} = \log a - b \log D_{ij} \qquad [9.11]$$

which should be recognized as a version of the simple linear

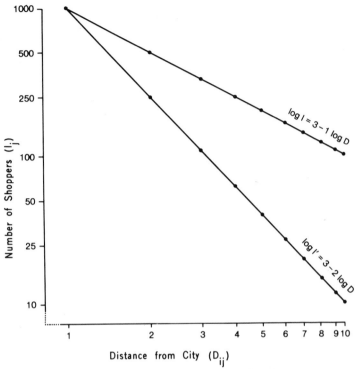

Figure 9.4　Shopping trip and distance relationships plotted on logarithmic graph paper.

regression equation discussed in the previous chapter. Stated in this way, the two parameters of the model may be estimated by regression analysis, given a set of observations on I and D converted into logarithms.

The reason why taking the logarithms of the two variables turns the basic potential or gravity formulation into a linear model can be explained quite easily. The kind of relationships between interaction and distance depicted in Table 9.1 (which are idealized versions of those found in reality) are in fact linear when plotted on logarithmic graph paper. The curves in Figure 9.3 turn into straight lines. This is illustrated in Figure 9.4, where the two sets of imaginary data are plotted and the lines drawn, along with their equations. In both cases the a parameter is 3 (i.e. log 1,000) because they have the same observation to begin with, but the top line has a b value of 1 compared with 2 for the other. The steeper the slope of the line, the greater the b parameter, which is of course the distance exponent. Plotting the logarithms of D and I on normal graph paper would also produce straight lines.

Models of this kind have been found to describe human interaction over distance very accurately, once the variables have been measured properly. Interaction does appear to fall away with distance, rapidly at first and then less rapidly as we get further away from the point of attraction. The equations provide close predictions of actual movements or flows, and the correlation coefficients between expected and actual interaction are generally highly significant.

As an actual example, data on trips to a new shopping centre in Sydney have been analysed. A sample of about 750 shoppers were interviewed to determine their places of residence, and this information was then aggregated by one-mile distance zones from the centre (Table 9.2). The data reveal the usual curvilinear falling

Table 9.2: Number of Customers Travelling Various Distances to Visit Chatswood Shopping Centre, Sydney

Distance (miles)		Customers (number)	
D	$\log D$	I	$\log I$
1	0·00	199	2·30
2	0·30	161	2·21
3	0·48	109	2·04
4	0·60	75	1·88
5	0·70	66	1·82
6	0·78	46	1·66
7	0·84	39	1·59
8	0·90	12	1·08
9	0·95	22	1·34
10	1·00	5	0·70
11	1·04	10	1·00
12	1·08	7	0·85

Source of data: sample survey by Wayne Bensley, Department of Geography, University of New England, 1973.

off of interaction as distance increases (see top of Figure 9.5). The data have been transformed by taking the logs of number of shoppers from each zone (I) and distance (D), and these can be subjected to a regression analysis. The result is as follows:

$$\log I = 2\cdot56 - 1\cdot42 \log D$$

The regression line is plotted on logarithmic scales in Figure 9.5, and the correlation coefficient of $r = -0\cdot878$ confirms the close fit. Taking the antilogarithm of the a parameter and using the b parameter as the distance exponent, the gravity formulation can now be written:

$$I = \frac{363}{D^{1.42}}$$

or
$$I = 363\, D^{-1.42}$$

This describes the observed behaviour of Chatswood shoppers quite accurately.

But is this necessarily the *best* fit to the data? An examination of the graphs in Figure 9.5 suggests that the logarithmic transformations may have 'gone too far', somewhat reversing the form of the original curve instead of making it very closely linear. In fact, a better fit can be obtained by transforming only distance into logs (Figure 9.6). The regression equation now becomes:

$$I = 195 - 185 \log D$$

and the correlation of $r = -0\cdot967$ confirms that we now have almost a perfect linear relationship. In research applications of the gravity model it may be necessary to experiment with different functions before the friction of distance is adequately measured.

The method outlined above applies to movement *to* a single focal point, *from* a number of other points. However, the model can easily be extended to accommodate two-way interaction within a system of nodes. In this formulation, two places interact with each other in proportion to the product of their respective attractive powers (i.e. sizes or 'masses'), and inversely to the intervening distance, as before. The equation is very similar to [9.9]:

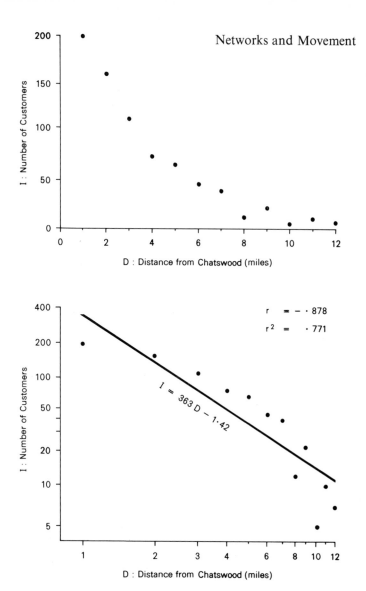

Figure 9.5   The relationship between number of customers and
distance from Chatswood shopping centre, Sydney:
top – original data; bottom – log-transformed data.
(Source of data: Table 9.2.)

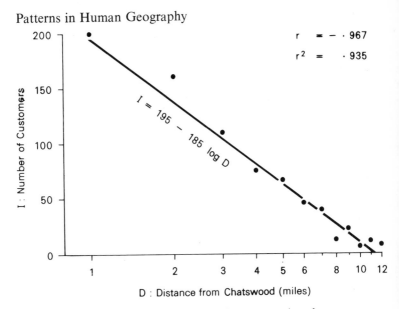

Figure 9.6 Another view of the relationship between number of customers and distance from Chatswood shopping centre: a logarithmic transformation of the distance variable alone. (Source of data: Table 9.2.)

$$I_{ij} = a \frac{P_i P_j}{D_{ij}^{\,b}} \qquad [9.12]$$

or alternatively:

$$I_{ij} = a P_i P_j D_{ij}^{-b} \qquad [9.13]$$

where I_{ij} is the total interaction between the two places in either direction, P_i and P_j are their mutual attractions, and D_{ij} is the distance between them. The letters a and b refer to the parameters to be estimated for best fit to the empirical situation, as before. The logarithmic version of this model, analogous to [9.11] above, can be used to find the parameter values by multiple regression analysis from sets of data on actual interaction, distance, and the attractive power of the nodes.

This gravity model has been used very extensively in research. It is popular as a descriptive device because it expresses inter-

294

action in terms of two variables with which it can be expected to relate in a functional sense, and it has been found to describe reality quite accurately once the appropriate attraction or mass variable has been properly identified and distance measured in suitable units. The gravity model has been found particularly useful in establishing the basic characteristics of existing patterns of movement, and using them to predict future patterns. In this form it is an essential component of a number of more complex models used in the planning of transportation systems and land use. These models are beyond the scope of the present discussion, but it is worth noting that to describe spatial patterns accurately enough to provide useful predictions for planning purposes is an attribute not enjoyed by many geographical techniques. Although it may well have been over-used, the gravity model has a rather special place in the geographer's bag of numerical tools.

Interaction and Spatial Organization

Interaction across distance is one of the ways in which man organizes geographical space. Some territories focus on one dominant node as the central point of the communications system and of the movement of things, while other territories look in a variety of different directions. Some nodes have wide spheres of influence; others are of only local significance, or dominated by major centres near by. It is useful to be able to describe the main features of this kind of dynamic spatial organization, as well as the specific patterns of human interaction within such a system.

One obvious approach is provided by simple cartography. If connections or flows between places are depicted on a map it is possible to identify the major focal points visually, and lines can be interpolated as boundaries between their spheres of influence. Some subjective judgement is involved, but the results can be quite effective as a sketch-map of the system.

The hosiery industry in the East Midlands can be used to demonstrate this technique. In the middle of the nineteenth century this industry was run almost entirely on a domestic system, with cottage workers in more than two hundred villages obtaining their materials periodically from the major organizing centres in the larger towns and cities, and taking a batch of finished product in at the same time. The report of a Parliamentary inquiry into the supposed exploitation of the workers provides information which may be used to reconstruct the spatial organization of the industry. In Figure 9.7 each reference in the report to people in a certain village working for a manufacturer or merchant in a certain town is depicted as a line drawn between the two places. The result is a connectivity map of the kind introduced above, though it is much more complex than the simple illustrations there. From the lines it is possible to interpolate rough boundaries to the catchment areas of the major centres 'putting out' work, and of certain secondary centres. Except for one substantial area of overlap across the Nottinghamshire–Derbyshire borderlands, the major putting-out centres appear to have had quite distinct spheres of influence, generally but not exclusively serving the villages closest to them.

Maps summarizing all manner of different patterns of movement can be constructed in a similar way. But there is a rather more precise numerical method which can be used if data are available in the right form. It is based on the gravity model. If the relationship with the two variables of attractive power and distance accurately describes patterns of spatial interaction, then it ought to be able to tell us towards which of the various alternative nodes or focal points a particular subordinate place should gravitate. If the pull (I) on any place j by a place i is in general described by:

$$_iI_j = \frac{P_i}{D_{ij}} \qquad [9.14]$$

where the two parameters a and b are unity, then evaluating this for all relevant nodes i should reveal the one with the strongest pull, i.e. where $_iI_j = $ max. If this is done for all places j, they can then be allocated to their respective dominant node (i) and boundaries between spheres of influence can be established. Alterna-

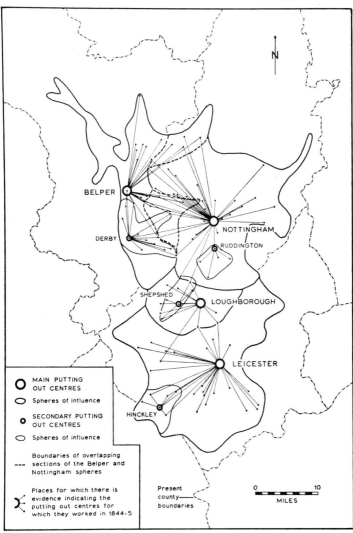

Figure 9.7 The nodal structure of the spatial organization of hosiery
manufacturing in the East Midlands in 1844. (Source:
D. M. Smith, 'The British Hosiery Industry at the Middle
of the Nineteenth Century', *Transactions and Papers*,
Institute of British Geographers, 32, 1963.)

tively, the position of the boundary between the spheres of any two nodes (i and j) with known P values can be found by calculating the distance from one of them which satisfies the condition that:

$$\frac{P_i}{D_{ij}} = \frac{P_j}{D_{ij}} \qquad [9.15]$$

in other words, the point where the pull of the two centres is the same. These methods are used quite commonly for defining market areas between trading centres on the basis of observed patterns of shopping trips. But it must be remembered that the gravity model is at best only a summary of interaction patterns, and that movement between some places may depart substantially from that predicted in the model, by virtue of special local circumstances. Like the regression model, the gravity formulation should have an error term, because actual human behaviour is seldom if ever simple enough to express with perfect accuracy as a simple function of a small number of variables.

An application to the identification of hinterlands is provided by Figure 9.8. This is taken from a study in which it was required to describe the existing spatial organization of retailing in North West England, as a preliminary to predicting the impact of a proposed regional shopping centre. The attractive power of each of three grades of shopping centre was measured by average sales of durable goods: £50.4M for grade I, £8·25M for grade IIA and £4·43M for grade IIB. Distance was measured by an estimate of travel time by car. Then the position of hinterland boundaries was found from the following modification of the gravity formula:

$$D_{I \to IIA} = \frac{T_{I\,IIA}}{1 + \sqrt{\dfrac{S_{IIA}}{S_I}}}$$

where $D_{I \to IIA}$ is the time-distance of the boundary from a grade I centre in the direction of a grade IIA centre,

$T_{I\,IIA}$ is the time-distance between the centres,

and S_I, S_{IIA} are the respective attractive powers in terms of durable goods sales.

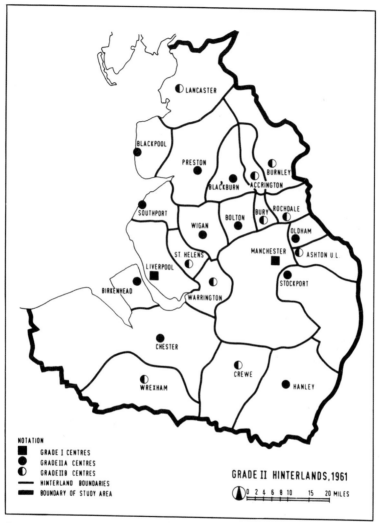

GRADE II HINTERLANDS, 1961

0 2 4 6 8 10   15   20 MILES

Figure 9.8   Shopping centre hinterlands in North West England,
derived from a version of the gravity model. (Source:
Regional Shopping Centres in North West England,
Department of Town and Country Planning, University
of Manchester, 1964.)

For example, the result for a grade I and grade IIA centre 25 minutes apart would be:

$$D = \frac{25}{1 + \sqrt{\dfrac{8 \cdot 25}{50 \cdot 14}}} = \frac{25}{1 + \sqrt{0 \cdot 165}} = 17 \cdot 8$$

The boundary line between these two centres would thus be drawn 17·8 minutes from the grade I centre, or 17·8/25 of the way to the smaller place. The rest of the boundaries would be found by repeating the calculation in appropriate directions.

If the central objective is to describe spatial organization as fully and accurately as possible, then the complete matrix of observed flows between points should be used, rather than a summary in the form of a map or equation. To this matrix may be applied a particularly effective technique developed by Nystuen and Dacey, based on graph theory. Imagine twelve cities with flows between them each way as illustrated in Table 9.3. The data may be taken to refer to telephone messages, the movement of goods, or any other such condition. The sum of all incoming messages is found for each city, and they are given a rank order on the basis of these figures. For each city the largest outward flow is identified. If this is to a place larger than the city of origin (as in the cases represented by the bold-type figures in Table 9.3), then the city of origin is deemed to be *subordinate* or satellite to the city of destination. Those cities with largest flows to a smaller or lower-ranked city (i.e. with numbers in italics in the table) are deemed *dominant*.

The results may now be depicted as graphs of the kind introduced in section 9.1. In Figure 9.9 each of the dominant nodes (*b*, *e*, *g* and *i*) has its own sub-graph, with the places subordinate to it connected by lines. This can now be converted into a conventional map, if the twelve cities are given a position in geographical space. Rough boundaries between spheres of influence of the dominant nodes can then be drawn, as in the hosiery industry example above. The city *k*, though defined as dominant, should be regarded as a secondary node, as it is itself subordinate to city *j*. The isolated city *e* may also have secondary status. This

Table 9.3: *Imaginary Data on the Flow of Messages Within a System of Cities, Used to Demonstrate the Graph Theory Approach to Spatial Organization*

		a	b	c	d	e	f	g	h	i	j	k	l
							Destination						
	a	—	75	15	20	28	2	3	2	1	20	1	0
	b	69	—	45	50	58	12	20	3	6	35	4	2
	c	5	51	—	12	40	0	6	1	3	15	0	1
	d	19	67	14	—	30	7	6	2	11	18	5	1
	e	7	40	48	26	—	7	10	2	37	39	12	6
Origin	f	1	6	1	1	10	—	27	1	3	4	2	0
	g	2	16	3	3	13	31	—	3	18	8	3	1
	h	0	4	0	1	3	3	6	—	12	38	4	0
	i	2	28	3	6	43	4	16	12	—	98	13	1
	j	7	40	10	8	40	5	17	34	98	—	35	12
	k	1	8	2	1	18	0	6	5	12	30	—	15
	l	0	2	0	0	7	0	1	0	1	6	12	—
Total		113	337	141	128	290	71	118	65	202	311	91	39
Rank		8	1	5	6	3	10	7	11	4	2	9	12

Source: J. D. Nystuen and M. F. Dacey, 'A Graph Theory Interpretation of Regions', *Papers*, Regional Science Association, 7, 1961.

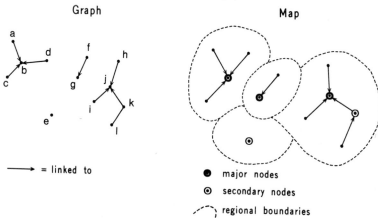

Graph   Map

⟶ = linked to

● major nodes

◉ secondary nodes

⌒ regional boundaries

Figure 9.9   The identification of nodes and regions from interaction data (Table 9.3), by the Nystuen and Dacey method.

Patterns in Human Geography

differentiation of nodes suggests a hierarchical arrangement, as found in real-world systems of central places and complementary regions.

An example of the application of this technique at a national level is provided in Figure 9.10. Here the flows of trunk telephone calls have been used to identify the nodal and regional structure of the South African system of cities, using the Nystuen and Dacey procedure. As in the imaginary case above, a hierarchy is suggested, with certain subsidiary centres having their own local regions within the territories dominated by the major national

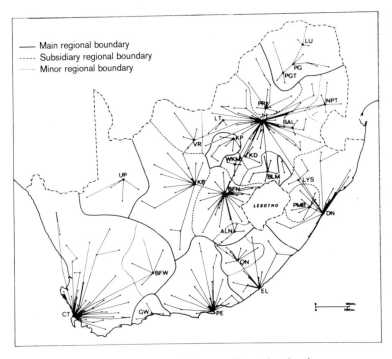

Figure 9.10   Nodal flows of trunk telephone traffic, and regional boundaries, in South Africa. (Source: C. Board, R. J. Davies and T. J. D. Fair, 'The Structure of the South African Space Economy: An Integrated Approach', *Regional Studies*, 4, 1970.)

nodes represented by such cities as Johannesburg, Durban and Cape Town.

The discussion of the spatial patterns adopted by human interaction has now brought us to the point of identifying regions. As man organizes his existence on the surface of the earth, his patterns of movement generate functional or dynamic regions centred on some focal point. In addition to those expressed through shopping trips, telephone calls and so on, patterns of commuting, journey to work, or periodic labour migrations are obvious examples. Such systems are an important part of our everyday life, as man (and his thoughts) becomes increasingly mobile and as our existence becomes increasingly organized about the major metropolitan centres where wealth, knowledge and culture are generated. However, this is but one aspect of the structure of regional systems, and it is to the more general question of areal classification and the identification of regions of homogeneous character that we must turn for the continuation and expansion of this theme.

10. Areal Classification and Regions

In this final chapter the attention shifts from the problem of describing specific geographical patterns to the broader question of synthesis. This involves areal classification, and application of the regional concept as a descriptive device. The identification of regions is a long-established mode of geographical synthesis, and the importance of this approach has in no way been diminished by the introduction of quantitative analysis. In fact, modern numerical methods have given regional geography a shot in the arm, providing means of analysing much larger amounts of information than could be used in the traditional summaries of areal differentiation. Unfortunately, most of the applications of modern methods have been in rather advanced research, and little has yet appeared in regional geography textbooks.

The Regional Approach

The essence of a regional approach is very simple and has changed little over the years. If some general summary description of the variable nature of life on part of the earth's surface is required, the most obvious procedure is to subdivide the territory on the basis of observed differences. The focus may be narrow and specific, perhaps concentrating on economic activity, or it can be broader and more general, relating to some higher abstraction like social well-being or the quality of life. Each subdivision can then be given some appropriate label, such as 'textile manufacturing district', 'service centre', or 'poverty region'. The outcome would be an areal classification, with all places or areas within the territory under study allocated to categories or classes on the basis of criteria relevant to the research topic.

The basic principles involved in establishing a sensible classification of places or areas are much the same as in any other classificatory problem. This question has already been considered in Chapter 1, so we can move directly to a discussion of methods of areal classification in current use. But before proceeding, it is necessary to distinguish between the identification of *regions* and other forms of areal classification. Some confusion exists, but most of this can be removed by regarding regional systems as special kinds of areal classifications, the main distinguishing feature of which is the spatial contiguity of the members of any given class. Thus a 'metal manufacturing region' or a 'depressed region' is usually a continuous piece of territory made up of contiguous areal observations, rather than a set of unconnected places scattered across a map but falling into the same class. Although it does not solve certain other methodological and philosophical problems which have surrounded the regional concept in the past, this distinction is sufficient for the purpose of this chapter: the term *areal classification* is used to denote a subdivision established without regard to the contiguity of members of the classes, while the term *region* is reserved for one which involves spatial continuity.

In a purely descriptive context, the importance of the contiguity of like areas is probably over-emphasized in geographical work on areal classification. Man seldom organizes his life in clearly-defined continuous areas of homogeneous character, and to construct systems of regions which create this impression is often a considerable distortion of reality. There may be some practical situations in which it is inconvenient to use an areal classification in which members of the same category are separated from each other; for example, governments may find it easier to plan the development of broad regions containing a number of depressed areas than to have to deal with each of these areas as an isolated entity. But the imposition of a contiguity constraint in the formation of an areal classification generally means some sacrifice in descriptive precision, and it should be done only where there are definite conceptual or practical advantages.

Patterns in Human Geography

Whatever the kind of subdivision used, the major technical objective of a good classification should be the same: to derive relatively homogeneous classes which are well differentiated from each other. Thus an areal classification or regional system based on the quality of human life would attempt to recognize groups of areas with closely similar character, or levels of living, each group markedly different from the others. The best classification from a purely technical point of view is usually one where the within-class differences are minimized and the between-class differences are maximized.

The delimitation of regions is a notoriously subjective activity. The discussion which follows is confined to reasonably objective numerical methods which make simultaneous use of a number of different variables. First, some fairly simple multi-criteria methods are reviewed, and this is followed by a fuller discussion of more advanced techniques developed in recent years. The chapter concludes with some practical applications in the identification of 'problem areas' where the nature of human existence leaves something to be desired.

Some Simple Multi-criteria Methods

Areal classification based on single criteria poses no great technical problems. To subdivide a piece of territory on the basis simply of percentage employed in a certain economic activity, for example, requires two decisions: the number of classes, and the values to be used to define their limits. The first of these problems is analogous to that of defining the classes in a histogram, and was discussed in Chapter 3. The choice of class limits can be based on obvious breaks in the frequency distribution of the values, on standard deviates, or on arbitrarily chosen regular intervals. All choropleth maps, as discussed in Chapter 2, comprise single-criteria areal classifications.

If a classification based on two or (at the most) three criteria is required, simple graphs can be used to find whether any clear groupings of areas exist. In effect, this places all observational units on a two-dimensional scale in which distance between them on the graph is a measure of dissimilarity. The closer together any two points, the more alike they are. This notion of proximity in some kind of non-geographical 'space' defined by the relevant criteria is central to modern methods of areal classification and regional delimitation.

As an example, an economic subdivision of Europe has been attempted, based on the sectorial origin of Gross Domestic Product (Figure 10.1). Alternative classifications are shown, one based on two criteria and the other on three. In the first, figures for the proportion of total GDP originating in the manufacturing and service sectors respectively are used, and the countries are plotted on a conventional graph with two axes. Three clear groups emerge: group *A* with generally high proportions in services and relatively low proportions in manufacturing, group *C* with the reverse, and group *B* occupying an intermediate position. These groups are distinct enough for there to be no doubt as to the appropriate number of classes or the allocation of individual nations between them. When mapped, two of the groups take on a clear geographical and political significance, for group *A* comprises the nations with relatively mature economies characterized by growing emphasis on services at the expense of the industrial sector, while group *C* is made up of six Eastern European countries where rapid industrialization which followed the introduction of Communist governments after the Second World War has produced a heavy emphasis on manufacturing.

The introduction of the proportion of GDP from agriculture and mining, as a third criterion, changes the classification in certain respects (Figure 10.1). The proportions accounted for by the three sectors have been plotted on a triangular graph with three axes. Now four groups can be recognized, although the distinction between two of them (I and II) is not very clear. The identification of group II focuses attention on five peripheral European nations in which agriculture is a relatively important contributor to GDP, with manufacturing correspondingly less prominent than in most other parts of Europe. The recognition of two groups in Eastern Europe now separates the four countries

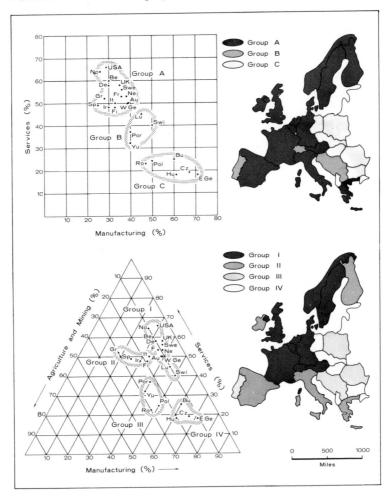

Figure 10.1 Two economic classifications of the countries of Europe, based on sectoral origin of Gross Domestic Product. Note: the figures for Bulgaria are estimates; no comparable data exists for Albania. (Source of data: *United Nations Year Book*, 1965.)

with the most intensive specialization in manufacturing (group IV) from those with relatively well-developed service sectors (group III).

If more than three criteria are needed in making a classification, conventional graphic methods cannot be employed. Various approaches to this kind of problem have been devised, ranging from the interpolation of regional boundaries based on super-imposition of maps of the individual variables to be taken into account, to the use of indices designed to combine information on a number of different conditions (as explained in Chapter 5). Two numerical methods of particular interest will be considered briefly by way of examples – an 'activity combination' method and the measurement of cross-boundary similarity.

The *activity combination method* is a generalization of a technique originally devised to classify agricultural areas, and is particularly applicable in economic geography. Given data on the proportion of total employment (or output, value added, etc.) in each sector of the economy, the technique classifies places or areas as 'one activity', 'two activity', 'three activity', and so on, specifying the activities or sectors in question. Its value appears to be confined to situations where the economy can be sensibly subdivided into at least four sectors and probably not more than six or seven.

As an example of this method, North West England has been subdivided on the basis of percentages employed in five broad industrial categories: (1) textiles and clothing, (2) engineering, vehicles and metals, (3) chemicals and ceramics, (4) coal mining, and (5) other industries. In order to classify each of ninety-five employment exchange areas in the region, their employment structures each have to be compared with 'ideal' or 'expected' structures which represent specific descriptive situations. Thus with a five-sector economy the ideal for a one-industry area is 100 per cent of total employment in one sector and none in the rest, for a two-industry area it is 50 per cent in each of two sectors and none in the rest, for a three-industry area the percentages are 33·3, 33·3, 33·3, 0 and 0, and so on. To make the comparison in any area, the sectoral divisions are placed in rank order and the sum of the squares of the deviations from the model ˙ ˙uctures is calculated in each case. This can be symbolized as follov. 3:

$$D_j = \sum_{i=1}^{N} (O_i - E_{ij})^2 \qquad [10.1]$$

where O_i (1, 2, . . ., 5 in this case) is the proportion employed in a given sector i and E_{ij} is the 'expected' proportion in sector i for model j, whatever it happens to be. The summation is over the N sectors (5 here). Each area is then classified according to the ideal structure it most closely resembles, i.e. the one for which D_j is least. For example, an area with 85 per cent in textiles, 6 in the engineering group, 5 in chemicals, 3 in coal mining and 1 in other industries would clearly be closest to the one-industry model and would be designated 'textile manufacturing area', while somewhere with, say, 50 per cent in engineering, 40 in chemicals, 5 in coal mining, 3 in other industries and 2 per cent in textiles would be a two-industry 'engineering and chemicals area'.

The results of the classification of North West England are shown in Figure 10.2. Only 'one-industry' and 'two-industry' areas are recognized, all other places being deemed to be of 'varied' industrial structure. Three kinds of one-industry area appear, specializing respectively in (i) textiles and clothing, (ii) engineering, vehicles and metals, and (iii) chemicals and ceramics. Five different combinations are represented in the two-industry category. The map shows that although there are some geographical groupings of areas in the same class, the dominant impression is one of spatial discontinuity. The technique has produced an areal classification and not a regional system.

The development of a system of regions comprising groups of contiguous areas can be facilitated if there is some method of measuring the similarity of adjoining areal units. This can be done by various techniques which establish *cross-boundary similarity*. These include Pearson's r and Spearman's r_S, and also the general similarity index based on the Gini coefficient discussed in earlier chapters. The procedure is simply to compare profiles of the economic structure (for example) of adjoining areas, with a high coefficient or index indicating close similarity. Cross-boundary

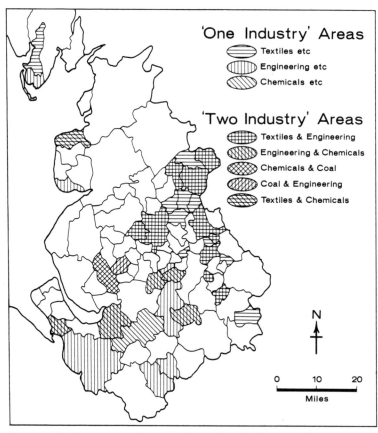

Figure 10.2   An areal classification of North West England based on
an 'industry combination' method. (Source: D. M. Smith,
Industrial Britain: The North West, David & Charles, 1969.)

correlation as an aid to regional delimitation was first used in the
1940s, but subsequent applications have been rather less frequent
than the technique justifies.

An industrial example will again be used to demonstrate this
method. First, an appropriate number of industrial categories
must be arrived at, with data compiled by areal units. Then
cross-boundary similarity is measured. Finally regional boundaries

311

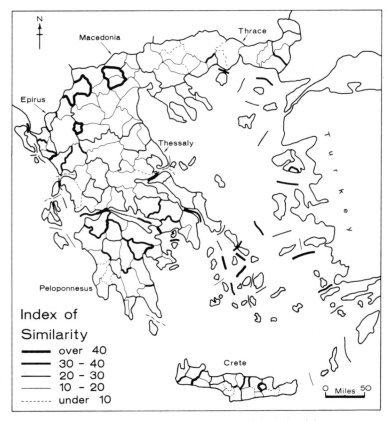

Figure 10.3   A cross-boundary similarity analysis of the industrial
structure of Greece at the eparchie level. (Source of
data: B. Kayser and K. Thompson, *Economic and Social
Atlas of Greece*, Centre of Economic Research, National
Statistical Service and Social Sciences Centre, Athens,
1966.)

are interpolated, along inter-areal boundaries across which the
degree of similarity of industrial structure is low. In Figure 10.3
this has been applied to the 146 eparchies of Greece, with industrial
employment subdivided into nine categories (Table 10.1). Similarity
has been measured by a coefficient which compares the two

312

Table 10.1: Subdivisions Used in the Analysis of the Industrial Structure of Greece

---

1. Food, beverages, tobacco, animal and vegetable oil
2. Textiles
3. Footwear and other wearing apparel
4. Wood, cork, furniture
5. Paper, paper products, printing, publishing
6. Chemicals, petroleum, coal mining
7. Non-metallic mineral products
8. Metal products, machines and appliances, transport equipment
9. Other manufacturing, including leather, rubber and basic metallurgy

---

percentage distributions, for each pair of adjoining areas. The similarity between adjoining eparchies i and j is thus:

$$S_{ij} = \sum_{k=1}^{N} |X_{ik} - X_{jk}|$$

[10.2]

where k is one of N ($= 9$) industrial classes, X_{ik} is the proportion ($\%$) employed in that class in eparchie i, and X_{jk} is the proportion employed in the adjoining eparchie j. The coefficient S is on the scale 0 to 100, and their values are indicated on the map by the boundary lines. The higher the coefficient and the thicker the line, the greater the structural dissimilarity between the areas in question.

The map reveals a number of interesting features of the industrial structure of Greece. Over much of Thrace and Macedonia, in the north east, the industrial character appears to change little across the boundaries of adjoining eparchies, and the same is true of much of Thessaly in central Greece. But to the south, in the Peloponnesus, much sharper differences are evident, as is also the case in Epirus and western Macedonia in the north west. The distinction appears to be between the relatively homogeneous industrial structure of largely domestic and small-scale activity in northern and central Greece and the greater diversity in the more developed south.

313

How far does Figure 10.3 really assist in the delimitation of industrial regions? With a little ingenuity some regional boundaries could be identified, but the final product would hardly constitute a set of neat and clearly defined groups of contiguous areas. Regional boundaries tend to be more strongly marked on some sides than others, and correlation bonding cannot create homogeneity where it does not exist in reality. However, this method can be quite useful as an aid to regional delimitation if not as the final answer. It can help to confirm the strength of boundaries suggested by other kinds of numerical analysis, and also adjudicate on the allocation of difficult cases between alternative regions.

'Multifactor' Areal Classification and Regionalization

Most work on areal classification and the identification of regional systems where a relatively large number of criteria are involved is now based on a package of statistical methods which are far more complex than those discussed above. It comprises the use of *factor analysis* (or *principal components analysis*), and related grouping procedures. This approach was first applied to areal data in sociology more than thirty years ago, but it received little attention in geography until the beginning of the 1960s. Since then it has been developed to a high degree of sophistication as a means of regional identification, in the classification of cities, and in urban social area analysis. It has also been applied to the problem of measuring spatial variations in economic and social health in different parts of the world. The rapidly growing literature in this fashionable field of research is reviewed in a number of the references in the Selected Reading to this chapter. The technique is demonstrated here mainly by example, concentrating on the results rather than the mechanics. The discussion of *how* it is done is brief, and avoids some of the technical questions reviewed in more advanced treatments such as are cited in the Selected Reading.

This 'multifactor' approach involves two main stages. The first reduces the data to more manageable proportions by extracting from it a relatively small number of *factors* or *components*, comprising composite variables which account for a large amount of the variability among the original criteria. This compression is possible because there is some overlap between what each variable accounts for in the total variance, just as in the case of the two distance variables in the trend surfaces explained in Chapter 7. In other words, some of the individual variables tell substantially the same story about areal differentiation. When this analysis has been done the areal units of observation can be given scores on the factors or components, and these can then be used for grouping areas into classes or regions. Because there will generally be substantially fewer factors than original variables, and because they identify underlying 'dimensions' of variation in the data by finding associated sets of characteristics, the process of classification is both simplified and more meaningful than if the data had all been used in their original form.

Before proceeding further, some explanation of factor analysis is required. Suppose that there are four spatially variable conditions with the following intercorrelation matrix (r):

	1	2	3	4
1	1·0			
2	1·0	1·0		
3	0·0	0·0	1·0	
4	0·0	0·0	1·0	1·0

Variables 1 and 2 are perfectly associated with one another ($r = 1\cdot0$) but not at all with the other two ($r = 0\cdot0$), while 3 and 4 are perfectly associated themselves but not with 1 and 2. Clearly, there are two quite independent dimensions of variation in the data, and in the interests of simplicity it would be possible to describe the geographical situation completely by taking just one of variables 1 and 2 and one of 3 and 4 because both variables in each pair tell us exactly the same thing about areal variation. There would thus be two factors here, each accounting for half the overall variation in the data as each variable incorporates a quarter of the total variance. Now, suppose that the correlation matrix had been as follows:

	1	2	3	4
1	1·0			
2	1·0	1·0		
3	1·0	1·0	1·0	
4	0·0	0·0	0·0	1·0

Here variables 1, 2 and 3 are perfectly correlated but uncorrelated with 4. Thus one dimension or factor now involves three of the variables telling the same story, and accounts for three quarters of the total variance. The areal scores on any of the first three variables could identify the nature of the areal variations which this factor describes, while variable 4 would represent a second (independent) dimension. This, very simply, is how factor analysis is able to compress data and eliminate redundancies.

The process of extracting factors can be explained by examining a somewhat more complex set of relationships. Imagine a matrix of correlations as follows:

	1	2	3	4
1	1·00			
2	0·57	1·00		
3	0·09	0·87	1·00	
4	−0·87	−0·91	−0·42	1·00

To understand how factor analysis operates some elementary geometry is helpful. Any pair of variables may be depicted graphically by lines or 'vectors' of the same unit length and with a common origin, and their strength of association can be represented by the angle between them. The angle can be anything from $0°$ to $180°$, and can be transformed into a correlation coefficient by taking its cosine. The cosines of angles from $0°$ to $180°$ range from 1·0 to −1·0, with $90°$ being 0. As an illustration, the relationship between variable 1 and the others in the matrix above are drawn in Figure 10.4a; 1 shows a moderate positive correlation

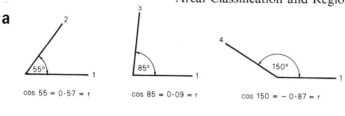

a

cos 55 = 0·57 = r   cos 85 = 0·09 = r   cos 150 = − 0·87 = r

b

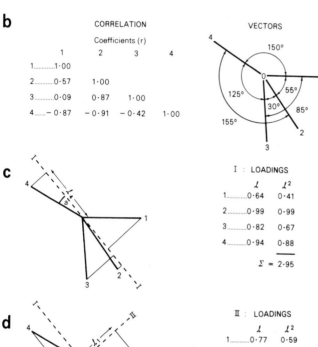

CORRELATION

Coefficients (r)

	1	2	3	4
1	1·00			
2	0·57	1·00		
3	0·09	0·87	1·00	
4	− 0·87	− 0·91	− 0·42	1·00

VECTORS

c

I : LOADINGS

	l	l^2
1	0·64	0·41
2	0·99	0·99
3	0·82	0·67
4	0·94	0·88
		$\Sigma = 2·95$

d

II : LOADINGS

	l	l^2
1	0·77	0·59
2	0·09	0·01
3	0·57	0·33
4	0·34	0·12
		$\Sigma = 1·05$

Figure 10.4   An imaginary case to illustrate the process of factor
analysis. (Note that the axes were drawn by eye and
have not been checked mathematically for goodness of
fit.)

with 2, a very low positive correlation with 3, and a high negative correlation with 4.

The four variables may be drawn together in the same way, with the common origin O (Figure 10.4b). For the purpose of this illustration the r values have been chosen so that the relationship between all pairs of variables can be depicted exactly by using no more than the 360° available in a two-dimensional diagram, though in reality more dimensions are generally needed. The angles shown in the diagram may be checked by looking up their cosines and verifying that these are the correlation coefficients in the matrix. The data are now ready for the first step in identifying the factors, which involves passing an axis of best fit through the common origin of the vectors so as to maximize the total variance accounted for. Geometrically, this requires maximizing the 'projection' lengths of the vectors (l – see Figure 10.4c) on to the axis, which are themselves equivalent to the cosines of the angles formed by the vectors with the axis (i.e. the correlation coefficients). Such a *principal axis* is plotted as the line I in Figure 10.4c. The projection of variable 4 is identified here as l_4; its length is 0·94 in vector units, which is the same as the angle a (20°) when converted into its cosine (0·94). These correlation coefficients with the axis are known as *factor loadings*. The four loadings on axis or factor I are listed in Figure 10.4c, the sum of their squares indicating the proportion (out of 4) of the variance in the original four variables accounted for; it is 2.95. This figure is the *eigenvalue*, and measures the 'strength' of the factor. A second axis can now be added perpendicular ('orthogonal') to the first. Loadings of the variables on this factor II are identified in the same way as explained above, from the vector projections or angles (e.g. l_1 and a in Figure 10.4d). The sum of l^2 or the eigenvalue for factor II is 1·05, which is the total variance of 4·0 less that accounted for already by factor I. Thus the four original variables can be replaced by two factors. Their identity is interpreted from the loadings: factor I represents variables 2 and 4 and to a slightly lesser extent 3, while factor II mainly reflects variable 1. Because the two factors account for all the variance in the data the sum of the l^2 values for any variable should be 1·0, a fact which can be verified from the data in Figure 10.4. The total variance in any variable accounted for by a given set of factors is known as the *communality*.

In reality, many axes or factors will be needed to account for all the variance in a large matrix of data. However, the first few factors can often extract a relatively large share, as will be shown in examples below. The total number of factors or components can be equal in number to the variables in the original matrix, but the procedure is usually stopped short of this. If the original variables are generally highly intercorrelated, the first factors will account for so much of the variability in the base data that they can be substituted for it without very much loss of information.

A helpful analogy to explain this process further is to compare it with a more conventional map analysis. If each of the original variables was displayed on a map some would show similar patterns and some would be different, and a careful comparison might enable them to be separated into sets which roughly correspond. In each set the patterns would be relatively highly correlated with each other. Factor analysis and its principal components version identify these different general patterns of variation, and summarize them in new indices which combine the original variables in proportion to how close their own patterns correspond with the general pattern.

A distinction must now be made between the two kinds of analysis which have so far been coupled together. *Principal components analysis* replaces the original variables by a new set of the same number of uncorrelated components, with the leading ones accounting for relatively large shares of the original variance. *Factor analysis* does basically the same thing, except that it extracts fewer factors than the original number of variables' and leaves some variance accounted for by an error term. Factor analysis is more properly used as a test procedure, when there is some *a priori* expectation as to the number of underlying factors and their composition. Principal components analysis is used more often as an empirical procedure seeking related groups of variables, and as a method of data reduction or compression. In practice, both methods often give substantially the same results. Components analysis is used more frequently in geography than factor analysis, and is the usual technique in areal classification.

There are many variations of factor or components analysis, useful in specific research situations. A popular application in areal classification is the *varimax rotation*, whereby the axes are rotated about the origin in such a way that each of the original variables tends to load high on only one factor. This creates a relatively simple factor structure in which giving some empirical identity or name to the dimensions recognized is made easier, usually at the cost of some explanatory power because eigenvalues on leading factors can be reduced. An alternative to the usual orthogonal solution is an *oblique rotation*, in which the second and subsequent axes can be at angles other than 90° to the principal axis. This has the advantage of avoiding forcing the data into an orthogonal structure if oblique axes would provide a better fit. To understand the various types of analysis available requires reference to a specialist text such as those of Guertin and Bailey, Harman and Rummel (see Selected Reading).

After the factor or components analysis has been undertaken the process of areal classification can be set in motion. This begins with the calculation of *factor scores* for each area on each of the major dimensions identified. The basic formula is:

$$F_{jk} = \sum_{i=1}^{m} l_{ik} Z_{ij} \qquad [10.3]$$

where F_{jk} is the score of area j on factor k,
  i is one of the m original variables,
  l_{ik} is the loading of factor k on variable i,
and Z_{ij} is the original observation (in standard form) for variable i in area j.

Thus each variable contributes to the score on each factor in accordance with how it loads on (i.e. correlates with) that axis. Variations on this formula are often used, the most common being transformations into Z-scores and weighting by the eigenvalue.

The factor scores establish the position of each area in k-

dimensional statistical space, where k is the number of factors or components in use. The allocation of areas to classes is generally accomplished by a stepwise grouping procedure, in which the most similar pair of observations (i.e. those closest together in the k-space) are grouped, then the two next closest, and so on until a convenient number of classes has been established. Computers can produce an areal classification which is as near optimal as possible with reference to some objective such as minimizing within-group variance and maximizing between-group variance. If a regional system is required rather than an areal classification, a contiguity constraint can be imposed to ensure that only adjoining areas are grouped together. Simpler methods include basing areal classifications on maps of scores on the leading factors and grouping on only two sets of scores graphically; both are shown in examples below.

The various steps in the application of multifactor areal classification are summarized in Figure 10.5. The original or base data take the form of a matrix $m \times n$, where n is the number of observations or areas to be classified and m is the number of variables or criteria to be used. The data are transformed into standard scores (Z), and an $m \times m$ matrix of correlation coefficients is computed. The coefficients are usually product moment (r), but they can be rank correlations or even phi coefficients derived from dichotomous variables. The factor or components analysis then produces the matrix of loadings (l) on the m or less dimensions extracted (the number is arbitrary, but a common rule of thumb is to stop when the eigenvalues begin to fall below 1·0, or $100/m$ per cent of the variance in the original data accounted for). The loadings and the original data combine to generate the new areal scores (F), which are used in grouping and the final formation of a classification or regional system. This can become geographical knowledge at a high level of synthesis, when careful interpretation of the factor structure with the assistance of the original correlations is brought together with maps of the geographical patterns of factor scores and perhaps graphic displays of the grouping procedure.

Two examples are provided to demonstrate the application of

321

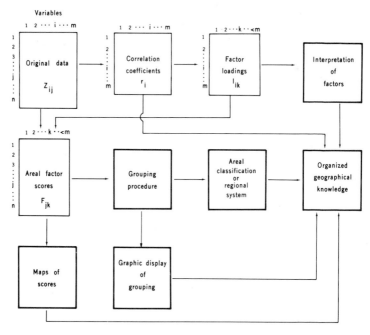

Figure 10.5   Stages in multifactor areal classification or regionalization
using factor analysis and related grouping methods.

this method. The first is a deliberately simplified case to clarify basic procedural questions. The second is a more sophisticated application to the development of areal social indicators – a problem for which the multifactor method is particularly suitable.

An Areal Classification Based on Industrial Employment

The first example reworks the data on the nine-sector subdivision of industrial employment in Greece used to show the cross-boundary similarity technique above (see Figure 10.3 and Table 10.1). These data are used for demonstration purposes only; a factor or components analysis requires more than nine variables for meaningful results. The 9×146 matrix of base data has been

Table 10.2: The Industrial Structure of Greece: Correlation Coefficients

Industry variable	1	2	3	4	5	6	7	8	9
1. Food etc.									
2. Textiles	−0·523								
3. Footwear etc.	−0·299	−0·228							
4. Wood etc.	−0·358	−0·157	0·115						
5. Paper etc.	−0·091	0·056	−0·084	−0·104					
6. Chemicals etc.	−0·050	0·007	−0·158	−0·118	0·008				
7. Non-metallic minerals	−0·292	0·147	−0·211	−0·050	−0·029	0·118			
8. Metal products etc.	−0·535	0·027	0·299	0·161	0·067	−0·031	0·208		
9. Other manufacturing	−0·236	−0·020	−0·081	0·134	0·038	0·111	−0·083	−0·150	

Source of data: B. Kayser and K. Thompson, *Economic and Social Atlas of Greece*, Centre of Economic Research, National Statistical Service and Social Sciences Centre, Athens, 1964.

subjected to a principal components analysis, the factors* first extracted being subsequently rotated according to the varimax criterion. The matrix of correlation coefficients on which the analysis was performed is shown in Table 10.2, which indicates relatively low levels of association between most of the industries. The factor analysis was reasonably effective in the circumstances, judged by data compression, for the two leading factors together account for just over 40 per cent of the original variance, and the next two raise the figure to 65 per cent.

The areal classification developed here is based on the first two factors alone, in order to make the example simple. Table 10.3 lists the loadings, together with communalities indicating the proportion of variance in each of the original variables accounted for by two factors together. The 'sum of squares' item in the first column of the table is the sum of the individual communalities, and for loadings it is the factor eigenvalue. The proportion of original variance accounted for by a factor is found by dividing the eigenvalue by m where m is the number of variables, and then multiplying by 100 to express it as a percentage.

The loadings indicate the structure or characteristics of the

---

* The term 'factor' tends to be used to denote the dimensions of variance extracted, irrespective of whether by factor or components analysis. Similarly, scores on these dimensions are usually called 'factor' scores.

Table 10.3: The Industrial Structure of Greece: Loadings on First Two
Factors

Industry variable	Communalities (Factors 1 and 2)	Loadings	
		Factor 1	Factor 2
1. Food etc	0·907	−0·809	−0·502
2. Textiles	0·541	0·149	0·720
3. Footwear etc	0·570	0·585	−0·477
4. Wood etc	0·368	0·541	−0·275
5. Paper etc	0·057	−0·019	0·238
6. Chemicals etc	0·186	−0·193	0·386
7. Non-metallic minerals	0·342	0·177	0·557
8. Metal products etc	0·591	0·762	0·100
9. Other manufacturing	0·094	−0·127	0·278
Total sum of squares	3·656	1·978	1·677
Proportion of variance accounted for (%)	40·6	22·0	18·6

Source of data: see Table 10.2.

dimensions which have been extracted. The interpretation and naming of the factors from the loadings is one of the most difficult aspects of this technique, and can involve considerable subjectivity. Table 10.3 shows that factor 1 has a very high negative loading on one variable – the food industries group – and a high positive loading on the metal products and machinery group. Food industries in Greece tend to be small-scale processing activities, while the metal industries are more representative of modern mechanized factory production. This factor thus appears to identify some aspect of the degree of contemporary industrialization. Factor 2 loads high only on textiles, which apart from the almost ubiquitous small-scale domestic production tends to be concentrated in the larger urban areas.

The next step is the calculation of factor scores for each eparchie. As expression [10.3] above indicates, the score for any area is obtained by combining the original data in Z-score form in proportions represented by the factor loadings. Thus an eparchie with high percentage employment in the food group will tend to get a high negative score on factor 1 because of the high negative loading on this variable, while an eparchie with a high proportion in metals, or in groups 3 and 4 which also have fairly high positive loadings, will tend to score high positively. Similarly the eparchies with high employment in the textiles group, or in non-metallic minerals (positive loading of 0·557), will have relatively high positive scores on factor 2.

The simplest way of arriving at an areal classification is to use scores on the first component only. These may be mapped, as in Figure 10.6, with classes established by mean and standard deviation, by quartiles, etc., or as in this case arbitrarily by the use of round figures. As the loadings suggest, this map is largely but not entirely a reflection of the employment patterns of the food and metals groups. High scores are concentrated in Macedonia and Thessaly, where the highest proportions in the metal industries are found, while the lowest (highest negative) scores pick out the nation's western and southern fringes, where food processing and in particular the production of olive oil dominates the industrial structure. In general, the industrial character is shown to change in a fairly regular manner from roughly north east to south west.

But this classification makes use of less than a quarter of the information provided by the original nine variables, for factor 1 accounts for only 22 per cent of the total variance. The inclusion of scores on factor 2 could raise the proportion to just over 40 per cent. The grouping of areas by scores on the two dimensions together can be done by plotting them both on a graph. Groups are formed in a stepwise manner, with the most similar pair of eparchies (as measured by linear distance on the graph) grouped together first and replaced by their mean centre, then the next two closest, and so on. (A full example of this method is described below.) In the present case the process was terminated when the 146 eparchies had almost all been reduced to five groups, to which were added a small number of isolated points on the graph not yet assigned to a group.

The five groups thus identified are mapped in Figure 10.7. A

325

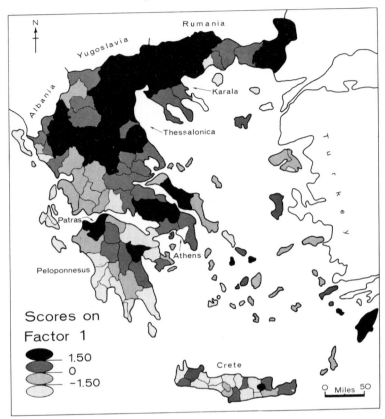

Figure 10.6   An areal classification of Greece, based on scores on the leading component extracted from industrial employment data by eparchies. (Source of data: see Figure 10.3.)

comparison with the previous map shows the effect of the introduction of the second set of scores. In Macedonia and parts of Thessaly and central Greece, group *A* tends to pick out the areas in which the metal industries are relatively well developed, with high scores on factor 1, while at the other end of the component 1 continuum group *E* finds the western and southern fringes where the food industries dominate the scene. Group *B* occupies an intermediate position with respect to factor 1. But the introduction of

326

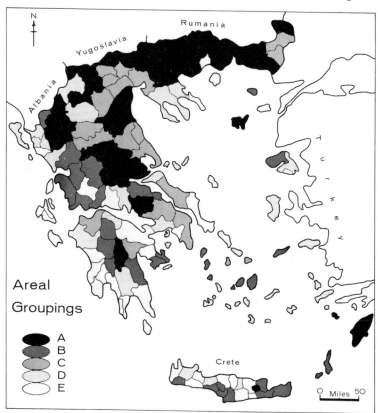

Figure 10.7   An areal classification of Greece, based on scores on the
two leading components extracted from eparchie
industrial employment data. (Source of data: see Figure
10.3.)

the second factor leads to a group *C*, which reflects the importance
of textile manufacturing in and around the cities of Thessalonica,
Larissa, Athens and Patras. Despite the absence of any contiguity
constraint in the formation of the groups, they do have a strong
element of geographical continuity, except in the case of group *D*.
This suggests that the industrial structure of Greece is quite uniform
over large areas.

327

The Regional Geography of Social Well-Being

The second example of multifactor areal classification addresses the problem of how the United States could be subdivided on the basis of the broad concept of social well-being.* Despite a growing interest in social aspects of areal differentiation, geography textbooks still largely confine themselves to physical and economic conditions in deriving systems of regions for the USA. To give adequate attention to the many facets of life which have a bearing on the well-being of society obviously requires masses of numerical information which is difficult to deal with by traditional methods of regional analysis. However, the multifactor technique offers a means by which underlying dimensions of areal variation can be extracted from a large data matrix and used in the identification of regions. Although demonstrated here in the context of social well-being, the technique can be just as effectively applied to the more traditional criteria of regional delimitation.

The first step is to establish an adequate definition of the guiding concept, a problem introduced in the first chapter of this book. Six general criteria of social well-being were arrived at from a survey of the literature, and these were further subdivided. Appropriate variables were then selected (see Table 10.4). The units of observation are the 48 contiguous states. The 47 variables selected are by no means a perfect representation of the concept of social well-being, which is in any event subject to value judgements, but they do get rather closer to the realities of life than is customary in traditional regional textbooks.

In Chapter 8 there was a discussion of a matrix of correlation coefficients between six social indicators and a general indicator (Table 8.9), derived from the data in the present example by summing standard scores. One indicator, representing social order or disorganization, seemed to be 'out of line' with the others, suggesting the existence of two major independent dimensions of

---

*This example is taken from a broader study: D. M. Smith, *The Geography of Social Well-being in the United States*, McGraw-Hill, 1973.

social well-being as a geographical variable. If this is so, it should be further clarified by principal components or factor analysis.

The technique used here to extract the leading dimensions of social well-being is the 'principal axis' solution. This tends to produce a first factor accounting for as high a proportion as possible of the original variance, and is a very effective method of data compression. The first factor in this case accounts for 38·56 per cent of the variance, and a second accounts for a further 13·74 per cent; subsequent factors are not considered here. The structure of the two leading dimensions, as revealed by the high-loading variables, is shown in Table 10.5. The first reflects variables representing all six of the major criteria of social well-being except for social order. Particularly prominent are conditions relating to poverty and affluence, with health and education also well represented. This dimension is therefore termed 'General Socio-Economic Well-Being'. It offers a very general and broadly defined indicator, in which high positive scores measure a good state of social well-being.

The second dimension is obviously associated with social order, which provides half the variables with loadings over 0·50; the prominence of venereal diseases, narcotics addiction and crime suggest the label 'Social Pathology'. This is basically the non-conforming indicator revealed by the correlations in Chapter 8. High positive scores clearly indicate poor conditions of social well-being on this component, as can be read from the signs on the loadings.

The geographical pattern of inter-state variations in social well-being may now be considered, through maps of the scores. The most prominent feature of the pattern of General Socio-Economic Well-Being (Figure 10.8) is the concentration of high negative (i.e. 'bad') scores in the South, in a belt running from Texas to the Virginias. Areas of relatively high positive (i.e. 'good') scores are found in the central mountain and western states, in the upper midwest, and in the eastern end of the major manufacturing belt. Parts of the south west, the plains, most of the manufacturing belt, the upper mountain states, northern New England and Florida all occupy intermediate positions. The highest state score (positive)

329

Patterns in Human Geography

Table 10.4: Criteria of Social Well-Being, and Variables Used in State State Analysis

Criteria and Variables	Direction of correlation with Social Well-Being
I Income, Wealth and Employment	
i *Income and Wealth*	
1 Per capita annual income ($) 1968	+
2 Families with annual income less than $3,000 (%) 1959	−
3 Total bank deposits per capita ($) 1968	+
ii *Employment Status*	
4 Public assistance recipients (% population) 1964	−
5 Union members per 1,000 non-agricultural employees 1966	+
6 White-collar employees (% of total) 1960	+
iii *Income Supplements*	
7 Average monthly benefit for retired workers ($) 1968	+
8 Average monthly AFDC payments per family ($) 1968	+
9 Average monthly aid to the disabled ($) 1968	+
10 Average monthly old age assistance ($) 1968	+
11 Average weekly state unemployment benefit ($) 1968	+
II The Environment	
i *Housing*	
12 Median value of owner-occupied houses ($) 1960	+
13 Houses dilapidated or lacking complete plumbing (%) 1960	−
14 Index of home equipment (max. = 600) 1960	+
III Health	
i *Physical Health*	
15 Households with poor diets (%) 1965	−
16 Infant deaths per 10,000 live births 1967	−
17 Tuberculosis deaths per million population 1967	−
18 Hospital expenses per patient day ($) 1965	+
ii *Access to Medical Care*	
19 Hospital beds per 10,000 population 1967	+
20 Physicians per 10,000 population 1967	+
21 Dentists per 10,000 population 1967	+
22 Persons covered by hospital health insurance (%) 1965	+
iii *Mental Health*	
23 Residents in mental hospitals etc per 100,000 population 1966	−
24 Patient days in mental hospitals per 1,000 population 1965	−
25 Mental hospital expenditures per patient day ($) 1965	+

330

Table 10.4: continued

IV Education

  i *Achievement*

    26 Illiterates per 1,000 population 1960   −

    27 Draftees failing armed services mental test (%) 1968   −

  ii *Duration*

    28 Median school years completed (×10) 1960   +

    29 Persons attended college per 1,000 population aged 25

            or over 1960   +

  iii *Level of Service*

    30 Pupils per teacher 1968   −

    31 Public school expenditures per pupil ($) 1967   +

V Social Disorganization

  i *Personal Pathologies*

    32 Alcoholics per 10,000 adults 1970   −

    33 Narcotics addicts per 10,000 population 1970   −

    34 Gonorrhoea cases per 100,000 population 1970   −

    35 Syphilis cases per million population 1970   −

    36 Suicides per million population 1967   −

  ii *Family Breakdown*

    37 Divorces 1966 per 1,000 marriages 1968   −

    38 Husband and wife households (% of total) 1966   +

  iii *Crime and Safety*

    39 Crimes of violence per 100,000 population 1969   −

    40 Crimes against property per 10,000 population 1969   −

    41 Motor vehicle accident deaths per million population 1967   −

VI Alienation and Participation

  i *Democratic Participation*

    42 Eligible voters voting (%) 1964   +

    43 Registered voters per 100 population of voting age 1968   +

  ii *Criminal Justice*

    44 Jail inmates not convicted (%) 1970   −

    45 Population per lawyer 1966   −

  iii *Racial Segregation*

    46 Negroes in schools at least 95% negro 1968   −

    47 City residential segregation index (max.=100) 1960   −

Sources of data: see D. M. Smith, *The Geography of Social Well-being in the United States,* McGraw-Hill, 1973.

Patterns in Human Geography

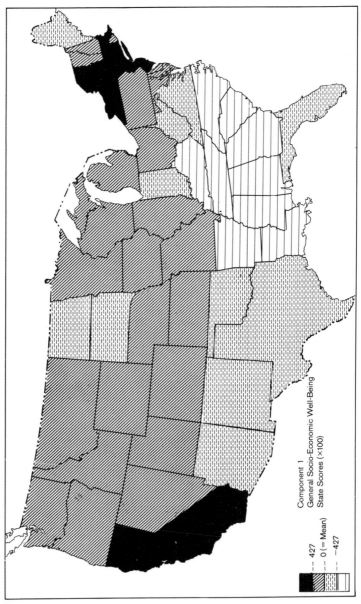

Component 1
General Socio-Economic Well-Being
State Scores (×100)

427
0 (= Mean)
−427

Figure 10.8   Scores on the leading component of social well-being
in the United States; see text for explanation. (Source:
D. M. Smith, *The Geography of Social Well-being in
the United States*, McGraw-Hill, 1973.)

*Table 10.5: Structure of Two Leading Components of Social Well-Being
at the State Level in the United States*

Component 1: *General Socio-Economic Well-Being*
(explained variance: 38·56%)
highest loadings: −0·9398 families with less than $3,000
                  −0·9083 houses dilapidated etc
                   0·8951 benefit for retired workers
                   0·8853 per capita income
                   0·8651 dentists/10,000 population
                   0·8556 AFDC payments
                   0·8086 state unemployment benefit
                   0·8065 value of owner-occupied houses
                  −0·7993 households with poor diets
                  −0·7993 infant deaths
                   0·7868 public school expenditures
                  −0·7834 mental test failures
                   0·7780 eligible voters voting
                   0·7749 white-collar employees
                   0·7615 physicians/10,000 population
                   0·7587 median school years completed

Component 2: *Social Pathology* (explained variance: 13·74%)
highest loadings: 0·8384 crimes of violence
                    0·7236 syphilis cases
                    0·6719 gonorrhoea cases
                    0·6528 narcotics addicts
                    0·6422 school segregation
                   −0·6325 registered voters
                    0·6043 crimes against property
                    0·5517 illiteracy
                    0·5413 tuberculosis deaths
                   −0·5329 index of home equipment

Source: D. M. Smith, *The Geography of Social Well-being in the
United States*, McGraw-Hill, 1973.

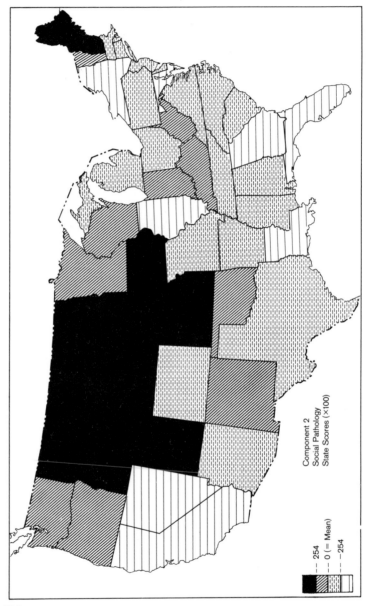

Component 2
Social Pathology
State Scores (×100)

254

0 (= Mean)

−254

Figure 10.9   Scores on the second component of social well-being
in the United States. (Source: see Figure 10.8.)

is in New York, followed by Connecticut, Massachusetts and California, while the highest negative is in Mississippi followed by South Carolina, Alabama and Arkansas.

Scores on Social Pathology (Figure 10.9) show a continuous belt of negative (i.e. below average) states extending from California and Nevada in the west, through the South, and up to New York and southern New England. The highest negative scores are in New York and California – two of the highest positive states on component 1 – followed by Louisiana, Nevada and Florida. These are all states with major cities containing populations subject to a high incidence of certain social problems. Positive scores appear in a belt from the north west to the upper midwest, in three New England states, and in Indiana–Kentucky–West Virginia. The highest positive scores, indicating lowest incidence of social pathologies, are in the Dakotas, Idaho and Iowa – farming states without urban concentrations.

Now an attempt can be made to classify the states on the basis of their performance on these two social indicators. The grouping is shown graphically in Figure 10.10, and Figure 10.11 illustrates a 'linkage tree' of the kind often used to demonstrate the formation of the groups. The step-by-step procedure can be followed by comparing these two diagrams; first the two closest (i.e. most similar) states of Minnesota and Wisconsin are grouped, then the next two, and so on. The grouping was terminated with the formation of the four shown in Figure 10.10, each of which occupies its own place in the two-dimensional social well-being 'space' represented by the graph. Group *A* includes states with relatively good performance on both General Socio-Economic Well-Being and Social Pathology; all have positive scores on the latter and all but three are above average on the former. States in group *B* do better on General Socio-Economic Well-Being than on Social Pathology; they tend to be highly urban and industrial compared to the general rural agricultural character of those in *A*, which occupy roughly the same position as *B* on the good to bad

335

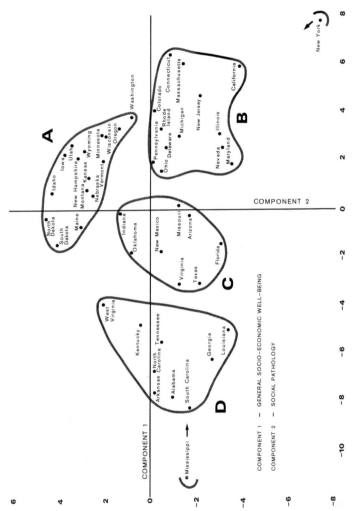

Figure 10.10 Grouping of states, based on scores on the two leading components of social well-being. (Source: see Figure 10.8.)

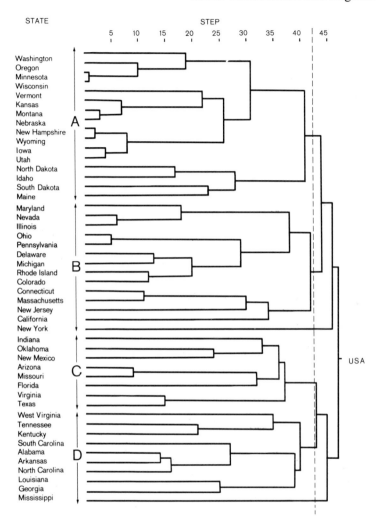

Figure 10.11   Steps in the grouping of states on the basis of scores
on the two leading components of social well-being, as
shown in Figure 10.10.

337

(i.e. top right to bottom left) continuum of social well-being. Group C is clearly worse off than A and B with respect to General Socio-Economic Well-Being, but on average slightly better than B though obviously worse than A on Social Pathology. Group D is very similar to C on Social Pathology, but markedly worse on General Socio-Economic Well-Being.

Membership of these four groups is mapped in Figure 10.12. Although no contiguity constraint was used in the grouping, a number of clear belts have emerged. The members of group A form a continuous belt from the Pacific north west to the Great Lakes, with an outlier in New England. At the other end of the continuum, the members of group D form a compact block in the South. Group C comprises five contiguous states, with the outlying members of Indiana, Virginia and Florida to the east. Group B has its main concentration in the major manufacturing belt, with outliers in Colorado and California–Nevada. The clear impression is of a core area of low social well-being in the South, a belt of high social well-being extending across the north of the country from coast to coast, and an intermediate or transitional zone separating them both geographically and socially. The regional homogeneity is interrupted only in the belt from Missouri to Maryland, where three of the four groups are represented.

The application of modern methods of multifactor areal classification to data on a wide range of human conditions thus reveals a pattern of regional differentiation different from those usually described in textbooks on the geography of North America. In clearly recognizing what may be called 'the Southern Region of Social Deprivation', the state classification here identifies an important piece of geographical reality which is often overlooked. The South has low levels of social well-being on most criteria, and it is this which distinguishes it from other regions rather than the old cotton belt with which it is still sometimes associated in textbooks. Moving away from the South social well-being generally improves at this broad state level. The division of the nation into the three major regions which emerge from this analysis thus appears to capture the essence of inter-state variations in social well-being.

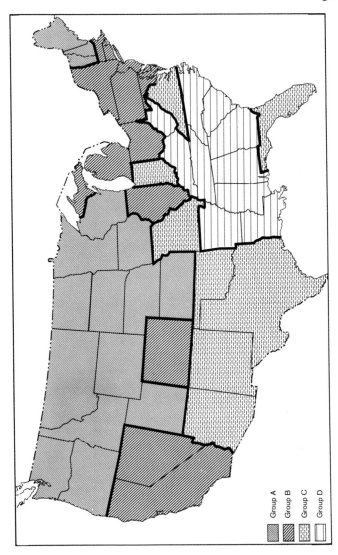

Figure 10.12   Membership of state groups arrived at by multifactor
classification: 'regions' of social well-being. (Source:
see Figure 10.8.)

The Identification of 'Problem' Areas and Regions

The multifactor approach to areal classification has some useful applications in the realm of public policy as well as in a more strictly academic context. With the capacity to develop territorial indicators of social well-being from data on a wide range of criteria, it can be used to identify 'problem' areas or regions for planning purposes. This can be particularly helpful when it is required to define areas for public investment or some remedial programme on the basis of the broadest possible definition of social well-being, poverty, economic health, or whatever the condition of concern might be.

The inter-state analysis of the United States summarized above can provide an example. If it was required to identify regional levels of 'social performance' or some such concept, the sets of state scores on the two leading components could both be interpreted as general social indicators. Both measure major dimensions of social well-being, and can be viewed normatively in the sense that scores at one end of the scale indicate a most desirable state of affairs while at the other end a most undesirable situation is identified. Each of the states was given a position on an interval scale representing a 'good' to 'bad' continuum. These figures permit fairly precise definition of America's major problem region, where many people (especially blacks) live in poverty.

But geographical units as large as American states are not really suitable for the definition of problem areas or regions. They have too much internal heterogeneity hidden in the averages, which in some states are largely a reflection of single major cities. In the USA much research has been done at the county level to identify areas of social or economic distress more exactly. This is an obvious application for multifactor areal classification, and a number of studies of this kind aimed at developing local indicators of 'economic health' have been undertaken.

A similar example from Britain may be described briefly. The North West is a major industrial region with adjustment problems arising from the decline of the old cotton industry; within it some

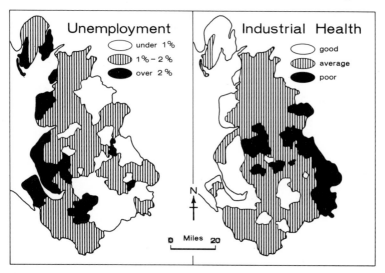

Figure 10.13 Two approaches to the identification of problem areas in North West England. (Sources of data: see D. M. Smith, 'Identifying the "Grey" Areas: A Multivariate Approach', *Regional Studies*, 2, 1968.)

areas have remained quite prosperous while others have been very seriously affected by changing economic conditions. In the design of public policy aimed at regional economic revival the identification and delimitation of the problem areas is a matter of great practical importance, providing obvious scope for the application of the geographer's new skills in areal classification.

Areas of economic deprivation can be identified in many different ways: two of these for North West England are shown in Figure 10.13. The left-hand map is based on the conventional criterion of percentage unemployment, and suggests that the problem areas are mainly along the coastal strip including Merseyside. By comparison, most of the eastern part of the region is apparently well off, with very low unemployment. The other map is based on a multifactor analysis of fourteen variables relating to industrial health, listed in Table 10.6. The pattern revealed by grouping on

Table 10.6: Fourteen Criteria of Industrial Health Used to Identify 'Problem' Areas in North West England

1. Changes in industrial employment 1959–65 (% per year)
2. Changes in industrial employment 1953–65 (% per year)
3. Changes in service employment 1953–65 (% per year)
4. Changes in total employment 1953–65 (% per year)
5. Industrial floor space built 1960–65 (square feet per industrial worker in 1959)
6. Index of structural change 1953–65
7. Average monthly unemployment 1966 (% insured employees)
8. Index of unemployment variability 1966 (highest month ÷ lowest month)
9. Females employed in industry 1965 (% of all employees)
10. Industrial employees 1965 (% of all employees)
11. Employment in engineering and metal industries 1965 (% of all industrial employees)
12. Employment in textile and clothing industries 1965 (% of all industrial employees)
13. Coefficient of industrial specialization 1965
14. Structural change in industrial employment 1953–65 (% industrial employees in 1953)

Source: D. M. Smith, *Industrial Britain: The North West*, David & Charles, 1969.

factor scores is quite different from the one suggested by unemployment, and focuses on the unsatisfactory state of the economy in the old cotton-manufacturing towns along the southeastern fringe of the region and in the coalmining area to the west. These are the areas in which the decline of the traditional industries has created serious problems of economic readjustment in the postwar years.

The reasons for the difference between these two maps has quite important public policy implications. Local economic stagnation is not necessarily accompanied by high unemployment in a reasonably prosperous nation, for people may simply move to jobs elsewhere, or leave the labour market altogether if they are women. This is what has happened in many of the Lancashire cotton and coal towns, and it helps to explain why unemployment is so low. Complementary to this, social conditions, such as a tradition of casual employment in the Liverpool docks and the seasonal nature of many jobs in the coastal resorts, contribute to the relatively high unemployment in some western parts of the region which seem prosperous by other criteria. By for so long concentrating their incentives for new industrial development on areas of high recorded unemployment, in particular the Merseyside conurbation, the government may have overlooked the problems of other parts of the region. This example helps to emphasize that single criteria may not be good measures of broad concepts like industrial or economic well-being, and that in isolation they may provide an incomplete and possibly misleading basis for the identification of problem areas. Definitions based on the examination of a wider range of variables provide a better basis for public policy involving large expenditures of money. The essence of the problem is to conceptualize the cause for concern, define it precisely, and then seek some accurate measurements.

The main criticism of the 'economic health' application of the multifactor approach to areal classification, as frequently conducted in the 1960s, is the restrictive nature of the concept. As a framework for the diagnosis of some unsatisfactory state of human affairs, a broader concept such as 'social health' or general social well-being would seem more appropriate. Improving economic health is a means to an end, not an end in itself. To concentrate on economic criteria in problem area identification for public policy carries with it the danger of overlooking more basic social ills.

The same general reservation is true of the multifactor areal classification approach as applied in 'factorial ecology' studies within individual cities. These have often been confined to easily accessible census variables, which means that demographic and 'socio-economic' conditions have often been given much greater weight than social problems. But the multifactor approach can accommodate all manner of variables if the data are available. The onus is on the user to make sure that the selection of variables is appropriate to the problem at hand, and that all relevant conditions are measured as far as possible.

As a final example, the identification of problem areas in a city may be demonstrated using Tampa, Florida. Like most major cities in America, Tampa has its ghetto area of slums and asso-

343

ciated social deprivation. In connection with the Model Cities programme initiated to improve conditions in the poor areas, a study was undertaken to develop some social indicators which could be used in defining urban problem areas. The spatial frame of reference was 71 census tracts, and the data were observations on almost fifty variables. The choice of variables was guided by the general concept of social well-being, and the major criteria and some of the individual measures used were the same as in the inter-state study summarized above.*

The data were subjected to a factor analysis. Four leading factors were extracted, and given the following names: Social Problems (17·8 per cent of variance accounted for), Socio-Economic Status (11·3), Racial Segregation (9·5), and Social Deprivation (8·3). Census tract scores (standardized) were calculated on each of these factors in such a way that in each case high positive scores could be interpreted as 'good' and high negative scores as 'bad'.

Problem areas may be identified by these scores. In Figure 10.14 tracts with scores worse than one standard deviation below the mean are mapped by the technique of superimposition of different types of shading illustrated earlier in this book (Figures 2.8 and 5.2). This method shows that the areas of worst performance on each of the four indicators generally coincide fairly closely. From this map a line could be drawn round the problem areas of the city with great confidence that this included the areas where social (and economic) well-being are at their lowest, by the criterion used in the analysis. The 'target areas' identified for planning purposes in Tampa in fact correspond very closely with the problem areas shown on this map.

These examples of problem area identification, together with the applications earlier in this chapter, should be sufficient to demonstrate the very considerable potential of factor analysis and the associated grouping techniques as means of describing areal

---

* Further particulars of the variables and results of this study, with the relevant background, will be found in D. M. Smith, *The Geography of Social Well-being in the United States*, McGraw-Hill, 1973, Chapter 9. The assistance of Mr Robert Gray in this project is gratefully acknowledged.

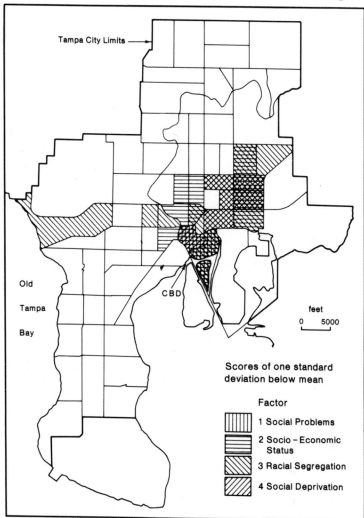

Tampa City Limits →

Old

Tampa

Bay

CBD

feet

0   5000

Scores of one standard
deviation below mean

Factor

1 Social Problems

2 Socio – Economic
  Status

3 Racial Segregation

4 Social Deprivation

Figure 10.14   Problem areas in the city of Tampa, Florida, based on
scores on four social well-being factors. (Source of
data: D. M. Smith and R. J. Gray, *Social Indicators for
Tampa, Florida*, Urban Studies Bureau, University of
Florida, 1972.)

345

variations in the nature and quality of human existence. They represent one of the highest orders of geographical synthesis yet devised. But it would be wrong to conclude without a warning again. Factor analysis is a highly sophisticated statistical procedure designed to reduce the complexity of multivariate problems, but, contrary to some expectations, it cannot perform magic. For example, if the initial data comprise a set of variables with a very low degree of intercorrelation, factor analysis will be unable to identify a small number of basic dimensions which can be substituted for the original with little loss of information. If the spatial patterns adopted by the data are obvious from the beginning, then the results of a multifactor areal classification may do little more than state the obvious.

One of the problems of the multifactor approach to areal classification is, paradoxically, the ease with which it can be carried out. Given an efficient computer system and some assistance with preparation of data input, a researcher could begin a day's work by extracting figures on a couple of dozen variables from the census, and end the day with a computer print-out of the factor loadings, scores, and even the linkage tree of step-by-step areal grouping. As a consequence, these techniques have been applied rather indiscriminately, particularly with respect to the choice of variables in the initial data matrix. To go beyond readily available data may involve more time and effort than the researcher is prepared to give the project, yet what is easily measured may reflect the reality of the problem imperfectly and incompletely. As long as the data are in the correct form and the computer is properly programmed some results will appear, and if sufficient care and skill is not exercised at the start the outcome may well exemplify the guiding axiom of quantitative analysis: 'garbage in, garbage out'. The grander the technique, the more important it is that the research problem should be carefully conceptualized, and that the variables chosen should be appropriate and accurately measured. Properly conducted, multifactor regionalization can lead to a high order of geographical description and point the way to real understanding; with poor conceptual guidance and inadequate data, the results may be meaningless.

Epilogue: On Patterns, Processes and Problems

A book on numerical methods inevitably immerses the reader in a mass of details. Before concluding, it may help to step back briefly from the numbers and equations, to consider some of the broader implications of the quantitative approach to human geography. These are matters which can be easily lost sight of in the preoccupation with techniques.

Great emphasis has been placed on the measurement of *location patterns* or *areal distributions* as a focal point of contemporary human geography. It has been shown that these patterns can be summarized in various ways, compared with one another, and ultimately used in the traditional process of regional synthesis. But what is actually achieved by more accurate description of the manner in which man arranges life on the surface of the earth? We may have been able to satisfy curiosity by reducing complex patterns to the simpler form of an equation, index or distribution map, and thus imposing intellectual order on the chaos of the world as we observe it. But where does this lead us? We may have a clearer impression of the way things are, but do we necessarily understand better why they are that way? And do we have any new visions as to how they ought to be?

A full discussion of such essentially philosophical issues is obviously beyond the scope of a book of this kind. But raising them briefly here should at least serve as a reminder that observing and measuring geographical patterns has limitations. To advance our understanding and promote human betterment, precise numerical description may be a necessary step, but in itself it is not sufficient to ensure that the end is attained.

The distinction between description and explanation has been stressed a number of times in the previous pages. A critical question in geography is the extent to which pattern might suggest process, or the links of cause and effect which lead things to be as they are. To identify and describe a pattern is not necessarily to know the process at work. The nature of a pattern might imply something of the process – that it makes for dispersal or concentration, or that it leads to regularity of spatial arrangement rather than clustering or randomness. But a nearest neighbour statistic, a centrographic measure or a trend surface equation explains nothing in itself. Only when these are set in a wider context can they contribute to the understanding of process.

Working from description towards explanation involves something more than the application of numerical methods of the kind reviewed in this book. It also requires some understanding of the way in which explanations are sought in the social sciences and the routes to understanding which others such as philosophers and logicians have found effective. David Harvey's *Explanation in Geography* is an obvious place to begin acquiring this kind of knowledge, supplemented by readings on the conduct of inquiry in the social or behavioural sciences at large. Some statistics texts provide limited background of this kind, but too often it is confined to an abstract account of the testing of statistical hypotheses without any reference to how these originate. To use quantitative techniques in a constructive and creative way it is necessary for them to be set within a research project carefully designed with a specific explanatory problem in mind. Employed in isolation, they achieve little. This book has been able to demonstrate a range of techniques and show something of the circumstances in which they are appropriate descriptive devices, but to make sound decisions on just when and how to apply a particular technique requires reference to the wider research context.

Explanation must begin with some hunches about the process at work, if only to narrow the choice of conditions to be observed. If an idea concerning cause and effect is based on a well-developed body of theory, or on previous research findings which have already revealed some capacity to account for reality, then plausible relationships between interconnected sets of conditions may be expressed quite precisely as expectations to be tested. From this it may be possible to deduce the geographical pattern which should be found if the hypothesized process actually operates, and then compare it with reality. Description in human geography perhaps achieves its highest scientific purpose when the discovery of a particular spatial pattern logically verifies some causal process thought to be at work, in a test of an observed pattern against a theoretical expectation. A fuller understanding is more likely to be advanced in this way than by attempts to infer process directly from pattern without the guidance of theory. Valuable contributions may emerge from the more empirical approach of taking observations on patterns which simply arouse curiosity and then using correlation analysis as a search for spatial associations, but such findings gain their real strength when related to other facts in a body of theory. Description thus occupies an important place in the continuing interplay between theory and observed reality.

But what is it that we should try to understand? What are the *fundamental* problems, the solution of which would be rightly regarded as a major advance in geographical learning or an important geographical contribution to knowledge in general? Much of the energy of the 'Quantitative Revolution' in geography was expended on the development and demonstration of techniques, with the general significance of the research problems often relegated to secondary importance. At times there was a danger of quantitative analysis becoming an end in itself, as geography was carried away by its newly found numerical dexterity. There has also been a perhaps unwarranted selectivity in the application of the quantitative approaches. In human geography the emphasis has been on the location of economic activity and on urban geography, while for example historical geography has received relatively little attention despite the wealth of numerical data in early census volumes. Basic social problems have generally attracted less interest than such narrow but highly fashionable topics as the diffusion of innovation and the analysis of point patterns. Indeed, it sometimes appeared that certain aspects of human geography have become popular fields of research more by virtue of convenient numerical data allied to particular techniques or an efficient computer program, than because they are fundamental to man's existence.

Epilogue

Now that the 'new' geography of the 1960s has become firmly established, it is time to pause for reflection. Questions are being asked about the 'significance' or 'relevance' of much work in the quantitative mould. Human geography has for a long time had its applied aspect – research connected with regional development problems, urban planning, and the like – as well as a deep concern with man's use or abuse of his natural resources. And the current public interest in environmental problems such as air and water pollution has provided special scope in recent years for practical research at the interface of human and physical geography. But there are many contemporary social issues with a strong geographical component which have been largely neglected until very recently, obvious examples being poverty, crime and other aspects of social deviance, and physical and mental health. The fact that these are matters of great social concern is leading to some vigorous questioning of the 'relevance' of contemporary geography, particularly in the United States, accompanied by a call for more professional involvement in the search for solutions to the problems of society. Many of the techniques of quantitative geography have already been applied to practical problems, but the kind of results which they produce may not always be what the planners or other public servants need. Such approaches to applied research may occasionally degenerate into just another demonstration of technical skill, which may impress for a while but which ultimately contributes little to the solution of real human problems. At a time when some geographers are saying that the 'Quantitative Revolution' has run its course, it is still often difficult to find convincing applications of many numerical methods in a context where some policy question in the spatial planning of human activity has been answered convincingly.

Although demonstration of the social relevance of numerical analysis in human geography has not been a primary aim of this book, the issue has not been entirely avoided. The description of spatial dimensions of contemporary societal problems such as regional poverty and the quality of urban life, which have featured in some of the examples, can contribute to their understanding and ultimately to the design of plans for their solution. In other examples of the application of particular techniques it has been

350

shown that such matters as crime, health, and general social well-being provide just as much grist to the quantitative mill as more conventional aspects of economic and urban geography. In particular, discussion of the development of *territorial social indicators* in a number of chapters should help to reveal the very great potential that exists for basic descriptive research on geographical variations in the quality of human existence. To 'quantify quality' seems an appropriate challenge to place before the geographer with skills in numerical methods. It is a necessary preliminary to improving the quality of life, and to reducing the spatial inequalities which are increasingly becoming matters of social concern.

The point has now been reached at which some knowledge of numerical methods and some degree of operational competence can be assumed in most people with a university degree in geography. That this is so, and that the present book is a review of existing techniques rather than offering a new set of tools, is due to the pioneers of the 1950s and 1960s who built new courses, wrote the first quantitative texts and conducted the basic research. By broad if not universal consensus, the development and demonstration of new techniques represented the highest professional achievement in geography during the past decade – a necessary phase for a discipline which had tended to lag behind other social sciences in the sophistication of its methodology and research design. The foundations were thus laid for a new geography, with a new professional paradigm and perhaps greater status within the scholastic world. But now there is another challenge to be met. As the geography of the 1970s emerges from its preoccupation with numerical techniques and enters what promises to be a more applied phase, fresh demands are being placed on the subject and new opportunities are being offered. The time is ripe for widespread demonstrations that the quantitative and model-building approach to human geography has a capacity to shed light on problems of great contemporary importance, and to help guide society towards their solution. It is in the ability to select the 'significant' problems from the trivial, and to distinguish the research tasks of real social relevance from those with only narrow academic interest, that the work of the next decade of geography should be judged.

Selected Reading

The following list, arranged by chapters, offers references on technical matters and on a selection of applications of the methods introduced in the text. The list is far from comprehensive, and readers should consult recent issues of major geographical journals for further examples and for the latest developments in quantitative human geography.

1. Compiling Geographical Information

CONTEMPORARY HUMAN GEOGRAPHY

Abler, R., Adams, J. S., and Gould, P., *Spatial Organisation: The Geographer's View of the World,* Prentice Hall, Englewood Cliffs, N.J., 1971, Chs. 1–4. (On science, geography and measurement.)

Bunge, W., *Theoretical Geography*, Lund Studies in Geography, Series C, No. 1, Gleerups, Lund, 1962. (Pioneer work in contemporary geography.)

Chorley, R. J., and Haggett, P. (eds.), *Models in Geography*, Methuen, London, 1967. (Extensive review of models and quantitative methods.)

Haggett, P., *Locational Analysis in Human Geography*, Edward Arnold, London, 1965. (First textbook on analytical human geography.)

Haggett, P., *Geography: A Modern Synthesis*, Harper & Row, New York, 1972. (An introduction to geography from a contemporary perspective.)

Harvey, D., *Explanation in Geography*, Edward Arnold, London, 1969. (Review of the conduct of inquiry in geography; Part V especially relevant to observation and measurement.)

Smith, D. M., *Industrial Location: An Economic Geographical Analysis*, John Wiley, New York, 1971, Ch. 9. (An introduction to the use of models in location analysis.)

Smith, D. M., *The Geography of Social Well-being in the United States*, McGraw-Hill, New York, 1973, Chs. 5 and 6. (The operational definition of an abstract concept.)

Selected Reading

STATISTICS AND QUANTITATIVE GEOGRAPHY

Berry, B. J. L., 'Approaches to Regional Analysis: A Synthesis', *Annals*, Association of American Geographers, 54, 1964, 2–11. (The geographical data matrix.)

Berry, B. J. L., and Marble, D. F. (eds.), *Spatial Analysis: A Reader in Statistical Geography*, Prentice Hall, Englewood Cliffs, N.J., 1968. (Background material and selected applications.)

Cole, J. P., and King, C. A. M., *Quantitative Geography*, John Wiley, London, 1968, Chs. 1–3. (Introduction to geography, mathematics and statistics.)

Duncan, O. D., Cuzzort, R. P., and Duncan, B., *Statistical Geography: Problems in Analysing Areal Data*, Free Press, New York, 1961, Ch. 3. (Difficulties of using geographical numerical data.)

Garrison, W. L., and Marble, D. F. (eds.), *Quantitative Geography, Part I: Economic and Cultural Topics*, Northwestern University, Studies in Geography No. 13, Evanston, Ill., 1967. (Selected applications.)

Greer-Wootten, B., *A Bibliography of Statistical Applications in Geography*, Association of American Geographers, Technical Paper No. 9, Washington, D.C., 1972. (Comprehensive bibliography with commentary; pp. 14–23 deal with the content of this chapter.)

Gregory, S., *Statistical Methods and the Geographer*, Longmans, London, 1968 (2nd edition). (General introduction to statistics for geographers.)

Hammond, R. and McCullogh, P. S., *Quantitative Techniques in Geography: An Introduction*, Clarendon Press, Oxford, 1974. (Introductory text for students with no mathematics but quite rigorous.)

King, L. J., *Statistical Analysis in Geography*, Prentice Hall, Englewood Cliffs, N.J., 1969. (Advanced text; Ch. 1 especially relevant to discussion of numerical data in geography.)

Kolstoe, R. H., *Introduction to Statistics for the Behavioral Sciences*, Dorsey Press, Homewood, Ill., 1969, Chs. 1–3. (Organizing data and using numbers in measurement.)

Lordahl, D. S., *Modern Statistics for Behavioral Sciences*, Ronald Press, New York, 1967, Ch. 1. (Introduction to numerical and statistical concepts.)

Theakstone, W. H., and Harrison, C., *The Analysis of Geographical Data*, Heinemann, London, 1970. (Brief elementary treatment.)

Yeates, M. H., *An Introduction to Quantitative Analysis in Economic Geography*, McGraw-Hill, New York, 1968. (Review and illustration of a wide range of applications.)

Selected Reading

Yeates, M. H., *An Introduction to Quantitative Analysis in Human Geography*, McGraw-Hill, New York, 1974. (Substantially revised and extended version of Yeates, 1968.)

2. Mapping Numerical Information
TECHNIQUES

Abler, R., Adams, J. S., and Gould, P., *Spatial Organization*, op. cit., pp. 72–82. (Relative space and cartograms.)

Board, C., 'Maps as Models', in R. J. Chorley and P. Haggett (eds.), *Models in Geography*, op. cit., Ch. 16. (General review from a contemporary perspective with extensive bibliography.)

Cole, J. P., and King, C. A. M., *Quantitative Geography*, op. cit., pp. 218–25. (Topology and map transformations.)

Dickinson, G. C., *Statistical Mapping and the Presentation of Statistics*, Edward Arnold, London, 1963. (General introductory treatment.)

Haggett, P., *Locational Analysis in Human Geography*, op. cit., Ch. 8, pp. 211–27. (Maps as descriptive devices in human geography.)

Harvey, D., *Explanation in Geography*, op. cit., pp. 219–23. (Projective geometry and transformations.) See also pp. 369–76. (Maps.)

Jenks, G. F., 'Generalisation in Statistical Mapping', *Annals*, Association of American Geographers, 53, 1963, pp. 15–26. (Discussion and illustration of techniques.)

Mackay, J. R., 'Some Problems and Techniques in Isopleth Mapping', *Economic Geography*, 27, 1951, pp. 1–9. (Classic paper on technique.)

Monkhouse, F. J., and Wilkinson, H. R., *Maps and Diagrams*, Methuen, London, 1964 (2nd edition). (Comprehensive text on cartographic methods.)

Muehrcke, P., *Thematic Cartography*, Commission on College Geography, Resource Paper No. 19, Association of American Geographers, Washington, D.C., 1972. (Review of data collection and mapping, including computer applications.)

Peucker, T. K., *Computer Cartography*, Resource Paper No. 17, Commission on College Geography, Association of American Geographers, Washington, D.C., 1972. (Thorough and up-to-date survey, full of examples.)

Robinson, A. H., *Elements of Cartography*, John Wiley, New York, 1960. (Standard textbook.)

Tobler, W. R., 'Geographic Area and Map Projections', *Geographical Review*, 53, 1963, pp. 59–78. (Cartograms and projections.)

Tobler, W. R., *Numerical Map Generalisation*, Discussion Paper No. 8,

Selected Reading

1966, Michigan Inter-University Community of Mathematical Geo-graphers. (Theoretical aspects.)

APPLICATIONS

Bashur, R. L., Shannon, G. W., and Metzer, C. A., 'The Application of Three-Dimensional Analogue Models to the Distribution of Medical Care Facilities', *Medical Care*, 8, 1970, pp. 395–407. (Examples of three-dimensional diagrams and maps generated by digital plotter.)

Johnston, B. L. C., 'The Distribution of Factory Population in the West Midlands Conurbation', *Transactions and Papers*, Institute of British Geographers, 25, 1958, 209–23. (Early application of quadrat mapping.)

Jones, E., and Sinclair, D. J., *Atlas of the London Region*, Pergamon Press, Oxford, 1968, Maps 43–7. (Quadrat mapping of land use and industrial data.)

Kingsbury, R. C., *An Atlas of Indiana*, Occasional Publication No. 5, Dept. of Geography, Indiana University, Bloomington, Ind., 1970. (Extensive use of computer maps.)

Lloyd, P. E., 'Industrial Changes in the Merseyside Development Area 1949–1959', *Town Planning Review*, 35, pp. 285–98. (Quadrat arrangement of industrial data.)

Rosing, K. E., and Wood, P. A., *Character of a Conurbation: A Computer Atlas of Birmingham and the Black Country*, University of London Press, 1971. (Major application of computer cartography.)

Smith, D. M., *Industrial Location: An Economic Geographical Analysis*, op. cit. (Examples of plotting industrial cost surfaces by computer mapping.)

Note: The more conventional methods of mapping numerical data can be found (used well or otherwise) in most geography textbooks and atlases.

3. Summarizing Sets of Observations

TECHNICAL

Gregory, S., *Statistical Methods and the Geographer*, op. cit., Chs. 1–7. (Review of descriptive and inferential statistics with some illustrations from human geography.)

Hammond, R. and McCullogh, P. S., *Quantitative Techniques in Geography*, op. cit., Chs. 4 and 5. (Probability distributions, sampling and estimates.)

Harvey, D., *Explanation in Geography*, op. cit., pp. 356–69. (Sampling in geographical research.)

Selected Reading

Huntsberger, D. V., *Elements of Statistical Inference*, Allyn & Bacon, Boston, 1961, Chs. 2 and 3. (Introduction to descriptive statistics.)

King, L. J., *Statistical Analysis in Geography*, op. cit., Chs. 3 and 4. (Probability functions, sampling and statistical inference.)

Kolstoe, R. H., *Introduction to Statistics for the Behavioral Sciences*, op. cit., Chs. 4–7. (Elementary introduction to descriptive and inferential statistics.)

Lordahl, D. S., *Modern Statistics*, op. cit., Ch. 2. (Descriptive statistics.)

Moroney, M. J., *Facts from Figures*, Penguin Books, Harmondsworth, 1951, Chs. 4–10. (Descriptive statistics, distributions and sampling.)

Theakstone, W. H., and Harrison, C., *The Analysis of Geographical Data*, op. cit., Chs. 3 and 4. (Distributions and sampling.)

Yeates, M. H., *Quantitative Analysis in Human Geography*, op. cit., Ch. 3. (Sampling in geography.)

Note: Most basic textbooks on statistics cover the subject matter of this chapter in detail. They also provide the theoretical background required for competent practical applications. The works cited here are simply those which the author has found particularly helpful.

APPLICATIONS

Berry, B. J. L., 'City Size Distributions and Economic Development', *Economic Development and Cultural Change*, 9, 1961, pp. 573–88. (Cumulative frequency distributions.)

Fuchs, R. J., 'Intraurban Variation of Residential Quality', *Economic Geography*, 36, 1960, pp. 313–25. (Use of coefficient of variation.)

Garrison, W. L., 'Some Confusing Aspects of Common Measurement', *Professional Geographer*, 8, 1956, pp. 4–5. (Use of standard deviation.)

Greer-Wootten, B., *A Bibliography of Statistical Applications in Geography*, op. cit., pp. 23–31. (Sample design and descriptive statistics.)

Hart, J. F., and Salisbury, N. F., 'Population Changes in Middle-Western Villages: A Statistical Approach', *Annals*, Association of American Geographers, 55, 1965, pp. 140–59. (Example of a square root transformation and the use of fractile diagrams.)

King, L. J., 'A Multivariate Analysis of the Spacing of Urban Settlements in the United States', *Annals*, Association of American Geographers, 51, pp. 222–33. (Use of fractile diagrams and log transformation.)

Thomas, E. N., 'Towards an Expanded Central-Place Model', *Geographical Review*, 51, 1961, pp. 400–11. (Example of use of probability paper and a log-log transformation.)

356

Yeates, M. H., 'Some Factors Affecting the Spatial Distribution of Chicago Land Values, 1910–1960', *Economic Geography*, 41, 1965, pp. 57–70. (Maps using class intervals based on the standard deviation.)

4. Comparing Sets of Observations

TECHNICAL

Chase, C. I., *Elementary Statistical Procedures*, McGraw-Hill, New York, 1967. (General introduction to statistical tests.)

Gould, P. R., 'Is *Statistix Inferens* the Geographical Name for a Wild Goose?', *Economic Geography*, 46, 1970, pp. 439–48. (The relevance of statistical inference in geography.)

Gregory, S., *Statistical Methods and the Geographer*, op. cit., Chs. 8, 9, and 10. (Comparison of sample values, analysis of variance and chi-square; illustrated by geographical applications.)

Haggett, P., *Locational Analysis in Human Geography*, op. cit., pp. 290–92. (Applications of comparison of means and ranks.)

Hammond, R., and McCullogh, P. S., *Quantitative Techniques in Geography*, op. cit., Ch. 6. (Hypothesis testing, including *t* test and various non-parametric methods.)

Lordahl, D. S., *Modern Statistics for Behavioral Sciences*, op. cit., Chs. 6, 7 and 9. (Analysis of variance and chi-square.)

Moroney, M. J., *Facts from Figures*, op. cit., Chs. 13, 14, 15, and 19. (General review of inferential statistics.)

Quandt, R. E., 'Statistical Discrimination Among Alternative Hypotheses and Some Economic Regularities', *Journal of Regional Science*, 5, 1964, pp. 1–23. (How to choose the distribution best fitting a set of observations.)

Siegel, S., *Nonparametric Statistics for the Behavioral Sciences*, McGraw-Hill, New York, 1956. (Basic text, with full discussion of chi-square, Mann–Whitney, Kolmogorov–Smirnov and other nonparametric tests.)

Walker, H., and Lev, J., *Statistical Inference*, Holt, Rinehart & Winston, New York, 1953, Ch. 4. (Chi-square.)

Yeates, M. H., *Quantitative Analysis in Human Geography*, op. cit., Ch. 6. (Geographical application of analysis of variance.)

Note: As in Chapter 3, the subject matter of this chapter is covered in almost all textbooks on statistics.

Selected Reading

APPLICATIONS

Dacey, M., 'An Empirical Study of the Areal Distribution of Houses in Puerto Rico', *Transactions and Papers*, Institute of British Geographers, 45, 1968, pp. 51–69. (Kolmogorov–Smirnov tests.)

Davis, J. T., 'Sources of Variation in Housing Values in Washington, D.C.', *Geographical Analysis*, 3, 1971, pp. 63–76. (Analysis of variance.)

Greer-Wootten, B., *A Bibliography of Statistical Applications in Geography*, op. cit., pp. 35–46. (References to further geographical research applications.)

Harvey, D. W., 'Geographic Process and the Analysis of Point Patterns', *Transactions and Papers*, Institute of British Geographers, 40, 1970, pp. 81–95. (Example of testing observed against expected theoretical frequencies.)

Lout, P., 'Testing the Significance of Formal Regions in the Macleay Valley, New South Wales', *Australian Geographical Studies*, 5, 1967, pp. 150–64. (Use of analysis of variance.)

Mackay, J. R., 'The Interactance Hypothesis and Boundaries in Canada', *The Canadian Geographer*, 11, 1958, pp. 1–8. (Testing goodness of fit of sample distributions.)

Mackay, J. R., 'Chi-Square as a tool for Regional Studies', *Annals*, Association of American Geographers, 48, 1958, p. 164. (Questions the method of Zobler; see below.)

Zobler, L., 'Statistical Testing of Regional Boundaries', *Annals*, Association of American Geographers, 48, 1958, pp. 43–4. (Use of chi-square test.)

Zobler, L., 'Decision Making in Regional Construction', *Annals*, Association of American Geographers, 48, 1958, pp. 140–48. (Use of analysis of variance and chi-square in testing regional boundaries.)

5. Transforming and Combining Data

TECHNICAL

King, L. J., *Statistical Analysis in Geography*, op. cit., pp. 113–15. (The Gini coefficient as a statistic.)

Lordahl, D. S., *Modern Statistics for Behavioral Sciences*, op. cit., Ch. 3. (Scale transformations.)

Schvessler, K., *Analysing Social Data: A Statistical Orientation*, Houghton Mifflin, Boston, 1971, Ch. 9. (Full discussion of the transformation of statistical data.)

Yeates, M. H., *An Introduction to Quantitative Analysis in Economic Geo-*

graphy, op. cit., pp. 89–94 and 153–7. (Indices of industrial diversification and income distribution explained and illustrated.)

APPLICATIONS

Conkling, E. S., 'South Wales: A Case Study in Industrial Diversification', *Economic Geography*, 39, 1963, pp. 258–72. (Diversification index and Lorenz curves.)

Coughlin, R. E., *Goal Attainment Levels in 101 Metropolitan Areas*, Regional Science Research Institute, Discussion Paper No. 41, 1970. (Use of Z-scores in the development of social indicators.)

Dickinson, J. C., Gray, R. J., and Smith, D. M., 'The "Quality of Life" in Gainesville, Florida: An Application of Territorial Social Indicators', *Southeastern Geographer*, 12, 1972, pp. 121–32. (Use of range standardization in the development of social indicators.)

Florence, P. S., Fritz, W. G., and Gillies, P. C., 'Measures of Industrial Distribution', in *Industrial Location and National Resources*, U.S. National Resources Planning Board, Washington, D.C., 1943, pp. 105–24. (The location quotient.)

Greer-Wootten, B., *A Bibliography of Statistical Applications in Geography*, op. cit., pp. 32–5. (Index construction.)

Lewis, G. M., 'Levels of Living in the North-Eastern United States *c.* 1960: A New Approach to Regional Geography', *Transactions and Papers*, Institute of British Geographers, 38, 1968, pp. 11–37. (Index based on standard score transformation.)

Smith, D. M., *The Geography of Social Well-being in the United States*, McGraw-Hill, New York, 1973, Chs. 7–9. (Illustrations of Z-scores and rankings in the development of territorial social indicators.)

Smith, D. M., *Crime Rates as Territorial Social Indicators*, Occasional Paper No. 1, Dept. of Geography, Queen Mary College, London, 1974. (Problems of data combination.)

Wilson, J. O., *Quality of Life in the United States – An Excursion into the New Frontier of Socio-Economic Indicators*, Midwest Research Institute, Kansas City, Mo., 1969. (Use of rankings and other techniques in the development of state social indicators.)

6. Measures of Geographical Patterns

TECHNICAL

Alexander, J. W., *Economic Geography*, Prentice Hall, Englewood Cliffs, N.J., 1963, pp. 407–10 and 594–9. (Review and illustration of coefficient of localization, etc.)

Selected Reading

Bachi, R., 'Standard Distance Measures and Related Methods for Spatial Analysis', *Papers*, Regional Science Association, 10, 1963, pp. 83–132. (Major technical source on centrographic methods, with many illustrations.)

Barton, D. E., and David, F. N., 'Tests for Randomness of Points on a Line', *Biometrika*, 43, 1956, 104–12. (Details of a number of methods.)

Clark, P. J., and Evans, F. C., 'Distance to Nearest Neighbour as a Measure of Spatial Relationships in Populations', *Ecology*, 35, 445–53. (Basic technical paper.)

Grieg-Smith, P., *Quantitative Plant Ecology*, Butterworth, London, 1957, Ch. 3. (Nearest neighbour analysis.)

Hammond, R., and McCullogh, P. S., *Quantitative Techniques in Geography*, op. cit., Chs. 2 and 9. (Measures and tests of spatial distributions.)

Isard, W., *Methods of Regional Analysis*, MIT Press, Cambridge, Mass., 1960, pp. 249–79. (General review of coefficient of localization and related measures.)

Lloyd, P. E., and Dicken, P., 'The Data Bank in Regional Studies of Industry', *Town Planning Review*, 38, 1968, pp. 304–16. (Comments on sensitivity of location indices to size of areal units.)

Neft, D. S., *Statistical Analysis for Areal Distributions*, Monograph No. 2, Regional Science Research Institute, 1967. (A comprehensive framework for 'geostatistics'.)

Pearson, E. S., 'Comparison of Tests for Randomness of Points on a Line', *Biometrika*, 50, 1963, 315–23. (More advanced methods.)

Sviatlovsky, E. E., and Eells, W., 'The Centrographic Method and Regional Analysis', *Geographical Review*, 27, 1937, pp. 240–54. (A very early paper in quantitative geography.)

APPLICATIONS

Dacey, M. F., 'Analysis of Central Place and Point Patterns by a Nearest Neighbour Method', *Lund Studies in Geography*, Series B, 24, 1962, pp. 55–75. (One of a number of papers by Dacey exploring the application of this technique.)

Dacey, M. F., 'The Spacing of River Towns', *Annals*, Association of American Geographers, 50, 1960, pp. 59–61. (Measurement of randomness of points on a line.) This should be read in conjunction with Burghardt, A. F., 'The Location of River Towns in the Central Lowlands of the United States', *Annals*, 49, 1959, pp. 305–23; and should be followed by Porter, P. W., 'Earnest and Orephagians: A Fable for the Instruction of Young Geographers', *Annals*, 50, 1960, pp. 297–9. Dacey attempted a quantitative response to Burghardt's traditional approach, and Porter questioned Dacey's method.

Getis, A., 'Temporal Land-Use Patterns Analysis with the use of Nearest Neighbour and Quadrat Methods', *Annals*, Association of American Geographers, 54, 1964, 391–9. (Interesting application.)

Greer-Wootten, B., *A Bibliography of Statistical Applications in Geography*, op. cit., pp. 32–5, 46–51. (References on index construction, geostatistics and measuring point patterns.)

Hägerstrand, T., *The Propagation of Innovation Waves*, Lund Studies in Geography, Series B, 4, 1952, pp. 3–19. (Use of median centre.)

King, L. J., 'A Quantitative Expression of the Pattern of Urban Settlements in Selected Areas of the United States', *Tijdschrift voor Economische en Sociale Geografie*, 53, 1962, pp. 1–7. (Application of nearest neighbour analysis.)

Murphy, R. E., and Spittall, H. E., 'Movements of the Center of Coal Mining in the Appalachian Plateaus', *Geographical Review*, 35, 1945, pp. 624–33. (Early application of shifting mean centre; see Fig. 1.)

Prunty, M. J., 'Recent Quantitative Changes in the Cotton Region of the Southeastern States', *Economic Geography*, 27, 1951, pp. 189–208. (Application of median centre; see Fig. 9.)

Shachar, A., 'Some Applications of Geo-Statistical Methods in Urban Research', *Papers*, Regional Science Association, 18, 1967, pp. 197–206. (Centrographic research in Israel for planning purposes.)

7. Areal Distributions as Surfaces

TECHNICAL

Chorley, R. J., and Haggett, P., 'Trend-Surface Mapping in Geographical Research', *Transactions and Papers*, Institute of British Geographers, 37, 1965, pp. 47–67. (Summary review.)

Cole, J. P., and King, C. A. M., *Quantitative Geography*, op. cit., Ch. 9. (Geography and three space dimensions, including an introduction to trend surfaces.)

Haggett, P., *Locational Analysis in Human Geography*, op. cit., pp. 269–76. (Introduction to trend surface analysis.)

Krumbein, W. C., 'Regional and Local Components of Facies Maps', *Bulletin of the American Association of Petroleum Geologists*, 40, 1956, pp. 2136–94. (Major technical contribution; includes 'expected value' method.)

Krumbein, W. C., 'Trend Surface Analysis of Contour-type Maps with

Selected Reading

Irregular Control-Point Spacing', *Journal of Geophysical Research*, 64, 1959, pp. 823–34. (Major technical contribution.)

Krumbein, W. C., and Graybill, F. A., *An Introduction to Statistical Models in Geology*, John Wiley, New York, 1965, Ch. 13. (Discussion of various aspects of trend surface analysis.)

Luckermann, F., and Porter, P. W., 'The Gravity and Potential Models in Economic Geography', *Annals*, Association of American Geographers, 50, 1960, pp. 493–504. (General review.)

Miller, R. L., 'Trend Surfaces: Their Application to Analysis of Description of Environments of Sedimentation', *Journal of Geology*, 64, 1956, pp. 425–46. (Appendix describes calculation methods.)

Neft, D. S., *Statistical Analysis for Areal Distributions*, op. cit. (Extensive discussion and numerous examples of potential surfaces; N.B. Figs. 16–22.)

Robinson, A. H., and Caroe, L., 'On the Analysis and Comparison of Statistical Surfaces', in Garrison, W. L., and Marble, D. F. (eds.), *Quantitative Geography, Part I*, op. cit., pp. 252–76. (See especially pp. 200–206 on best fit surfaces.)

Smith, D. M., *Industrial Location: An Economic Geographical Analysis*, op. cit., pp. 297–304. (Review of market potential concept and aggregate travel, with examples of surfaces.)

Stewart, J. Q., 'The Development of Social Physics', *American Journal of Physics*, 18, 1950, pp. 239–52. (The potential concept.)

Yeates, M., *Quantitative Analysis in Human Geography*, op. cit., Ch. 6. (Potential, and trend surfaces.)

APPLICATIONS

Fairburn, K. J., and Robinson, G., 'Towns and Trend-Surfaces in Gippsland, Victoria', *Australian Geographical Studies*, 5, 1967, pp. 125–34. (Application of trend surface analysis to residuals from regression.)

Greer-Wootten, B., *A Bibliography of Statistical Applications in Geography*, op. cit., pp. 80–83. (Trend surface analysis.)

Haggett, P., 'Trend-Surface Mapping in the Interregional Comparison of Intra-Regional Structures', *Papers*, Regional Science Association, 20, 1967, pp. 19–28. (Major research application in human geography; see also comments in Macomber, L., 'Utility of Trend Surfaces in Interregional Map Comparisons', *Journal of Regional Science*, 11, 1971, pp. 87–90.)

Haggett, P., and Bassett, K. A., 'The Use of Trend-Surface Parameters in Inter-Urban Comparisons', *Environment and Planning*, 2, 1970, pp.

225–37. (One of the few recent applications of trend surfaces in human geography.)

Harris, C., 'The Market as a Factor in the Localization of Industry in the United States', *Annals*, Association of American Geographers, 44, 1954, pp. 315–48. (Classic early application of the market potential concept.)

Warntz, W., *Towards a Geography of Price*, University of Pennsylvania Press, Philadelphia, 1959. (Major application of the market potential concept.)

8. Association between Patterns

TECHNICAL

Abler, R., Adams, J. S., and Gould, P., *Spatial Organisation*, op. cit., Ch. 5. (Introduction to correlation, regression, and other ways of structuring geographical relationships.)

Cole, J. P., and King, C. A. M., *Quantitative Geography*, op. cit., Chs. 6 and 7. (Discussion and illustration of various correlation methods.)

Dogan, M., and Rokkan, S. (eds.), *Quantitative Ecological Analysis in the Social Sciences*, MIT Press, Cambridge, Mass., 1969. (Contains a number of contributions dealing with ecological correlation applications and problems.)

Ezekiel, M., and Fox, K. A., *Methods of Correlation and Regression Analysis*, John Wiley, New York, 1959 (3rd edn). (Basic text on simple and multiple correlation.)

Gregory, S., *Statistical Methods and the Geographer*, op. cit., Chs. 11 and 12. (Introduction to correlation and regression in geographical problems.)

Hammond, R., and McCullogh, P. S., *Quantitative Techniques in Geography*, op. cit., Chs. 7 and 8. (Correlation and regression analysis, with geographical illustrations.)

Huntsberger, D. V., *Elements of Statistical Inference*, op. cit., pp. 190–206. (Correlation.)

King, L. J., *Statistical Analysis in Geography*, op. cit., Ch. 6. (Spatial relationships and the measurement of areal association by correlation methods.)

Lordahl, D. S., *Modern Statistics for Behavioral Sciences*, op. cit., Ch. 11. (Correlation techniques.)

Poole, M. A., and O'Farrell, P. N., 'The Assumptions of the Linear Regression Model', *Transactions and Papers*, Institute of British Geographers, 52, 1971, pp. 145–58. (Basic reading prior to attempting research applications.)

Selected Reading

Robinson, A. H., 'The Necessity of Weighting Values in Correlation Analysis of Areal Data', *Annals*, Association of American Geographers, 46, 1956, pp. 233–6. (The affect of the varying size of areal units of observation.)

Siegel, S., *Nonparametric Statistics for the Behavioral Sciences*, op. cit., pp. 195–239. (Correlation by chi-square, and by the Spearman and Kendall rank coefficients.)

Thomas, E. N., *Maps of Residuals from Regression: Their Characteristics and Uses in Geographical Research*, Department of Geography, University of Iowa, 1960. (Basic technical contribution; see especially pp. 25–58.)

Thomas, E. N., and Anderson, D. L., 'Additional Comments on Weighting Values in Correlation Analysis of Areal Data', *Annals*, Association of American Geographers, 55, 1965, pp. 492–505. (An inferential approach to the problem of size of areal units.)

Walker, H. M., and Lev, J., *Statistical Inference*, op. cit. (Good general reference on measures of association, including chi-square and the point biserial correlation.)

Yeates, M., *Quantitative Analysis in Human Geography*, op. cit., Chs. 4 and 5. (Simple and multiple correlation and regression, with details of the mathematics involved.)

Note: Most statistics textbooks provide an adequate treatment of simple correlation and regression, and the use of chi-square and rank correlation; their choice is largely a personal matter.

APPLICATIONS

Britton, J. N. H., *Regional Analysis and Economic Geography: A Case Study of Manufacturing in the Bristol Region*, Bell, London, 1967. (Use of correlation analysis.)

Brunn, S. D., and Hoffman, W. L., 'The Spatial Response of Negroes Toward Open Housing: The Flint Referendum', *Annals*, Association of American Geographers, 60, 1970, pp. 18–36. (Stepwise regression analysis.)

Greer-Wootten, B., *A Bibliography of Statistical Applications in Geography*, op. cit., pp. 51–6 and 67–76. (Correlation techniques, ecological correlation, and regression analysis.)

Logan, M. I., 'Manufacturing Decentralisation in the Sydney Metropolitan Area', *Economic Geography*, 40, 1964, pp. 151–65. (Correlation analysis, including mapping of residuals from regression.)

McCarty, H. H., Hook, J. C., and Knos, D. S., *The Measurement of Association in Industrial Geography*, Department of Geography, University of Iowa, 1956. (Early geographical application, comparing different methods.)

Olsson, G., 'Distance and Human Interaction: A Migration Study', *Geografiska Annaler*, 47B, 1965, pp. 3–43. (Stepwise regression analysis.)

Stafford, H. A., 'Factors in the Location of the Paperboard Container Industry', *Economic Geography*, 36, 1960, pp. 260–66. (An early application of multiple correlation and regression in human geography.)

Note: The above are a brief selection of some of the better known applications. See Greer-Wootten's bibliography (op. cit.) for a more extensive list.

9. Networks and Movement

TECHNIQUES

Abler, R., Adams, J. S., and Gould, P., *Spatial Organisation*, op. cit., Chs. 7 and 8. (Comprehensive review of the contemporary approach to spatial interaction, movement and transport systems; particularly useful on potential and gravity models.)

Carrothers, G. A. P., 'An Historical Review of the Gravity and Potential Concepts of Human Interaction', *Journal of the American Institute of Planners*, 22, 1956, 94–102. (Brief survey.)

Cole, J. P., and King, C. A. M., *Quantitative Geography*, op. cit., pp. 539–74. (Introduction to network analysis.)

Haggett, P., *Locational Analysis in Human Geography*, op. cit., Ch. 3 and pp. 236–40. (General discussion of networks with introduction to measurement.)

Haggett, P., 'Network Models in Geography', in Chorley and Haggett (eds.), *Models in Geography*, op. cit., pp. 609–68. (General review.)

Haggett, P., and Chorley, R. J., *Network Analysis in Geography*, Edward Arnold, London, 1969. (Definitive text on networks in human and physical geography.)

Isard, W., *Methods of Regional Analysis*, MIT Press, 1960, Ch. 11. (General survey of gravity, potential and spatial interaction models.)

Nystuen, J. D., and Dacey, M. F., 'A Graph Theory Interpretation of Nodal Regions', *Papers*, Regional Science Association, 7, 1961, pp. 29–42. (Major technical contribution to the analysis of spatial organization.)

Yeates, M. H., *An Introduction to Quantitative Analysis in Economic Geography*, op. cit., Ch. 8. (Introduction to the measurement of transport systems.)

APPLICATIONS

Board, C., Davies, R. J., and Fair, T. J. D., 'The Structure of the South

Selected Reading

African Space Economy: An Integrated Approach', *Regional Studies*, 4, 1970, pp. 367–92. (Examples of the analysis of flows and a number of other techniques.)

Garrison, W. L., 'Connectivity of the Interstate Highway System', *Papers*, Regional Science Association, 6, 1960, pp. 121–37. (Early application of graph approach.)

Kansky, K. J., *Structure of Transportation Networks*, Dept of Geography, University of Chicago, Research Paper No. 84, 1963. (Classic study of network measures and relationships.)

Kariel, H. G., and Kariel, P. E., *Explorations in Social Geography*, Addison-Wesley, 1972, Ch. 11. (Review of spatial interaction techniques, including the gravity model with examples.)

King, L. J., Casetti, E., and Jeffrey, D., 'Economic Impulses in a Regional System of Cities: A Study of Spatial Interaction', *Regional Studies*, 3, 1969, pp. 213–18. (Use of regression in fitting interaction model parameters.)

Taaffe, E. J., 'The Air Traffic Pattern of Chicago', *Tijdschrift voor Economische en Sociale Geografie*, April/May 1965, pp. 82–5. (Application of gravity model.)

10. Areal Classification and Regions

TECHNICAL (GENERAL)

Abler, J., Adams, J. S., and Gould, P., *Spatial Organisation*, op. cit., Ch. 6. (Introduction to methods of classification.)

Berry, B. J. L., 'A Method for Deriving Multifactor Uniform Regions', *Przeglad Geograficzny*, 33, 1961, pp. 263–82. (Paper which initiated factor-analytical areal classification in geography.)

Berry, B. J. L., 'Grouping and Regionalisation: An Approach to the Problem using Multivariate Analysis', in W. L. Garrison and D. F. Marble (eds.), *Quantitative Geography, Part I*, Studies in Geography No. 13, Northwestern University, Evanston, Ill., pp. 214–51. (General overview.)

Haggett, P., *Locational Analysis in Human Geography*, Ch. 9. ('Region-building' – an introduction to contemporary methods.)

King, L., *Statistical Analysis in Geography*, op. cit., Chs. 7 and 8. (More advanced treatment of factor analysis, principal components analysis and areal classification in geography.)

Spence, N. A., and Taylor, P. J., 'Quantitative Methods in Regional

Taxonomy', in C. Board *et al.* (eds.), *Progress in Geography*, 2, Edward Arnold, London, 1970, pp. 1–63. (Overview of current methods.)

TECHNICAL (FACTOR ANALYSIS)

Armstrong, J. S., 'Derivation of Theory by Means of Factor Analysis, or Tom Swift and his Electric Factor Analysis Machine', *The American Statistician*, Dec. 1967, pp. 17–21. (A note of caution.)

Guertin, W. H., and Bailey, J. P., *Introduction to Modern Factor Analysis*, Edwards Bros., Ann Arbor, Mich., 1970. (Recent text.)

Harman, H. H., *Modern Factor Analysis*, Chicago University Press, Chicago, 1966 (2nd edn). (Definitive work.)

Rummel, R. J., 'Understanding Factor Analysis', *Journal of Conflict Resolution*, 11, 1967, pp. 444–80. (Helpful introductory treatment.)

Yeates, M., *Quantitative Analysis in Human Geography*, op. cit., Ch. 9. (Brief review of factorial analysis.)

Note: Recent issues of geographical periodicals such as *Area* and *Professional Geographer* contain papers dealing with various problems in the application of factor analytical methods.

APPLICATIONS

Ahmad, Q., *Indian Cities: Characteristics and Correlates*, Research Papers No. 102, Dept of Geography, University of Chicago, 1966. (Major application of multivariate city classification.)

Berry, B. J. L., 'The Identification of Declining Regions: An Empirical Study of the Dimensions of Rural Poverty', in R. S. Thoman and W. D. Wood (eds.), *Areas of Economic Stress in Canada*, Queens University Press, Kingston, Ont., 1965, pp. 22–66. (Major application of multivariate areal classification.)

Cole, J. P., and King, C. A. M., *Quantitative Geography*, op. cit., Ch. 6. (Areal classification by cross-boundary correlation and factor analysis: examples of France and USA.)

Giggs, J. A., 'Socially Disorganised Areas in Barry: A Multivariate Approach', in A. Carter and W. K. D. Davies (eds.), *Urban Essays: Studies in the Geography of Wales*, Longmans, London, 1970, pp. 101–43. (Application of factor analysis and areal classification.)

Greer-Wootten, B., *A Bibliography of Statistical Applications in Geography*, op. cit., pp. 57–67, pp. 86–8. (Factor analysis, principal components analysis and classification; many applications listed.)

Selected Reading

Hadden, J. K., and Borgatta, E. F., *American Cities: Their Social Characteristics*, Rand McNally, Chicago, 1965. (Major factor-analytical study.)

Moser, C. A., and Scott, W., *British Towns: A Statistical Study of their Social and Economic Differences*, Oliver & Boyd, Edinburgh, 1961. (First major application of factor analysis to city classifications.)

Rees, P. H., 'Concepts of Social Space: Toward an Urban Social Geography', in B. J. L. Berry and F. Horton (eds.), *Geographical Perspectives on Urban Systems*, Prentice Hall, Englewood Cliffs, N.J., 1970, pp. 265–330. (Review of areal classification within the city.)

Robson, B. T., *Urban Analysis: A Study of City Structure*, Cambridge University Press, Cambridge, 1969. (Major factor-analytical study of intra-city spatial structure.)

Smith, D. M., *Industrial Britain: The North West*, David & Charles, Newton Abbot, Devon, 1969. (Applications of regional definition and the identification of problem areas.)

Smith, D. M., *The Geography of Social Well-being in the United States*, McGraw-Hill, 1973, Chs. 7 and 9. (Use of factor analysis in regional definition and problem area identification.)

Spence, N. A., 'A Multifactor Uniform Regionalisation of British Counties on the Basis of Employment Data for 1961', *Regional Studies*, 2, 1968, pp. 87–104. (Application of multifactor approach.)

Thompson, J. H. *et al.*, 'Towards a Geography of Economic Health: the Case of New York State', *Annals*, Association of American Geographers, 52, 1962, pp. 1–20. (First application of this popular technique of the 1960s.)

Weaver, J. C., 'Crop Combination Regions in the Middle West', *Geographical Review*, 44, 1964, pp. 175–200. (A useful technique with general application.)